Athlete Learning i

Elite athletes lead a particular way of life, which creates significant learning and shapes their selves. This is the first sociological-pedagogical text to conceptualise athlete learning in elite sport and across athletic careers. It outlines theories of learning and argues for a cultural perspective capturing contextual influence, temporal changes, individual dispositions, and subjectivity.

Presented in three parts—landscaping elite sport and theorising athlete learning; showcasing athletes' learning in elite sport; and informing research and practice—the book features nine international, multi-contextual, and multi-experience case studies of athlete careers, experiences, and learning across individual and team sports such as boxing, rugby, basketball, hockey, and gymnastics.

This is fascinating reading for students, researchers, and practitioners in sport organisations, sports coaching, coach education, and sport sociology and pedagogy.

Natalie Barker-Ruchti is Associate Professor at the School of Health Sciences, Division of Sport, University of Örebro, Sweden. Prior to this appointment, and during the time of writing this book, Natalie was Associate Professor at the Department of Food and Nutrition and Sport Science at the University of Gothenburg. Her research focuses on coaches and coaching and on athletes and athlete learning. Examining specific elite sport contexts, coaching practices, and athletes' experiences, Natalie's research offers insight into the influence sport and coaches have on athletes' performance, selves, and lives.

Routledge Research in Sports Coaching

The *Routledge Research in Sports Coaching* series provides a platform for leading experts and emerging academics in this important discipline to present ground-breaking work on the history, theory, practice and contemporary issues of sports coaching. The series sets a new benchmark for research in sports coaching, and offers a valuable contribution to the wider sphere of sports studies.

Available in this series:

Sport Coaching Research and Practice
Ontology, Interdisciplinarity and Critical Realism
Julian North

Leadership in Sports Coaching
A Social Identity Approach
Paul Cummins, Ian O'Boyle and Tony Cassidy

Learning to Mentor in Sports Coaching
A Design Thinking Approach
Edited by Fiona C. Chambers

Care in Sport Coaching
Pedagogical Cases
Edited by Colum Cronin and Kathleen Armour

Professional Advances in Sport Coaching
Research and Practice
Edited by Richard Thelwell and Matt Dicks

Athlete Learning in Elite Sport
A Cultural Framework
Edited by Natalie Barker-Ruchti

Athlete Learning in Elite Sport

A Cultural Framework

Edited by
Natalie Barker-Ruchti

Routledge
Taylor & Francis Group
LONDON AND NEW YORK

First published 2019
by Routledge
2 Park Square, Milton Park, Abingdon, Oxon OX14 4RN

and by Routledge
52 Vanderbilt Avenue, New York, NY 10017

First issued in paperback 2020

Routledge is an imprint of the Taylor & Francis Group, an informa business

British Library Cataloguing-in-Publication Data
A catalogue record for this book is available from the British Library

Library of Congress Cataloging-in-Publication Data
A catalog record has been requested for this book

ISBN 13: 978-0-367-66147-2 (pbk)
ISBN 13: 978-1-138-08641-8 (hbk)

Typeset in Goudy
by Cenveo® Publisher Services

Contents

Table

List of contributors

Natalie Barker-Ruchti is Associate Professor at the School of Health Sciences, Division of Sport, University of Örebro, Sweden. Prior to this appointment, and during the time of writing this book, Natalie was Associate Professor at the Department of Food and Nutrition and Sport Science at the University of Gothenburg. Her research focuses on coaches and coaching and on athletes and athlete learning. Examining specific elite sport contexts, coaching practices, and athletes' experiences, Natalie's research offers insight into the influence sport and coaches have on athletes' performance, selves, and lives.

Francesca Cavallerio is a Senior Lecturer in Sport and Exercise Sciences (Sport Psychology and Qualitative Research Methods) at the School of Psychology and Sport Science, Anglia Ruskin University, UK. She is a former rhythmic gymnastics coach. Her research uses qualitative methodologies to explore the psychosocial aspects affecting youth elite athletes' well-being and overall development during and following their sport career. She is also interested in the areas of diversity and inclusion in coaching and in high-performance gymnasts' experiences of the gymnastics culture.

Georgia Cervin is an Honorary Research Fellow in History at the University of Western Australia. She is a former international gymnast, and her doctoral research examined women's artistic gymnastics during the Cold War. She is particularly interested in the intersection of sport, politics, and culture in history, as well as issues of sports governance and gender. She is currently editing a book of biographies of women leaders in international sport.

Ali Greey is currently pursuing a master's degree at the University of Toronto in the Faculty of Kinesiology and Physical Education. Her research centres upon social justice in sport, with a particular focus on identifying strategies for making locker rooms safer and more inclusive for the LGBTTIQQ2SA community. She retired from the Canadian National Boxing Team after winning three consecutive national titles.

Gretchen Kerr is a Professor in the Faculty of Kinesiology and Physical Education and Vice-Dean of the School of Graduate Studies at the University of Toronto. Her research expertise includes the psychosocial aspects of youth participation in high-performance sport and athlete maltreatment. She has a long history in women's gymnastics, first as a competitive athlete and then as a coach and sport psychology consultant. She also serves as a volunteer Athlete Welfare Officer for sport organizations, receiving and investigating complaints of athlete maltreatment and providing educational programmes. In 2010, she was a recipient of the Canadian Association of Women and Sport and Physical Activity's "Most Influential Women" award.

Roslyn Kerr is a Senior Lecturer in Sociology of Sport and the Head of the Department of Tourism, Sport and Society at Lincoln University, New Zealand. She has published a wide range of articles in sport, particularly examining issues in sports governance, high performance, coaching, and sports history. She is particularly interested in the French school of sociology, with previous publications having utilised the work of Foucault, Latour, and Bourdieu.

Koji Kobayashi is a Lecturer in the Department of Tourism, Sport and Society at Lincoln University, New Zealand. His research interests include globalisation, cultural production, practice of representation, and identity politics as they relate to sport and recreation. His work has appeared in journals such as *Sociology of Sport Journal*, *International Review for the Sociology of Sport*, *Sport in Society*, *Managing Sport and Leisure*, and *Consumption Markets and Culture*.

Geoff Kohe's research has predominantly focused on the historical, political, and sociocultural dimensions of the Olympic movement and sport organisations. In particular, he has examined sport museums and heritage, Olympic legacy initiatives in education, sport workers' welfare, and aspects of athletic body politics.

Christopher R. Matthews is a Senior Lecturer in Sociology in the School of Science and Technology at Nottingham Trent University, UK. He has published widely on topics relating to sport, violence, gender studies, social theory, and teaching in higher education.

Katrina McDonald is a Senior Lecturer in Sports Coaching and Physical Education at Anglia Ruskin University, UK. Her research interests are in the areas of qualitative research methods, specifically with and around athletes and their education and learning. She was an international judo competitor and then later went to work as a coach in a performance environment; this experience she brings to her research.

Myrian Nunomura is a Professor at the University of São Paulo, Brazil. She has published on various aspects of artistic gymnastics and sport pedagogy, including coaching and coach education, and is currently interested in the culture of high-performance gymnastics. The majority of her research is qualitative in nature, focusing on interviews, documents, and observational field studies. She is also interested in publishing books for coaches and teachers involved in gymnastics teaching and has published *Gymnastics Foundations*, *Understanding Artistic Gymnastics*, and *High Performance Gymnastics*.

Rūtenis Paulauskas works at Lithuanian University of Educational Sciences and Lithuania Sports University. His central areas of teaching and research pertain to coaching high-performance basketball players, teaching sport concepts and skills, and the physical fitness of youth and adolescents.

Laura G. Purdy's research focuses on the careers and lives of sport workers in elite/professional sport. Her recent projects have examined the welfare, representation, and advocacy of sport workers in European contexts. She works at Edge Hill University, UK.

Astrid Schubring is a Senior Lecturer in Sociology of Sport at the University of Gothenburg, Sweden. She teaches in the Sports Coaching, Physical Education Teacher, and Sport Science Master programme and leads the university's dual career scheme for elite athletes. Her research focuses on social dimensions of health and illness, youth sport, sustainable career development, and coaching in elite sport.

Anne Tjønndal has a PhD in Sociology and an MSc in Sport Science and is an Associate Professor in Research Methods and Methodology in the Social Sciences at the Faculty of Social Science, Nord University, Norway. Her research interests include sport leadership and coaching, social inclusion and exclusion in sport, sport and gender, and sport innovation and technology. She is also a certified AIBA 1 Star Boxing Coach, a competitive boxer, and the former national champion in the women's lightweight division.

Acknowledgements

My thanks goes out to Routledge's Simon Whitmore and his team for their invitation to and support of writing this book. I also thank the authors of Chapters 4–12 for providing excellent case studies. The contributions make the book unique and compelling. I further thank Claes Annerstedt, Dean Barker, Klara Boije af Gennäs, and Pär Rylander for providing feedback on chapter drafts. Lastly, I am grateful to the Faculty of Education, University of Gothenburg, for the grant for research visits at academic institutions abroad they awarded me in 2017. During my stay at the University of Toronto and University of Lausanne in 2018, I was able to write much of the book's contents.

Introduction

Natalie Barker-Ruchti

The purpose of this book is to present a cultural framework that can be used to think about and research athlete learning in elite sport. The book covers the contemporary elite sport context and theories that researchers have employed to understand learning in elite sport. It develops a cultural perspective of learning, which the authors of the nine case studies have employed to examine athletes' learning in elite sport. In bringing together the cultural perspective of learning and a case study methodology, the book offers a unique resource for scholars, students, and practitioners interested in understanding athletes' learning in elite sport and advancing sport coaching science, coaching practice, and coach education.

Many scholars have given learning scientific attention. Despite the extensive literature that has emerged from this research, definitions either are basic or differ depending on scientific perspective. A basic definition that many social scientists have adopted is that learning is a continuous social process that is influenced by many sources and generates durable change to a person's beliefs, conduct, and self (Säljö, 2009). While such change can be of a practical or cognitive nature, research has shown that it has a dispositional dimension; that is, it affects what individuals typically or habitually believe, assume, and do. Often, this dispositional learning occurs unnoticed, yet it is important, as it defines people's sense of who they are. For this book, I term this learning *learning as self-development*.

With relevance to elite sport, research has shown that contemporary elite sport ideals, norms, and practices create specific ways of life. These ways of life shape athletes to *become and be* elite athletes, a learning that is significant and durable, constituting elite sport performance, health and well-being, and lives after retiring from sport (Barker-Ruchti, Rynne, Lee, & Barker, 2014). In this book, the effects the elite sport ways of life have on athletes' learning as self-development represent the core topic.

My motivation to write a book on elite athletes' learning is threefold. First, my motivation stems from the sociocultural case study research that I have accomplished over the past eight years and that has generated unique insights into elite sport realities. This research aimed to understand how athletes learn to be elite athletes (e.g., Andersson & Barker-Ruchti, 2018; Barker-Ruchti et al., 2014; Barker-Ruchti & Schubring, 2016). In studying cases of elite athletes' lives and focusing on their elite sport settings, life phases and events, and experiences, the questions that I considered in this research included these: What *is* being an elite athlete? How do athletes *learn to be* elite athletes? What affects elite athletes' learning? And why may elite athletes' sense of self *change* over time? The answers that I have developed from the research made me realise that learning is a continuous process of self-development that is influenced by contextual norms and ideals; organisations and systems, spaces, and material objects; relationships and practices; athletes' backgrounds, life phases, and experiences; serendipitous events; and individual meaning making. It is my hope that by leading into this book with these questions about being and learning, its contents can generate cultural understanding of athlete learning in elite sport.

Second, my motivation for this book stems from my ambition to develop a theoretical perspective that allows thinking about and generates understanding of the experiences and learning of elite athletes. It felt to me as though the multitude of available theories, many of them capturing different aspects of learning, does not provide adequate tools to think about the complex and diverse athlete learning that I had come to recognise. One perspective that did help me to interpret elite athletes' learning as self-development was Hodkinson, Biesta, and James's (2008) cultural theory of learning. While not without limitations and critique (Enright & Gard, 2016), I found that the theory has potential to create a *cultural framework* with which to understand athlete learning in elite sport. It is thus that readers should see this book in its entirety as a resource that allows scholars, students, and practitioners interested in sport organisations, sports coaching, coach education, and sport sociology and pedagogy to think about and research athlete learning in elite sport.

Lastly, I was motivated to compile this book because I believe that research on elite athletes' learning can advance sport coaching science. At present, coaching research foregrounds the coach, coaching practice, and sporting contexts. Rarely do scholars consider how athletes' learning can inform coaching practice. While coach/coaching research produces important knowledge, I agree with education scholars that to develop teaching (read coaching), 'a prerequisite must be an appropriate understanding of the nature of learning and of learning careers, and the wider lives of the young people we are trying to help' (Bloomer & Hodkinson, 2000, p. 74). I thus intended to connect athlete learning research to sport coaching science and demonstrate how thinking and knowing about learning can inform coaching practice.

Contents and structure of the book

The book is organised in three parts. The first part grounds elite athletes' learning through three chapters. *Chapter 1* landscapes the nature of contemporary elite sport. It outlines how the demands of elite sport, including its competitive pressures, intensity of training, behavioural demands, and long-term commitment, create a precarious environment that may be detrimental to athletes' health, education, and social life. *Chapter 2* outlines three theoretical perspectives that researchers have used to understand learning. It does this by adopting three metaphors of learning—learning as acquisition, learning as participation, and learning as storying. *Chapter 3* proposes the cultural perspective of learning that I have developed to think about learning. It presents the conceptions of 'learning culture', 'becoming', 'horizons for action' and 'horizons of learning', and 'turning points' and conceptualises how these interact to influence learning as self-development.

The book's second part exemplifies elite athlete learning. *Chapters 4* through *12* contain nine case studies of female and male elite athletes and their learning as self-development. These cases represent different sports from around the globe and capture learning relative to diverse elite sport experiences and career pathways.

Lastly, the book's third part brings together the cultural perspective of learning and case study methodology. *Chapter 13* outlines the methodology I regard suitable for athlete learning research and presents how the cultural understanding of learning can inform coaching research, coach education, and coaching practice. *Chapter 14* concludes the book by providing final reflections on learning as self-development and researching athlete learning.

References

Andersson, R., & Barker-Ruchti, N. (2018). Career paths of Swedish top-level women soccer players. *Soccer and Society*, 1–15.

Barker-Ruchti, N., Rynne, S. B., Lee, J., & Barker, D. M. (2014). Athlete learning in Olympic sport. *Sports Coaching Review*, *3*(2), 162–178.

Barker-Ruchti, N., & Schubring, A. (2016). Moving into and out of high-performance sport: The cultural learning of one women's artistic gymnast. *Physical Education and Sport Pedagogy*, *21*(1), 55–68.

Bloomer, M., & Hodkinson, P. (2000). Learning careers: continuity and change in young people's dispositions to learning. *British Educational Research Journal*, 26(5), 583–597.

Enright, E., & Gard, M. (2016). Media, digital technology and learning in sport: A critical response to Hodkinson, Biesta and James. *Physical Education and Sport Pedagogy*, *21*(1), 40–54.

Hodkinson, P., Biesta, G., & James, D. (2008). Understanding learning culturally: Overcoming the dualism between social and individual views of learning. *Vocations and Learning*, *1*, 27–47.

Säljö, R. (2009). Learning, theories of learning, and units of analysis in research. *Educational Psychologist*, *44*(3), 202–208.

Part I

Landscaping elite sport and theorising athlete learning

Chapter 1

Contemporary elite sport landscape

Natalie Barker-Ruchti

The purpose of this chapter is to sketch the 'landscape' of contemporary elite sport. I understand this landscape to consist of the elite sport governing bodies and stakeholders (e.g., sponsors, policy writers, administrators, spectators), elite athletes and their families, spaces and material objects (e.g., swimming pool, sport equipment), social memory that those participating in or consuming elite sport carry, and relationships and activities that elite sport stakeholders participate in. The aim with this landscaping is to create a macro-level perspective of elite sport, similar to a map that illustrates the topographic, climatic, economic, political, and sociocultural features of a geographical location. To achieve this landscaping, I first discuss the commodification of sport and then consider how the commodity orientation shapes the purpose, view, and knowledge of elite sport. I then reflect on effects this landscape has on elite sport practice.

Commodification of elite sport

Since the 1990s, the commodification of elite sport has developed at a fast pace. The past 20 to 30 years, in particular, have seen 'greater professionalization and global migration of players [read also athletes], the corporatization of clubs, the proliferation of merchandising, rule-changes to draw in new customers, and a general redefinition of the competitive structures and *ethos* [read logic or character] of sport' (Walsh & Giulianotti, 2001, p. 53). This commodification has turned (elite) sport into a multi-billion-dollar industry (Jeanrenaud & Késenne, 2006; Milano & Chelladurai, 2011), which in most Western countries, through sales from media rights, event tickets, merchandise, and sponsorship deals, significantly contributes to national economies and employment opportunities (Commission of the European Communities, 2007).

The commodification has also created a global medal market. While initially amateur sport emphasised individual effort and did not allow athletes and coaches to receive monetary rewards for their successes, competition for world supremacy through medals became serious when Eastern and Western countries were embroiled in Cold War politics (Riordan, 2002). Since the dissolution and fragmentation of East European states and of the Soviet Union particularly, the medal market has intensified to a global sporting arms race (Oakley & Green, 2001). Winning medals at major sporting events such as the Olympic Games and placing in the top ranks of international medal tallies are perceived as important and drive national governments and sport governing bodies to value and invest in elite sport. The common justification these organisations offer for their investments is that international representation and national success convey to citizens social values, encourage participation in physical activities, and contribute to feelings of national identity and social cohesion (Haut, Prohl, & Emrich, 2016).

Many scholars are, however, critical of these positive effects in terms of both whether medals can actually achieve social and health outcomes and whether the means to reach such athletic success are ethical and sustainable (Barker, Barker-Ruchti, Wals, & Tinning, 2014). Walsh and Giulianotti (2001) even document how elite sport's commodity orientation has pathological effects, such as the loss of sport's core ethos of skill development, decreased enjoyment and sportsmanship, heightened inequalities because of national differences in resources to produce elite sport success, and unethical practices such as doping and match-fixing.

Commodity-driven elite sport and its effects on practice

According to a number of scholars, an orientation towards and the importance of commodities have infiltrated and changed our understanding of life, humans, the economy, and knowledge (Peters & Wals, 2013). This infiltration has become evident in most public spheres, including education, science, and health. Schools and universities, for instance, evaluate themselves and are being evaluated against performance and productivity criteria, and a ranking system determines the 'best' educational institutions. The well-being of pupils and students, their development as people, and the community impact they may generate receive much less attention. With regard to elite sport, Barker-Ruchti, Barker, and Annerstedt (2014) have adopted Wals and Jickling's (2002) commodity and community thinking to show how the commodity orientation has shaped the purpose of sport, the view of athletes, the coach-athlete relationship, the purpose of training, and the type of knowledge employed to understand coaching and sport performance (see Table 1.1).

How do the five commodity characteristics affect elite sport and its athletes? Research shows that with regard to the *purpose of sport*, athletes follow a performance narrative, which Douglas and Carless (2014) define as the 'single-minded dedication to sport performance that justifies, and even demands, the exclusion or relegation of all other areas of life and self' (p. 73). Commonly, performance-driven athletes regard their participation in sport, particularly the necessary extensive training, as an investment that is made in return for enhanced performance and (future) competitive success (Barker, Barker-Ruchti, Rynne, & Lee, 2014). Research shows the extreme relegation and performance investment strategies that athletes (and often also parents) adopt, including moving away from home and sometimes even country, postponing or ignoring education and/or professional training, risking

Table 1.1 Underlying assumptions and practices of commodity-oriented elite sport

Purpose of sport	*Sport for market and international comparison* Emphasis is on financial gain and international medals; has an outcome orientation; reflects a 'market' and 'marketability'
View of athletes	*Efficiency* Athletes are seen in mechanistic terms; talented vs untalented; body-as-machine and resource for economic gains and ranking; tight time frames; cause-effect relationship between training and performance gain
	Spectating pleasure and social benefit Athletes serve others' pleasurable looking; athletes' achievements are used for greater social benefit (i.e., national pride/identity, gender ideals/roles)
	Athlete self-regulation Athletes view their bodies as machines; athletes risk their health; athletes are over-conforming
Coach-athlete relationship	*Instrumentality* Coach is knower—athlete is learner; one-coach authority; coaching is treated as transfer of predetermined and fixed goals
Purpose of training	*Focus on continuous growth* Purpose of training is athletic progress and normative targets; all aspects of life are planned in the pursuit of performance enhancement; athletes are socially isolated
Epistemological orientation	*Empirical rationalism* Scientific knowledge represents truth; biomedical knowledge is key; trust is placed in technology; control and elimination of 'distractions' are important
	Scientific and technical knowledge Used to predict, control and intervene in athletic training; trust is placed in science; particular technical knowledge and technology/equipment override other ways of knowing and doing

Source: Adapted with permission from Barker-Ruchti, Barker, & Annerstedt (2014).

health and well-being, limiting family and social life, and adopting illegal actions (Andersson & Barker-Ruchti, 2018; Barker-Ruchti, Barker, Rynne, & Lee, 2012; Carless & Douglas, 2013; McMahon & Penney, 2012; Schubring & Thiel, 2015).

In terms of *how athletes are viewed*, scholars have linked the commodity orientation to the objectification of athletes (Cassidy, Jones, & Potrac, 2016). At the levels of coaching and training, this objectification turns athletes into resources that are often 'measured' before being included in a (junior) elite sport program. If identified as having the 'right' physical dispositions and talents, the athletes are selected to be prepared for elite athletic success. Most Western countries employ or are presently implementing and refining systems to produce predominantly physical and psychological measurements (e.g., body weight, height, predicted growth; psychological measurement) and use performance results to distinguish among athletes and predict future athletic performance (Barker-Ruchti, Schubring et al., 2017). A number of scholars have, however, critiqued the focus sport organisations and actors place on talent. The basis for their criticism is that research refutes the belief that measuring certain characteristics can predict future performance success (Anshel & Lidor, 2012; Collins & Bailey, 2013). In response, a number of researchers argue that talent identification and development is unethical because it violates the child's right to an open future (Miah & Rich, 2006) and that attention should instead be placed on the effective development of sport participants (Martindale, Collins, & Daubney, 2005; Martindale & Mortimer, 2011). The conception of 'talent' and the importance of physical and performance characteristics, however, remain deep-seated and influence sport organisations and actors to differentiate between potential and non-potential elite athletes.

At the level of spectators, athletes are also objectified. Research shows that both male and female spectators watch sport because it allows the (illicit) gazing at bodies and performance, satisfies needs and obsessions, and generates identification with athletes (Duncan & Brummett, 1989; Toffoletti & Mewett, 2012). Research further documents how the media represents predominantly successful athletes from a small range of sports (e.g., soccer players in Europe, rugby players in New Zealand, ice hockey players in Canada) (Cooky, Messner, & Musto, 2015). These athletes represent their country's most popular sport and are heroified for their strength, courage, and athletic performance because it is believed that they provide citizens with 'feel-good' moments (e.g., national identity, pride, positive mood) and images of national success (Grix, 2010). The celebration of male athletic success, however, marginalises others, including female, disabled, and LGBTQ+ individuals (Daddario, 1998; Markula, 2009). Generally speaking, the media narrative of non-male athletes centres around difference (rather than ability) by highlighting women's sexual appeal and need for (male) support (Barker-Ruchti, 2009), spectacularising freakishness and overcoming personal tragedy (for disabled athletes) (Beacom, French, & Kendall, 2016), and focusing on LGBTQ+ athletes' coming out (Chawansky & Francombe, 2011). In addition, as the media rarely reports on the actual struggles of becoming an elite athlete and leaves out representations of athletes who do not reach elite-level sport, its reports create an unrealistic view of what it means to become an elite athlete (Chambliss, 1989).

Lastly, at the level of athletes, most will accept that they need to adjust to rules and expectations, come to know and adapt to local sporting contexts (i.e., club rules, a coach's coaching philosophy), and endeavour to 'do their best'. Young elite athletes are particularly likely to conform to expectations, especially when moving from junior to senior performance levels. Hughes and Coakley (1991) even write, as do others (Johns & Johns, 2000; Pettersson, Pipping Ekström, & Berg, 2013), that such athletes may over-conform to norms and values, a positive deviance that includes such practices as accepting risks, training and competing with pain, and (over-)regulating their diet.

With regard to the *coach-athlete relationship*, scholars have linked the commodity orientation to an unequal power distribution between coaches and athletes.

If coaches regard their athletes as objects or resources, they tend to adopt the position of the expert and leader and treat their athletes as learners and followers. The coaching pedagogy involves instructions and manipulation, with some researchers equating this type of coaching to a process that normalises hierarchy between coaches and athletes (Jacobs, Smits, & Knoppers, 2016; Lang, 2010). In sports that practice early specialisation and are shaped by traditional gender ideals, such as women's artistic gymnastics, figure skating, and swimming, power inequalities are particularly pronounced, and athletes in these sports are at risk of experiencing violence (read also abuse) (McMahon & Penney, 2013; Smits, Jacobs, & Knoppers, 2016; Stirling & Kerr, 2009).

In terms of the *intended purpose of training*, the commodity orientation drives market-oriented training. Such training focuses on progression and performance, which in some sports are tightly prescribed with performance targets and even age categories (Barker-Ruchti, Kerr, Schubring, Cervin, & Nunomura, 2017). Slow or late learning is not part of this linear view of athlete development. The focus is predominantly on the individual and less so on coaching, resources, and the individual support and care that athletes may need in order to manage demanding training, schooling, and competition schedules. Particularly in sports where athletic performance success is associated with physical maturation (e.g., strength- and collision-based sports) and in artistic sports where maturation is considered a career-ending factor (i.e., women's artistic gymnastics), the focus on individual dispositions is pronounced. Research shows that athletes may be selected because of early maturation (Ashworth & Heyndels, 2007), excluded because of 'maturational deficits' (Malina, 2011), and asked to retire because they are perceived 'too old' (Kerr, Barker-Ruchti, Schubring, Cervin, & Nunomura, 2015).

Lastly, with regard to *epistemological orientation*, the commodity orientation takes empirical rationalism as a starting point to privileging scientific and technical knowledge. This means that today's coaches increasingly rely on specialized scientific training methods, particularly those derived from physiology, biomechanics, and equipment development (Svensson, 2016). An effect of this scientisation of training and coaching is that experiential, local, and intuitive knowledge is devalued (Kohe & Purdy, 2018). A further consequence is that the pedagogy of coaching is losing importance in comparison to the fact-driven analyses of performance. Certainly, the demands sport organisations and often also athletes place on coaches to work 'scientifically' can reduce coach confidence and motivation and can change the coach-athlete relationship.

Elite sport as a precarious context

The commodity orientation of (elite) sport and the influence it has on our understanding of its actors, relationships, practices, and knowledge have not gone without criticism. Importantly, scholars have outlined how the commodity orientation heightens risks of a context that is inherently fickle. Overbye (2018), for instance, outlines the internal and external risks elite sport entails, including the inherent competitiveness, performance pressure, risk of replacement, culture of risk-taking, physical and mental stress, financial instability, risk of injury, illness, declining performance, limited career frame, and stakeholder dependence. As a result, elite sport, by its nature, places athletes in precarious situations. Indeed, abundant scientific literature reveals the serious detriments elite sport precarity can have on athletes' health, well-being, retirement, and lives after sport (Baker, Safai, & Fraser-Thomas, 2014).

In addition to problematising elite sport's inherent risks, scholars and sport governing bodies have for many years debated elite sport's purpose of producing medals, especially in relation to national governing bodies' mandate to develop sport for all (Collins, 2009; Hanstad & Skille, 2010), problematic and illegal coaching and training practices (e.g., doping, different forms of abuse, match-fixing, corruption) (Barker et al., 2014; Cleret, McNamee, & Page, 2015), effects on athletes' health and well-being and on their identity (Baker et al., 2014; Barker-Ruchti, Rynne, Lee, & Barker, 2014), and consequences for knowledge and coaching (Kohe & Purdy, 2018). This body of literature agrees that elite sport is an 'expensive' phenomenon that serves few.

Lastly, research has recently started to critique commodity-driven elite sport by showing that not all elite sport settings are driven by a market logic. Research into Swedish elite sport, for instance, has shown that elite sport settings can focus on long-term athletic development, holistic athlete development, and enjoyment (Annerstedt & Lindgren, 2014; Barker-Ruchti et al., 2015; Grahn, 2014). However, the Swedish elite sport setting and, to a certain extent, those in other Nordic countries (Andersen & Ronglan, 2012) are unique, as they are shaped by socialist history and politics, a strong focus on sport-for-all, and a lack of centralised sport systems. Most other countries that value and invest in elite sport are not influenced by a socialist legacy. Thus, the global sporting arms race is dominated by economic revenue and medal tallies.

Conclusion

Contemporary elite sport is shaped by a commodity orientation that focuses on money and medals. This outcome logic shapes the purpose of sport and the views, relationships, practices, and knowledge that organisations and actors adopt and participate in. The resulting landscape is precarious and risks athletes' health, well-being, and lives after sport. Athletes and other participants that enter and perform the activities of this landscape, however, will learn to adapt to elite sport and the way of life this context demands. The learning this adaptation entails (read learning as self-development) 'makes' elite athletes.

References

Andersen, S. S., & Ronglan, L. T. (2012). Elite sports in Nordic countries: Perspectives and challenges. In S. S. Andersen & L. T. Ronglan (Eds.), *Nordic elite sport: Same ambitions—Different tracks* (pp. 11–24). Oslo: Universitetsforlaget.

Andersson, R., & Barker-Ruchti, N. (2018). Career paths of Swedish top-level women soccer players. *Soccer & Society*, 1–15.

Annerstedt, C., & Lindgren, E.-C. (2014). Caring as an important foundation in coaching for social sustainability—A case study of a successful Swedish coach in high performance sport. *Reflective Practice*, *15*(1), 27–39.

Anshel, M. H., & Lidor, R. (2012). Talent detection programs in sport: The questionable use of psychological measures. *Journal of Sport Behavior*, *35*(3), 239.

Ashworth, J., & Heyndels, B. (2007). Selection bias and peer effects in team sports: The effect of age grouping on earnings of German soccer players. *Journal of Sports Economics*, 8(4), 355–377.

Baker, J., Safai, P., & Fraser-Thomas, J. (2014). *Health and elite sport: Is high performance sport a healthy pursuit?* London: Routledge.

Barker, D., Barker-Ruchti, N., Rynne, S. B., & Lee, J. (2014). 'Just do a little more': Examining expertise in high performance sport from a sociocultural learning perspective. *Reflective Practice*, *15*(1), 92–105.

Barker, D., Barker-Ruchti, N., Wals, A. E. J., & Tinning, R. (2014). High performance sport and sustainability: A contradiction of terms? *Reflective Practice*, *15*(1), 1–11.

Barker-Ruchti, N. (2009). The media as an authorising practice of femininity: Swiss newspaper coverage of Karin Thürig's bronze medal performance in road cycling. In P. Markula (Ed.), *Olympic women and the media: International perspectives* (pp. 214–231). New York: Palgrave.

Barker-Ruchti, N., Barker, D., & Annerstedt, C. (2014). Techno-rational knowing and phronesis: The professional practice of one middle-distance running coach. *Reflective Practice*, *15*(1), 53–65.

Barker-Ruchti, N., Barker, D., Rynne, S. B., & Lee, J. (2012). 'One door closes, a next door opens up somewhere': The learning of one Olympic synchronised swimmer. *Reflective Practice*, *13*(3), 373–385.

Barker-Ruchti, N., Kerr, R., Schubring, A., Cervin, G., & Nunomura, M. (2017). 'Gymnasts are like wine, they get better with age': Towards a pedagogy of effective athlete development in women's artistic gymnastics. *Quest*, 69(3), 345–365.

Barker-Ruchti, N., Rynne, S. B., Lee, J., & Barker, D. (2014). Athlete learning in Olympic sport: A cultural analysis. *Sports Coaching Review*, *3*(2), 162–178.

Barker-Ruchti, N., Schubring, A., Aarresola, O., Kerr, R., Grahn, K., & McMahon, J. (2017). Producing success: A critical analysis of athlete development governance in six countries. *International Journal of Sport Policy and Politics*, *10*(2), 215–234.

Beacom, A., French, L., & Kendall, S. (2016). Reframing impairment? Continuity and change in media representations of disability through the Paralympic Games. *International Journal of Sport Communication*, 9(1), 42–62.

Carless, D., & Douglas, K. (2013). Living, resisting, and playing the part of athlete: Narrative tensions in elite sport. *Psychology of Sport and Exercise*, *14*(5), 701–708.

Cassidy, T., Jones, R. L., & Potrac, P. (2016). *Understanding sports coaching: The pedagogical, social and cultural foundations of coaching practice* (3rd edition) [Electronic version]. New York: Routledge.

Chambliss, D. F. (1989). The mundanity of excellence: An ethnographic report on stratification and Olympic swimmers. *Sociological Theory*, *7*(1), 70–86.

Chawansky, M., & Francombe, J. M. (2011). Cruising for Olivia: Lesbian celebrity and the cultural politics of coming out in sport. *Sociology of Sport Journal*, 28(4), 461–477.

Cleret, L., McNamee, M., & Page, S. (2015). 'Sports integrity' needs sports ethics (and sports philosophers and sports ethicists too). *Sport, Ethics and Philosophy*, 9(1), 1–5.

Collins, D., & Bailey, R. (2013). 'Scienciness' and the allure of second-hand strategy in talent identification and development. *International Journal of Sport Policy and Politics*, 5(2), 183–191.

Collins, M. (2009). Public policies on sports development: Can mass and elite sport hold together? In V. Girginov (Ed.), *Management of sports development* (pp. 59–88). Oxford, UK: Elsevier.

Commission of the European Communities. (2007). *White paper on sport.* Retrieved from https://eur-lex.europa.eu/legal-content/EN/TXT/HTML/?uri=LEGISSUM:l35010&from=EN. Brussels:

Cooky, C., Messner, M. A., & Musto, M. (2015). 'It's dude time!': A quarter century of excluding women's sports in televised news and highlight shows. *Communication and Sport*, 3(3), 261–287.

Daddario, G. (1998). *Women's sport and spectacle: Gendered television coverage and the Olympic Games*. Westport, CT: Praeger.

Douglas, K., & Carless, D. (2014). *Life story research in sport: Understanding the experiences of elite and professional athletes through narrative*. London: Routledge.

Duncan, M. C., & Brummett, B. (1989). Types and sources of spectating pleasure in televised sports. *Sociology of Sport Journal*, 6(3), 195–211.

Grahn, K. (2014). Alternative discourses in the coaching of high performance youth sport: Exploring language of sustainability. *Reflective Practice*, 15(1), 40–52.

Grix, J. (2010). From hobbyhorse to mainstream: Using sport to understand British politics. *British Politics*, 5(1), 114–129.

Hanstad, D. V., & Skille, E. Å. (2010). Does elite sport develop mass sport?: A Norwegian case study. *Scandinavian Sport Studies Forum*, 1, 51–68.

Haut, J., Prohl, R., & Emrich, E. (2016). Nothing but medals? Attitudes towards the importance of Olympic success. *International Review for the Sociology of Sport*, 51(3), 332–348.

Hughes, R., & Coakley, J. (1991). Positive deviance among athletes: The implications of overconformity to the sport ethic. *Sociology of Sport Journal*, 8(4), 307–325.

Jacobs, F., Smits, F., & Knoppers, A. (2016). 'You don't realize what you see!': The institutional context of emotional abuse in elite youth sport. *Sport in Society*, 20(1), 126–143.

Jeanrenaud, C., & Késenne, S. (2006). *The economics of sport and the media*. Cheltenham, UK: Edward Elgar.

Johns, D. P., & Johns, J. S. (2000). Surveillance, subjectivism and technologies of power: An analysis of the discursive practice of high-performance sport. *International Review for the Sociology of Sport*, 35(2), 219–234.

Kerr, R., Barker-Ruchti, N., Schubring, A., Cervin, G., & Nunomura, M. (2015). *Coming of Age: Towards Best Practice is Women's Artistic Gymnastics*. LEaP Research Report Nr. 37, Lincoln University, Canterbury, New Zealand. http://researcharchive.lincoln.ac.nz/bitstream/10182/6515/3/Leap%2037-Coming-of-age.pdf.

Kohe, G. Z., & Purdy, L. G. (2018). Analytical attractions and the techno-continuum: Conceptualising data obsessions and consequences in elite sport. *Sport, Education and Society*, 1–14.

Lang, M. (2010). Intensive training in youth sports: A new abuse of power. In K. K. P. Vanhoutte, G. Fairbairn, & M. Lang (Eds.), *Bullying and the abuse of power* (pp. 57–64). Freeland, UK: Inter-Disciplinary Press.

Malina, R. M. (2011). Skeletal age and age verification in youth sport. *Sports Medicine*, *41*(11), 925–947.

Markula, P. (2009). *Olympic women and the media: International perspectives*. New York: Palgrave.

Martindale, R., Collins, D., & Daubney, J. (2005). Talent development: A guide for practice and research within sport. *Quest*, *57*(4), 353–375.

Martindale, R., & Mortimer, P. (2011). Talent development environments: Key considerations for effective practice. In D. J. Collins, A. Abbott, & H. Richards (Eds.), *Performance psychology: A practitioner's guide* (pp. 65–84). London: Churchill Livingstone.

McMahon, J. A., & Penney, D. (2012). (Self-) surveillance and (self-) regulation: Living by fat numbers within and beyond a sporting culture. *Qualitative Research in Sport, Exercise and Health*, *5*(2), 1–22.

McMahon, J. A., & Penney, D. (2013). Body pedagogies, coaching and culture: Three Australian swimmers' lived experiences. *Physical Education and Sport Pedagogy*, *18*(3), 317–335.

Miah, A., & Rich, E. (2006). Genetic tests for ability?: Talent identification and the value of an open future. *Sport, Education and Society*, *11*(3), 259–273.

Milano, M., & Chelladurai, P. (2011). Gross domestic sport product: The size of the sport industry in the United States. *Journal of Sport Management*, *25*(1), 24–35.

Oakley, B., & Green, M. (2001). The production of Olympic champions: International perspectives on elite sport development systems. *European Journal for Sports Management*, 83–105.

Overbye, M. (2018). An (un) desirable trade of harms? How elite athletes might react to medically supervised 'doping' and their considerations of side-effects in this situation. *International Journal of Drug Policy*, 55, 14–30.

Peters, S., & Wals, A. E. J. (2013). *Learning and knowing in pursuit of sustainability: Concepts and tools for trans-disciplinary environmental research*. New York: Peter Lang.

Pettersson, S., Pipping Ekström, M., & Berg, C. (2013). Practices of weight regulation among elite athletes in combat sports: A matter of mental advantage? *Journal of Athletic Training*, *48*(1), 99–108.

Riordan, J. (2002). *The international politics of sport in the twentieth century*. London: Routledge.

Schubring, A., & Thiel, A. (2015). Coping with growth in adolescent elite sport. *Sociology of Sport Journal*, *31*(3), 304–326.

Smits, F., Jacobs, F., & Knoppers, A. (2016). 'Everything revolves around gymnastics': Athletes and parents make sense of elite youth sport. *Sport in Society*, *20*(1), 66–83.

Stirling, A. E., & Kerr, G. A. (2009). Abused athletes' perceptions of the coach-athlete relationship. *Sport in Society*, *12*(2), 227–239.

Svensson, D. (2016). Technologies of sportification: Practice, theory and co-production of training knowledge in cross-country skiing since the 1950s. *European Studies in Sports History*, *9*(1), 141–160.

Toffoletti, K., & Mewett, P. (2012). 'Oh yes, he is hot': Female football fans and the sexual objectification of sportsmen's bodies. In K. Toffoletti & P. Mewett (Eds.), *Sport and its female fans* (pp. 99–114). London: Routledge.

Wals, A. E. J., & Jickling, B. (2002). 'Sustainability' in higher education: From doublethink and newspeak to critical thinking and meaningful learning. *International Journal of Sustainability in Higher Education*, *3*(3), 221–232.

Walsh, A. J., & Giulianotti, R. (2001). This sporting mammon: A normative critique of the commodification of sport. *Journal of the Philosophy of Sport*, *28*(1), 53–77.

Chapter 2

Existing theories of learning

Natalie Barker-Ruchti

In this chapter, I present three learning conceptualizations that have guided research on athlete learning in elite sport. I use three metaphors to present these conceptualizations: *learning as acquisition*, *learning as participation*, and *learning as storying*. The use of the acquisition and participation metaphors has been a popular way to illustrate basic assumptions of learning (for a detailed discussion of the metaphoric understanding of cognitive and participatory learning theories, see Sfard, 1998); learning as storying is an emerging metaphor in elite sport research. In what follows, I use the three learning metaphors as starting points to demonstrate how the theories' different scientific traditions—positivism, social constructivism, and socio-narratology, respectively—conceptualise knowledge, process of learning, and knowledge transfer and to discuss the athlete learning research that the traditions have generated. In doing this below, I employ the vocabularies researchers have used to write about learning from their different scientific vantage points.

Acquisition metaphor—Learning as individual cognition

Acquisition represents the historically dominant metaphor that scientists have used to understand learning. A central assumption that underlies this metaphor is that knowledge is 'an entity that is acquired in one task setting and conveyed to other task settings' (Cobb & Bowers, 1999, p. 5). This view of knowledge as an obtainable, possessable, and transferable commodity has theorised learning as an 'accumulation of material goods', the learner as 'a container to be filled with certain materials', and the leader as an expert who imparts these commodities (Sfard, 1998, p. 5).

The acquisition metaphor suggests that learning is a cognitive-neural process. The brain represents the location of learning, with the central nervous system being the mode that transports information to the brain. At its basis, this mode is understood to include an internal information-processing mechanism that follows a stimulus-mediation-response scheme, which relates stimuli in the form of instructions, descriptions, and demonstrations to individuals' responses (Anderson, Reder, & Simon, 1997). Through accumulation, refinement, and combination of such stimuli, individuals develop physical cognitive structures in the brain (Sfard, 1998). These structures explain how a person can come to own knowledge, skills, concepts, ideas, and schema. Some cognitive researchers acknowledge that personal traits enhance individuals' possible stimulus-mediation-responses. For those with favourable traits (e.g., intelligence), the acquisition perspective accepts that individuals can come to excel in grasping knowledge and developing skills (Sfard, 1998). For those with traits that constrain acquisition responses, learning may be limited, requiring significant time, support, and effort in order to achieve progression.

Cognitive scholars recognise the influence of contextual factors (Cobb & Bowers, 1999). These factors include learners' interactions with experts, literal positioning in formalised learning contexts, relationships with others, the time and opportunities provided for learning, and the scope and quality of the instruction they receive during a time of learning or training (Cobb & Bowers, 1999). The overarching assumption is that if a learning situation provides these conditions, the development of cognitive structures is possible.

In terms of transfer of knowledge, the acquisition metaphor assumes that, as described above, transfer of knowledge and skills is possible from one person to another, commonly through instruction and demonstration by an expert. The second form of transfer refers to individuals taking knowledge/skills from place to place or from situation to situation. As individuals are seen to develop cognitive structures in their brain, which remain inscribed in healthy individuals, they are thought to carry these structures to other locations, where they are able to recall and use the inscribed knowledge and skills.

The acquisition metaphor represents the most popular perspective researchers have used to understand elite athletes' learning; specifically, they have looked at this learning in terms of (a) movement capability, (b) sport expertise, and (c) life skills. With regard to *movement capability*, motor learning science equates learning to computer programming and most closely adopts the stimulus-mediation-response scheme. The notion is essentially the idea that through instructions, demonstrations of desired outcomes, repetitive exercises, and corrective feedback, athletes acquire 'sets of cognitive instructions, or "schema", which they can then "run" at the appropriate time' (Barker, Bergentoft, & Nyberg, 2017, p. 6). Scholars suggest that this encoding process begins when children's movement programs are immature or rudimentary, at which time the practice of fundamental motor or movement skills is seen as necessary to develop more complicated physical skills later on (Baker, Côté, & Abernethy, 2003b; Côté, Baker, & Abernethy, 2003).

Researchers have also given attention to the development of *sport expertise* in order to understand how some athletes can excel and others are not able to reach elite sport standards. In this research, scholars focus on physiological and cognitive adaptations, with the former relating to movement capability and skill acquisition and the latter to information-processing strategies. For perceptual or cognitive sports in particular, expertise is hailed as important, as athletes must plan, act, monitor, evaluate, adapt, predict, and anticipate while performing, each of which requires a number of skills, mechanisms, and processes in order to achieve proficiency (Ericsson & Delaney, 1999; Ericsson & Kintsch, 1995).

Both movement capability and sport expertise build on the idea of 'step-by-step' learning (Abbott, Collins, Martindale, & Sowerby, 2002; Gagné, 2004; Martindale, Collins, & Daubney, 2005). This association with movement progression portrays learning as incremental and the amount of training, immediate practice-related factors (e.g., quality of instruction and feedback, opportunities to practice), and physical and personal traits as influencing learning tempo and outcomes (Baker, Horton, Robertson-Wilson, & Wall, 2003). The 10-year rule, which refers to a long-term commitment to intense training, has been proposed as a minimum requirement of time to reach elite-level performance (Ericsson, Krampe, & Tesch-Römer, 1993). In more recent years, scholars have moved away from the argument of time to that of practice needing to be deliberate, meaning it 'demands full concentration and often requires problem-solving and better methods of performing the tasks' (Ericsson, 2008, p. 991). Deliberate practice strategies that research has shown to have beneficial effects are video training, competition, group exercises, and individualised coach instruction (Baker, Côté, & Abernethy, 2003a). Further, to prevent learning plateauing, Ericsson (1996) proposed that training should consist of well-defined tasks, appropriate levels of difficulty, informative feedback, opportunities for repetition, and correction.

With regard to physical and personal traits, a number of factors have received scientific attention. Research has shown, for instance, that athletes' month of birth influences movement learning (Helsen, Hodges, Van Winckel, & Starkes, 2000). This 'relative age effect' (Nolan & Howell, 2010) is particularly relevant for sports where size and strength matter, as it allows those born early in the year more time to grow and mature, and to practice and thus receive more coaching attention, than those born later on. In contrast to these positive age effects, growth and maturation may disrupt progression because they can cause injuries and growth problems (Committee on Sports Medicine Fitness, 2000; Schubring & Thiel, 2014). During an adolescent growth spurt, for instance, the immature skeleton is 'less resistant to tensile, shear and compressive forces than either mature bone or more immature prepubescent bone' (DiFiori et al., 2014, p. 287). Gallahue and Donnelly (2003) consider such health problems to cause 'proficiency barriers', which may restrict an athlete's learning and progression to more specialized sports skills.

A further assumption is that talent or giftedness determines learning extent and outcome (Helsen et al., 2000; Tranckle & Cushion, 2006; van Rossum & Gagné, 2005). The underlying assumption is that humans inherit genetic dispositions that favour certain activities, such as the perfect or absolute pitch that may predispose individuals for music (Gregersen, Kowalsky, Kohn, & Marvin, 2001) or the aerobic fitness and cardiac performance that may predispose others for certain sports (Bouchard, Malina, & Pérusse, 1997). As a result, a large body of literature proposes systems, models, and procedures to identify and develop athletic talent

(Abbott et al., 2002; Andersen, Bjorndal, & Ronglan, 2015; De Bosscher, Shibil, Westerbeek, & van Bottenburg, 2015; Henriksen, Stambulova, & Roessler, 2010). The Long-Term Athlete Development Model (Ltad Model) (Balyi & Hamilton, 2004), the Foundations, Talent, Elite, Mastery Framework (FTEM Framework) (Gulbin, Croser, Morley, & Weissensteiner, 2013), and the Developmental Model of Sport Participation (DMSP) (Côté & Vierimaa, 2014) are three popular conceptions that model performance development by building on the acquisition understanding.

Lastly, with regard to *life skills*, scholars have defined such skills as positive youth development, social-emotional growth, and life skills development (Gould & Carson, 2008). Within these understandings, research has focused on practical and cognitive skills such as stress management (Gould, Eklund, & Jackson, 1993), decision-making (Davids, Araújo, Correia, & Vilar, 2013), teamwork (Bloom & Stevens, 2004), motivation (Naber, 2006), and sport-specific cognitive skills (Ward et al., 2008). Life skills development research has also examined interpersonal competencies, including caring and ethical values, self-worth, and positive future outlook (Gould & Carson, 2008). As with movement capability and expertise, the learning of life skills is understood to require intentional teaching and fostering through demonstration, modelling, and practice. Gould and Carson's (2008) model of coaching life skills through sport acknowledges the direct influence that coach characteristics, teaching strategies, and indirect contextual factors (e.g., demands of a sport, modelling by others) have on athletes' identities, sense of belonging, self-worth, and perception of life skill utility. The assumption is that, should the direct and indirect effects be low, positive learning and utilisation outside of sport are reduced and may actually cause negative outcomes such as injury, disordered eating, dropping out, stress, and burnout (Gould & Carson, 2008). Formal interventions to teach life skills have thus been popular. Consensus on how sport-based programs can effectively teach life skills, however, is still missing (Holt & Neely, 2011).

With regard to transfer, cognitive sport scientists argue that since skills can be obtained (i.e., engraved in the brain), they allow individuals to transport them from one place or situation to another. Some research has shown, however, that the transfer of skills between motor tasks is small and only the case if activities are very similar (Schmidt & Young, 1987). The transfer of perceptual and cognitive expertise in particular depends on skill simplicity and similarity of domains and situations (Baker et al., 2003b). Indeed, life skills research shows that transferability cannot be assumed; rather, it requires transferability skills (e.g., utilisation knowledge, confidence in ability to apply skills elsewhere) and transfer support.

In summary, the acquisition metaphor of learning creates a cognitive view of learning. It focuses on the mind as the location of learning, the neurological system as the mode through which learning takes place, and the learning outcomes as knowledge and skill acquirement. While dominant, this perspective has received criticism. At a philosophical level, a key critique is that the acquisition metaphor implicitly splits the mind from the body and therefore excludes the individual's embodied experiences of perceiving herself, other persons and things, and the learning and the identities (or selves) this constructs (Illeris, 2018). From an epistemological perspective, the criticism has been that the acquisition metaphor disregards the (reflexive) influence ideologies, social structures, relations of power, *and* individuals have on the construction of identities (or selves) (Hodkinson, Biesta, & James, 2008). Lastly, scholars have criticised the acquisition understanding because they regard it as being unable to account for social learning and thus the shaping of individuals' sense of who they are.

Participation metaphor—Learning as situational

The understanding of learning as situational emerged during the early to mid-20th century from scholars such as John Dewey, Jean Piaget, and Lev Vygotsky. Following are the key ways in which the participation metaphor differs from the acquisition metaphor: Scholars' understanding of learning as situational defines knowledge as socially constructed, the mind as not separate from the body, and learning as a continuous social process that applies to everybody (Hodkinson, Biesta, & James, 2008). In her in-depth discussion of the acquisition and participation metaphors, Sfard (1998) notes that the emergence of learning as participation changed the vocabulary used to describe learning from a reception of commodities to a 'doing and knowing' and 'knowing and doing'.

A key theory that emerged from the view of learning as knowing-doing is the 'social theory of learning' or 'situated learning theory' (Lave & Wenger, 1991; Light, 2011). This social conceptualisation assumes that learning occurs in 'communities of practice', which represent 'groups of people who share a concern or a passion for something they do and learn how to do it better as they interact regularly' (Wenger, 2011, p. 1). In these communities, levels of expertise position individuals. Metaphorically speaking, individuals with limited expertise are positioned at the periphery of a community, while experts enjoy a more central or influential position. These positions are not fixed, and as learning occurs continuously, they may change as novices develop into experts. Lave and Wenger (1991) understand this change in positioning as a *movement* from the periphery (being a novice) to the centre of a community of practice (being an expert). This movement is likened to apprenticeship learning, which conceptualises how a beginner may experience her participation in a community until she is a fully independent participant (Fuller, Hodkinson, Hodkinson, & Unwin, 2005). This learning gives community members a sense of belonging, commitment, and identity. These effects relate to a particular community of practice and may converge or conflict with the effects of other communities, a challenge participants must negotiate in order to create a coherent sense of self (Handley, Sturdy, Fincham, & Clark, 2006).

Learning as participation in communities of practice is understood as progressive in terms of improvement as learners develop expertise based on experiences and learning, in terms of social immersion as learners become full members of a social context, and, lastly, in terms of distancing when experts lose social importance (Hager & Hodkinson, 2009). As a result, rather than defining learning as a temporally fixed process of obtaining specific commodities, the participation metaphor describes learning as a continuous social process in which individuals subsume learning through practices without predetermined learning outcomes. This interaction allows focus on how individuals continuously adapt to, fit into, and affect constantly changing contexts, particularly regarding the initiation and education of learners in professional contexts or workplaces (Hodkinson & Hodkinson, 2004; Lave & Wenger, 1991). Metaphors to describe learning that emerged from this understanding include 'learning as activity', 'apprenticeship learning', 'legitimate peripheral participation', and 'generational encounters' (Lave & Wenger, 1991; Wenger, 1998).

In terms of transfer, the participation metaphor does not assume that individuals transport knowledge or skills from one context to another. In fact, a number of scholars have critiqued the idea of transportation (Lobato, 2006). Rather, scholars advocating learning as participation propose that instead of the theoretical point of departure being cognitive inscriptions, it is a location within which an individual has participated. For individuals that move to another social context, even if this context is similar to any previous ones, learning will be necessary. Transfer concepts that scholars have developed from the situated perspective are 'movement' (Lave & Wenger, 1991) and 'transition' (Beach, 1999).

In sport science, a number of researchers have drawn on the participation metaphor to understand elite athletes' learning. Informal learning in relation to cultural ideals and expectations, as well as others within sport communities of practice, has received particular attention (Fitzclarence, Hickey, & Matthews, 1997; Galipeau & Trudel, 2006). This research demonstrated that the participants in a community of practice learn by getting to know its cultural specificities, by participating in its activities, and by interacting with those within the community as they observe one another, communicate with one another, work together, and take on different roles and responsibilities. This research has examined different types of sporting communities. At the level of a sports club, Light's (2006, 2010) research demonstrated that training, competitions, and social events (e.g., fund-raising events, end-of-year celebrations) represent cultural activities that teach participants social skills, moral values, and life skills. With regard to specific sport teams, Christensen, Laursen, and Sørensen (2011) and Hegde and Standal (2013) found that belonging represents an important characteristic of a community of practice. On the one hand, the scholars found that belonging meant that new members of teams underwent a period of being a 'rookie', which only ended once older players retired and the novices could move into freed positions (Hegde & Standal, 2013). On the other hand, subcommunities of practice specific to player positions (e.g., goalie community of practice) influenced how players belonged (Christensen et al., 2011). The sense of belonging the players experienced influenced their feelings of communal acceptance, the roles that they felt they could accept and execute, and their athletic performance trajectories.

A community of practice can also be a two-athlete unit. Lund, Ravn, and Christensen (2012, 2013), in studying the learning of synchronised trampoline jumpers and double scull rowers, found that the athletes learnt from each other, particularly through synchronising their movements. Jumping and rowing both demand rhythm, which required heightened awareness of one's own and one's partner's actions. These kinaesthetic and empathic demands affected the interactions between the sets of athletes, providing a source of learning that the athletes described as having instilled a 'sixth sense' necessary for peak performance. In both the trampoline and the rowing cases, however, one athlete was experienced and one a novice. The 'generational encounters' (Wenger, 1998) this created also caused different degrees of independence, as well as interpersonal hierarchies and friction (Lund et al., 2012). In so doing, the encounter affected both the experts and the novices, influencing them to learn from each other in unexpected ways (Downey, 2005).

With regard to transfer between communities of practice, research on athletes moving from one context to another, including out of sport, confirms that athletes cannot simply leave their athletic selves in elite sport. If the communities differ considerably, adjustment will be significant. Research I have conducted with Schubring (2016) followed a young gymnast who needed to leave her home club's athlete-centred atmosphere for her country's national training centre. The move required her to make considerable changes to self and practices (i.e., learning) in order to adjust to the national team coach's authoritarian coaching style. In a similar case, an elite softballer, during a break from her sport, participated in lower-level field hockey. She experienced both alienation because her fellow hockey players did not take training as seriously as she did and frustration because she could not effectively engage in the hockey community (Barker-Ruchti, Rynne, Lee, & Barker, 2014). The research into both the gymnast's and the softballer's experiences of participation in new communities showed how their identities required adjustment. For athletes who retire from sport, this lack of fit and need for adaptation and learning are heightened (Barker-Ruchti, Barker, Rynne, & Lee, 2012; Barker, Barker-Ruchti, Rynne, & Lee, 2014). In many cases, athletes experience their movement out of sport and the necessary learning as difficult.

In summary, the participation metaphor of learning represents a social view of learning. It considers local contexts and the social relations and practices within these and provides a perspective for thinking about how individuals continuously learn through their participation in such settings. In so doing, the metaphor describes the learner as an integral part of communities of practice and learning and knowing as connected to context. With regard to sport, this perspective has stimulated research on particular cases of sporting settings, people units, and individuals' positions within sporting contexts. While this insight illuminates the complex and contextually influenced nature of athlete learning, the participation metaphor has limitations. For one, the metaphor's focus on location overlooks individual subjectivity (i.e., life histories, dispositions, intelligible action). This omission limits the theory's capacity to conceptualise how individuals' meaning making relates to learning (Billett, 2001; Hodkinson & Hodkinson, 2004). For two, the participation understanding underestimates the importance of direct and effective coaching and repetitive practice, which represent important aspects of elite sport training (Owen-Pugh, 2013). For three, the learning as participation metaphor pays little attention to the embodied learning process and thus does not provide a micro-level perspective of learning (Rambusch & Ziemke, 2005). Lastly, much of the existing research has adopted 'a thin temporal slice of human experience rather than a longitudinal perspective' (Bloomer & Hodkinson, 2000, p. 584), thus omitting the nature and processes of cultural and individual change.

Narration metaphor—Learning as storying

Narrative sociologists began to recognise the importance of individuals' storying during the 1980s. The idea of 'homo narrans' (Fisher, 1984) assumes that humans are storied beings and that stories represent a primary form of knowledge through which humans organize their experiences into temporally meaningful episodes. Healthy individuals story their lives coherently and causally. This narration represents a means for individuals to learn, understand, and make sense of their social worlds (Hydén, 1997; Somers, 1994) and to see possibilities for life through extending and developing their identities and horizons.

In terms of the process of learning, narrative learning theory assumes that individuals learn as they make meaning of the stories they hear and as they story and re-story their lives. This storying has several effects: For one, it brings 'coherence to the chaos of experience that bombards us daily' (Clark & Rossiter, 2008, p. 62). For two, creating 'narrative threads' crafts sense of self (Carless & Douglas, 2013; Clark & Rossiter, 2008). This crafting is, on the one hand, collective, as the stories individuals hear inform them of dominant 'social, public, and cultural narratives' that they have available (Somers, 1994, p. 614). Once individuals have learnt what narrative scripts they can and should follow, they align their stories to these threads. On the other hand, narrative learning theory posits that individuals do not follow *the* narrative but rather continuously re-create their narratives as they enter, move within, and exit social contexts; hear stories; and story their lives (Hydén, 1997). Clark and Rossiter (2008) call this 'work to story a story', which individuals do through thinking, talking to others, or writing about stories.

Narrative disruption is an important concept within the narration metaphor. Much research has focused on how unexpected events dislocate individuals' narratives, the reactions they may adopt in response, and the 'narrative wreckage' this may cause (Frank, 1995). The idea is that individuals are bound to experience disruptions (e.g., illness, injuries, misfortune), and while some events create minor deviations or temporary dislocations from the narrative script being followed, others demand individuals to re-create their narratives. In such cases, Carless and Douglas (2013) see two possible responses: The individual modifies her behaviour to fit the dominant narrative, *or* she modifies the story by creating an alternative thread. Neither option is easy and without personal consequences.

In terms of transfer, and similar to the acquisition and participation metaphors, the narration metaphor theorises narrative transfer between people: As a narrator tells a story, those who listen to the story create meaning and understanding (Clark & Rossiter, 2008). This transfer of knowledge, however, represents a process through which those telling and those listening to stories co-construct what a story means to them. The narration metaphor also conceptualises transfer in terms of an individual moving from one social context to another. Similar to the participation metaphor, the 'abandoning of a narrative' (Douglas & Carless, 2009) when moving from one context to another requires individuals to let go of one narrative thread and to find and adapt other (suitable) threads (for an in-depth description of narrative thread, see Whiffin, Bailey, Ellis-Hill, & Jarrett, 2014). Such transitions can be laborious and time-consuming.

In sport science, researchers have employed the narrative metaphor to understand how athletes (a) experience injuries, (b) develop athletic careers, and (c) retire from elite sport. Kleiber and Brock (1992; Brock and Kleiber, 1994) were among the first to use narratology to examine athletes' *injuries*. Their research showed that injuries threaten and even disrupt athletes' identities but that through the narration of an injury as a commonplace phenomenon in sport, they can maintain their athletic identity, position, and status within the sporting community. In terms of how *athletes develop athletic careers*, narrative research has shown that it is important for elite athletes to develop and maintain athletic identity. Douglas and Carless (2014) are key authors who have identified several narrative scripts that athletes follow when preparing for and participating in elite sport. The dominant script these two authors recognised is the 'performance narrative', which is the 'single-minded dedication to sport performance to the exclusion of other areas of life and self' (Douglas & Carless, 2009, p. 215). Research has demonstrated the extreme lengths athletes go to in order to align their lives to the performance script, with results indicating that the alignment forecloses identity, compromises education, limits family time and social relationships, and harms long-term well-being (Barker-Ruchti & Schubring, 2016; Carless & Douglas, 2013; Kuhlin, Barker-Ruchti, & Stewart, submitted). The other two narratives Douglas and Carless (2006) identify, the discovery and relational narratives, are much less common.[1] However, Carless and Douglas (2013) show that athletes resist the performance narrative either by explicitly following the discovery or the relational narrative or by moving between narrative scripts depending on what stories others consider most appropriate.

Narrative researchers have also studied how athletes *retire from elite sport*. Again, Douglas and Carless (2009; Carless & Douglas, 2009) have demonstrated, as have other researchers (Barker-Ruchti & Schubring, 2016; Barker et al., 2014; Cavallerio, Wadey, & Wagstaff, 2017; Kuhlin et al., submitted), that elite athletes who identify with and follow the performance narrative experience narrative wreckage when withdrawing from the sporting contexts they participate in. This period of still living the performance narrative but having left the elite sport context was evidenced as traumatic in the researched cases, and significant support was required in order to find a new narrative script to align with.

In summary, the narration metaphor represents both cognitive and social perspectives of learning as together they point to the individual process of storying as the learning process and to the dominant narrative scripts that are available. In this sense, these perspectives provide a bridge between the stories told by specific persons and 'the dominant discourses and narratives [i.e., narrative threads or scripts] within which we all collectively live our lives' (McLeod, 2006, p. 207). However, the narration metaphor can be regarded as limited: Although it theorises the learning process through aspects of storying, this form of learning does not explicitly focus on the embodying nature of learning or identity formation (Bresler, 2006). Similar to the participation metaphor, existing literature is limited in providing a cognitive perspective of learning. Lastly, as pointed out by Nünning (2012), narratology is still limited in providing a narrative or narrativist theory of culture or a cultural theory of narrative.

Conclusion

In this chapter, I have presented three learning metaphors that have been influential in guiding research on learning in elite sport: learning as acquisition, learning as participation, and learning as storying. For each of these metaphors, its underlying assumptions of knowledge, learning process, and transfer of knowledge have allowed sport science researchers to produce knowledge about learning, yet each perspective has limitations. The acquisition metaphor provides a cognitive perspective that shows individual cognition and neurological functioning. The participation metaphor, in contrast, prioritises local contexts and communities, creating a social view of learning. Lastly, the narration metaphor provides both an individual and a social perspective by understanding learning as influenced by socially constructed narrative scripts and individual storying; yet it comes up short regarding the embodied and cultural nature of learning. On this basis of possibilities and limitations, I present in the following chapter a fourth metaphor of learning, *learning as becoming*, to develop a means to think about athletes' learning in elite sport.

Note

1. The relational narrative tells of athletes participating in elite sport for social reasons; the discovery narrative attributes participation to personal development purposes. These two narratives are much less common compared to the performance narrative (Carless & Douglas, 2012).

References

Abbott, A., Collins, D., Martindale, R. J., & Sowerby, K. (2002). *Talent identification and development: An academic review*. Edinburgh: sportscotland.

Andersen, S. S., Bjorndal, C. T., & Ronglan, L. T. (2015). The ecology of talent development in the Nordic elite sport model. In S. S. Andersen, B. Houlihan, & L. T. Ronglan (Eds.), *Managing elite sport systems: Research and practice* (pp. 49–66). London: Routledge.

Anderson, J. R., Reder, L. M., & Simon, H. A. (1997). Situative versus cognitive perspectives: Form versus substance. *Educational Researcher, 26*(1), 18–21.

Baker, J., Côté, J., & Abernethy, B. (2003a). Learning from the experts: Practice activities of expert decision makers in sport. *Research Quarterly for Exercise and Sport, 74*(3), 342–347.

Baker, J., Côté, J., & Abernethy, B. (2003b). Sport-specific practice and the development of expert decision-making in team ball sports. *Journal of Applied Sport Psychology, 15*(1), 12–25.

Baker, J., Horton, S., Robertson-Wilson, J., & Wall, M. (2003). Nurturing sport expertise: Factors influencing the development of elite athlete. *Journal of Sports Science and Medicine, 2*(1), 1–9.

Balyi, I., & Hamilton, A. (2004). Long-term athlete development: Trainability in childhood and adolescence. *Olympic Coach, 16*(1), 4–9.

Barker, D., Barker-Ruchti, N., Rynne, S., & Lee, J. (2014). Moving out of sports: A socio-cultural examination of Olympic career transitions. *International Journal of Sports Science and Coaching*, 9(2), 255–270.

Barker, D., Bergentoft, H., & Nyberg, G. (2017). What would physical educators know about movement education? A review of literature, 2006–2016. *Quest*, 1–17.

Barker-Ruchti, N., Barker, D., Rynne, S. B., & Lee, J. (2012). 'One door closes, a next door opens up somewhere': The learning of one Olympic synchronised swimmer. *Reflective Practice, 13*(3), 373–385.

Barker-Ruchti, N., Rynne, S. B., Lee, J., & Barker, D. M. (2014). Athlete learning in Olympic sport. *Sports Coaching Review, 3*(2), 162–178.

Barker-Ruchti, N., & Schubring, A. (2016). Moving into and out of high-performance sport: The cultural learning of one women's artistic gymnast. *Physical Education and Sport Pedagogy, 21*(1), 55–68.

Beach, K. (1999). Consequential transitions: A sociocultural expedition beyond transfer in education. *Review of Research in Education, 24*(1), 101–139.

Billett, S. (2001). *Learning at the workplace: Strategies for effective practice*. Sydney: Allen & Unwin.

Bloom, G. A., & Stevens, D. E. (2004). Case study: A team-building mental skills training program with an intercollegiate equestrian team. *Online Journal of Sport Psychology, 4*(1), 1–16.

Bloomer, M., & Hodkinson, P. (2000). Learning careers: Continuity and change in young people's dispositions to learning. *British Educational Research Journal, 26*(5), 583–597.

Bouchard, C., Malina, R. M., & Pérusse, L. (1997). *Genetics of fitness and physical performance*. Champaign, IL: Human Kinetics.

Bresler, L. (2006). Embodied narrative inquiry: A methodology of connection. *Research Studies in Music Education, 27*(1), 21–43.

Brock, S. C., & Kleiber, D. A. (1994). Narrative in medicine: The stories of elite college athletes' career-ending injuries. *Qualitative Health Research, 4*(4), 411–430.

Carless, D., & Douglas, K. (2009). 'We haven't got a seat on the bus for you' or 'all the seats are mine': Narratives and career transitions in professional golf. *Qualitative Research in Sport and Exercise, 1*(1), 51–66.

Carless, D., & Douglas, K. (2012). Stories of success: Cultural narratives and personal stories of elite and professional athletes. *Reflective Practice, 13*(3), 387–398.

Carless, D., & Douglas, K. (2013). 'In the boat' but 'selling myself short': Stories, narratives, and identity development in elite sport. *Sport Psychologist, 27*(1), 27–39.

Cavallerio, F., Wadey, R., & Wagstaff, C. R. (2017). Adjusting to retirement from sport: Narratives of former competitive rhythmic gymnasts. *Qualitative Research in Sport, Exercise and Health*, 9(5), 533–545.

Christensen, M. K., Laursen, D. N., & Sørensen, J. K. (2011). Situated learning in youth elite football. *Physical Education and Sport Pedagogy*, *16*(2), 163–178.

Clark, M. C., & Rossiter, M. (2008). Narrative learning in adulthood. *New Directions for Adult and Continuing Education*, *2008*(119), 61–70.

Cobb, P., & Bowers, J. (1999). Cognitive and situated learning perspectives in theory and practice. *Educational Researcher*, *28*(2), 4–15.

Committee on Sports Medicine Fitness. (2000). Intensive training and sports specialization in young athletes. *Pediatrics*, *106*(1), 154–157.

Côté, J., Baker, J., & Abernethy, B. (2003). From play to practice: A developmental framework for the acquisition of expertise in team sports. In J. Starkes & K. A. Ericsson (Eds.), *Expert performance in sports: Advances in research on sport expertise* (pp. 89–110). Champaign, IL: Human Kinetics.

Côté, J., & Vierimaa, M. (2014). The developmental model of sport participation: 15 years after its first conceptualization. *Science and Sports*, *29*, s63–s69.

Davids, K., Araújo, D., Correia, V., & Vilar, L. (2013). How small-sided and conditioned games enhance acquisition of movement and decision-making skills. *Exercise and Sport Sciences Reviews*, *41*(3), 154–161.

De Bosscher, V., Shibil, S., Westerbeek, H., & van Bottenburg, M. (2015). *Successful elite sport policies: An international comparison of the Sports Policy factors Leading to International Sporting Success (SPLISS 2.0) in 15 nations*. Aachen, Germany: Meyer & Meyer Verlag.

DiFiori, J. P., Benjamin, H. J., Brenner, J. S., Gregory, A., Jayanthi, N., Landry, G. L., & Luke, A. (2014). Overuse injuries and burnout in youth sports: A position statement from the American Medical Society for Sports Medicine. *British Journal of Sports Medicine*, 48, 287–288.

Douglas, K., & Carless, D. (2006). Performance, discovery, and relational narratives among women professional tournament golfers. *Women in Sport and Physical Activity Journal*, *15*(2), 14–27.

Douglas, K., & Carless, D. (2009). Abandoning the performance narrative: Two women's stories of transition from professional sport. *Journal of Applied Sport Psychology*, *21*(2), 213–230.

Douglas, K., & Carless, D. (2014). *Life story research in sport: Understanding the experiences of elite and professional athletes through narrative*. London: Routledge.

Ericsson, K. A. (2008). Deliberate practice and acquisition of expert performance: A general overview. *Academic Emergency Medicine*, *15*(11), 988–994.

Ericsson, K. A., & Delaney, P. (1999). Long-Term Working Memory as an Alternative to Capacity Models of Working Memory in Everyday Skilled Performance. In A. Miyake & P. Shah (Eds.), *Models of Working Memory: Mechanisms of Active Maintenance and Executive Control* (pp. 257–297). Cambridge: Cambridge University Press.

Ericsson, K. A., & Kintsch, W. (1995). Long-term working memory. *Psychological Review*, *102*(2), 211–245.

Ericsson, K. A., Krampe, R. T., & Tesch-Römer, C. (1993). The role of deliberate practice in the acquisition of expert performance. *Psychological Review*, *100*(3), 363–406.

Fisher, W. R. (1984). Narration as a human communication paradigm: The case of public moral argument. *Communications Monographs*, *51*(1), 1–22.

Fitzclarence, L., Hickey, C., & Matthews, R. (1997). Getting changed for football: Challenging communities of practice. *Curriculum Perspectives*, *17*(1), 69–73.

Frank, A. W. (1995). The wounded storyteller: Body, illness, and ethics. In. Chicago: University of Chicago Press.

Fuller, A., Hodkinson, H., Hodkinson, P., & Unwin, L. (2005). Learning as peripheral participation in communities of practice: A reassessment of key concepts in workplace learning. *British Educational Research Journal*, *31*(1), 49–68.

Gagné, F. (2004). Transforming gifts into talents: The DMGT as a developmental theory. *High Ability Studies*, *15*(2), 119–147.

Galipeau, J., & Trudel, P. (2006). Athlete learning in a community of practice: Is there a role for the coach? In R. L. Jones (Ed.), *The sports coach as educator: Reconceptualising sports coaching* (pp. 77–94). London: Routledge.

Gallahue, D., & Donnelly, F. (2003). *Development of physical education for all children*. Champaign, IL: Human Kinetics.

Gould, D., & Carson, S. (2008). Life skills development through sport: Current status and future directions. *International Review of Sport and Exercise Psychology*, *1*(1), 58–78.

Gould, D., Eklund, R., & Jackson, S. (1993). Coping strategies used by U.S. Olympic wrestlers. *Research Quarterly for Exercise and Sport*, *64*(1), 83–93.

Gregersen, P. K., Kowalsky, E., Kohn, N., & Marvin, E. W. (2001). Early childhood music education and predisposition to absolute pitch: Teasing apart genes and environment. *American Journal of Medical Genetics Part A*, 98(3), 280–282.

Gulbin, J. P., Croser, M. J., Morley, E. J., & Weissensteiner, J. R. (2013). An integrated framework for the optimisation of sport and athlete development: A practitioner approach. *Journal of Sports Sciences*, *31*(12), 1319–1331.

Hager, P., & Hodkinson, P. (2009). Moving beyond the metaphor of transfer of learning. *British Educational Research Journal*, *35*(4), 619–638.

Handley, K., Sturdy, A., Fincham, R., & Clark, T. (2006). Within and beyond communities of practice: Making sense of learning through participation, identity and practice. *Journal of Management Studies*, *43*(3), 641–653.

Hegde, E., & Standal, O. (2013). Learning to become a team player: Situated learning in Paralympic sledge hockey. *European Journal of Adapted Physical Activity*, 6(1), 30–42.

Helsen, W. F., Hodges, N. J., Van Winckel, J., & Starkes, J. L. (2000). The roles of talent, physical precocity and practice in the development of soccer expertise. *Journal of Sports Sciences*, *18*(9), 727–736.

Henriksen, K., Stambulova, N., & Roessler, K. K. (2010). Holistic approach to athletic talent development environments: A successful sailing milieu. *Psychology of Sport and Exercise*, *11*(3), 212–222.

Hodkinson, H., & Hodkinson, P. (2004). Rethinking the concept of community of practice in relation to schoolteachers' workplace learning. *International Journal of Training and Development*, 8(1), 21–31.

Hodkinson, P., Biesta, G., & James, D. (2008). Understanding learning culturally: Overcoming the dualism between social and individual views of learning. *Vocations and Learning*, *1*, 27–47.

Holt, N. L., & Neely, K. C. (2011). Positive youth development through sport: A review. *Revista Iberoamericana de psicología del ejercicio y el deporte*, 6(2), 299–316.

Hydén, L. C. (1997). Illness and narrative. *Sociology of Health and Illness*, *19*(1), 48–69.

Illeris, K. (2018). A comprehensive understanding of human learning. In K. Illeris (Ed.), *A comprehensive understanding of human learning* (pp. 7–20). London: Routledge.

Kleiber, D. A., & Brock, S. C. (1992). The effect of career-ending injuries on the subsequent well-being of elite college athletes. *Sociology of Sport Journal*, 9(1), 70–75.

Kuhlin, F., Barker-Ruchti, N., & Stewart, F. (submitted). Growing up as a figure skater: Storying the influence of the coach-athlete relationship. *Qualitative Research in Sport, Exercise and Health.*

Lave, J., & Wenger, E. (1991). *Situated learning: Legitimate peripheral participation in communities of practice.* New York: Cambridge University Press.

Light, R. (2006). Situated learning in an Australian surf club. *Sport, Education and Society, 11*(2), 155–172.

Light, R. (2010). Children's social and personal development through sport: A case study of an Australian swimming club. *Journal of Sport and Social Issues, 34*(4), 379–395.

Light, R. L. (2011). Opening up learning theory to social theory in research on sport and physical education through a focus on practice. *Physical Education and Sport Pedagogy, 16*(4), 369–382.

Lobato, J. (2006). Alternative perspectives on the transfer of learning: History, issues, and challenges for future research. *Journal of the Learning Sciences, 15*(4), 431–449.

Lund, O., Ravn, S., & Christensen, M. K. (2012). *Learning by joining the rhythm: Apprenticeship learning in elite double sculler rowing.* Paper presented at the Scandinavian Sport Studies Forum, 2012, Vol 3, pp. 167–188.

Lund, O., Ravn, S., & Christensen, M. K. (2013). Jumping together: Apprenticeship learning among elite trampoline athletes. *Physical Education and Sport Pedagogy, 19*(4), 383–397.

Martindale, R., Collins, D., & Daubney, J. (2005). Talent development: A guide for practice and research within sport. *Quest, 57*(4), 353–375.

McLeod, J. (2006). Narrative thinking and the emergence of postpsychological therapies. *Narrative Inquiry, 16*(1), 201–210.

Naber, J. (2006). From high school to the Olympic Games: Learning from a variety of swimming coaches. *International Journal of Sport Science and Coaching, 1*(2), 125–126.

Nolan, J. E., & Howell, G. (2010). Hockey success and birth date: The relative age effect revisited. *International Review for the Sociology of Sport, 45*(4), 507–512.

Nünning, A. (2012). Narrativist approaches and narratological concepts for the study of culture. In B. Neumann & A. Nünning (Eds.), *Traveling concepts for the study of culture* (pp. 145–183). Berlin: Walter de Gruyter.

Owen-Pugh, V. (2013). Theorizing sport as a community of practice: The coach-athlete relationship in British professional basketball. In J. Hughes, N. Jewson, & L. Unwin (Eds.), *Communities of practice: Critical perspectives* (pp. 93–105). London: Routledge.

Polkinghorne, D. E. (1995). Narrative configuration in qualitative analysis. *International Journal of Qualitative Studies in Education, 8*(1), 5–23.

Rambusch, J., & Ziemke, T. (2005). *The role of embodiment in situated learning.* Paper presented at the 27th Annual Conference of the Cognitive Science Society (pp. 1803–1808). Mahwah, NJ: Lawrence Erlbaum.

Schmidt, R. A., & Young, D. E. (1987). Transfer of movement control in motor skill learning. In S. M. Cormier & J. D. Hagman (Eds.), *Transfer of learning: Contemporary research and applications* (pp. 47–79). Amsterdam: Elsevier.

Schubring, A., & Thiel, A. (2014). Coping with growth in adolescent elite sport. *Sociology of Sport Journal, 31*(3), 304–326.

Sfard, A. (1998). On two metaphors for learning and the dangers of choosing just one. *Educational Researcher, 27*(2), 4–13.

Somers, M. R. (1994). The narrative constitution of identity: A relational and network approach. *Theory and Society, 23*, 605–649.

Tranckle, P., & Cushion, C. J. (2006). Rethinking giftedness and talent in sport. *Quest*, 58(2), 265–282.

van Rossum, J. H. A., & Gagné, F. (2005). Talent development in sports. In F. A. Dixon & S. M. Moon (Eds.), *The handbook of secondary gifted education* (pp. 281–316). Waco, TX: Prufrock Press.

Ward, P., Farrow, D., Harris, K. R., Williams, A. M., Eccles, D. W., & Ericsson, K. A. (2008). Training perceptual-cognitive skills: Can sport psychology research inform military decision training? *Military Psychology*, 20, 71–102.

Wenger, E. (1998). *Communities of practice: Learning, meaning, and identity*. Cambridge: Cambridge University Press.

Wenger, E. (2011). *Communities of practice: A brief introduction*. https://scholarsbank.uoregon.edu/xmlui/bitstream/handle/1794/11736/A%20brief%20introduction%20to%20CoP.pdf?sequence=1&isAllowed=y.

Whiffin, C. J., Bailey, C., Ellis-Hill, C., & Jarrett, N. (2014). Challenges and solutions during analysis in a longitudinal narrative case study. *Nurse Researcher*, *21*(4), 20–26.

Chapter 3

Cultural perspective of learning

Natalie Barker-Ruchti

In this chapter, I aim to develop a cultural perspective from which to think about athlete learning in elite sport. I base this perspective on a cultural theory of learning (Hodkinson, Biesta, & James, 2008), which defines learning as that which occurs through the activities individuals perform in the contexts they participate in, in interaction with others, in reaction to unexpected events, and in making sense of their experiences. This definition of learning means that regardless of context or situation, people learn (Säljö, 2003) and that although learning develops individuals' knowledge and skills, it entails continuous personal development. This *learning as self-development* shapes individuals' visions for action and of learning, conduct, and sense of self.

Background to the cultural perspective of learning

My proposition of a cultural perspective has its starting point in the research British education scholar Phil Hodkinson led during the late 1990s[1] (Hodkinson & James, 2003). This longitudinal research focused on individuals' learning as part of moving into, within, and out of a variety of educational settings. A major finding of this research was the insight into the interrelationships among participation in a formal learning context, development of sense of self, and individual agency. The empirical results demonstrated that the research's pupils, students, and adult learners developed sense of self in relation to (a) the social ideals and expectations of the educational contexts they participated in, (b) the backgrounds and experiences they brought to the educational settings, (c) the life events they experienced, and (d) the meaning they made of their contexts, life events, and learning (Goodson, Hodkinson, Field, Biesta, & Macleod, 2011). In order to conceptualise these elements of learning, Hodkinson, Biesta and James (2008) developed two interrelated and complementary theories: the *Theory of Learning Cultures*, which conceptualises the *modes* of learning, and the *Cultural Theory of Learning*, which theorises the *processes* of learning.

Hodkinson, Biesta, and James's (2008) attempt to integrate the mode and process of learning builds on (a) an anthropological definition of culture, (b) a Deweyian perspective of education; and (c) a Bourdieuian understanding of socialisation.

The *anthropological definition of culture* terms culture not as an artistic, spiritual or intellectual activity (Williams, 1983) and does not bind it by a particular cultural space or location, such as a museum, theatre or school class. Rather, culture is defined as a way of life. This way of life consists of 'human *activity*, often but not exclusively collective activity,' which is meaningful for groups of individuals, commonly during a particular period in time (Hodkinson, Biesta, & James, 2008, p. 33, emphasis mine). Human activity entails all that individuals do: (1) practical action such as the professional activities that people engage in at work or the movements a group of kids executes when they practice a sport, (2) interactions and communication that take place between individuals and groups of individuals, and (3) individual cognitive and emotional engagement, which includes such 'intelligible thought' activities as anticipation, deliberation, interpretation, and judgement. Most people continuously perform practical, social, and intelligible activities, some of which they perform spontaneously, perhaps in reaction to an unexpected event. Most human activity, however, is performed routinely, as it is driven by a complex assemblage of unquestioned social ideals and expectations, institutionalised structures, unequal social positioning, access to resources, governing rules, and material objects.

The *Deweyian perspective of education* (Dewey, 2002, 2007) has been influential in arguing that learning is

> life-long, crucial to the inter-generational transmission of cultural practices and occurred within and outside of educational institutions and the workplace. [Dewey] also insisted learning was an embodied process—making his work directly relevant to scholars of body pedagogics—while acknowledging that it occurred at distinctive sensory, kinaesthetic, pre-reflective and conscious 'levels' within individuals. (Shilling, 2017, p. 1208)

Dewey's insistence that individuals' thinking is deliberate, although influenced by context, was particularly guiding for Hodkinson and colleagues' conceptualisation of learning as cultural.

The *Bourdieuian understanding of socialisation* (e.g., Bourdieu, 1977), particularly this scholar's concepts of 'field' and 'habitus', further supported Hodkinson and colleagues' efforts to conceptualise the embodied nature of learning. *Field* is a concept that Bourdieu (1977) compared to a 'market', which he understood to consist of actors that mutually depend on one another but that are unequally positioned according to, and in competition with, the ideals and expectations meaningful in this context and the individual purchasing power individuals have. Hodkinson, Biesta, and James (2008) adopted the notion of field in terms of the 'forces' it entails—that is, the complex power relations that exist among actors, groups of actors, institutions, objects, and ideals and expectations (Bourdieu, 1985). *Habitus*, which Bourdieu (1977) defined as a battery of durable, transposable, but also mutable dispositions to all aspects of life that are often subconscious or tacit, is a concept that explains how individuals, within markets, develop their sense of self and conduct. A key Bourdieuian argument is that the formation of habitus entails an internalisation process through which social structures become embodied and operate within and through individuals (Hodkinson, Biesta, & James, 2008). Hodkinson and colleagues drew on habitus in preference to identity, which they regarded as too narrow to explain how individuals are shaped by, but also can shape, context.

In this chapter, I base the cultural perspective of athlete learning in elite sport on Hodkinson and colleagues' anthropological, Deweyian, and Bourdieuian conceptualisations of learning. Specifically, I draw on the Theory of Learning Cultures (TLC) and the Cultural Theory of Learning (CTL) and wish to develop these two theories with a perspective that combines career development (Hodkinson, 2008; Hodkinson & Sparkes, 1997) and disposition of learning (Bloomer & Hodkinson, 2000a; Bloomer & Hodkinson, 2000b). I believe that the resulting perspective allows longitudinal contextualised thinking on how elite sport cultures and learning processes integrate to shape elite athletes' learning as self-development. In the following, I begin by sketching how the cultural perspective of learning centralises human activity as the mode through which learning occurs. I use Hodkinson and colleagues' metaphor of 'learning culture' as a macro means to understand this mode of learning, and I use their metaphors of 'becoming' and 'horizon for action'/'horizon of learning' to demonstrate the continuous and ubiquitous, yet idiosyncratic, process of learning. I then adopt Hodkinson and Sparkes's (2008; 1997) idea of turning points, which they theorised in the sociological career theory 'careership', and Bloomer and Hodkinson's (2000b) conception of 'learning career', which they developed to conceptualise dispositions of learning. Lastly, I draw on Enright and Gard's (2016) response to Hodkinson, Biesta, and James's (2008) theorisation to critically engage with the cultural perspective of learning.

Theory of learning cultures

Based on the background outlined above, Hodkinson, Biesta, and James (2008) suggest that cultural contexts, within which multiple participants routinely perform institutionalised and meaningful activities (i.e., adopt certain ways of life), represent *learning cultures*. Learning cultures are common in formal workplaces and institutions but can also emerge informally as when individuals meet to pursue a particular activity (e.g., when kids play football on a neighbourhood street). In either case, the anthropological understanding defines culture not by the context's physical boundaries—the walls of a factory building, the edges of a swimming pool, or the neighbourhood street that a group of children uses to play soccer—but by 'the actions, dispositions and interpretations of the participants' (Hodkinson, Biesta, & James, 2008, p. 34). A number of written and unwritten rules govern these activities. With regard to the former, and specific to elite sport, international governing agencies such the World Anti-Doping Agency and the International Olympic Committee and national and local sport organisations govern elite sport. With regard to the latter, sport- or training-specific traditions and ideologies are significant. The pixie-style model of coaching women's artistic gymnastics, for instance, which prescribes that gymnasts must be short, thin, and physically undeveloped to learn gymnastics skills, represents an unwritten rule that has shaped the ideal age of gymnasts and authoritarian coaching practices since the late 1960s and 1970s (Kerr, Barker-Ruchti, Schubring, Cervin, & Nunomura, 2017). Such formal and informal rules mean that learning cultures produce certain *ways of life* and certain *types of athletes*—not just in terms of their athletic training and performances but also in terms of their sense of self and general conduct (Larsson & Quennerstedt, 2012). Consider, for instance, how a Paris St. Germain soccer player from Brazil, a Bulgarian rhythmic gymnast, and an Australian weightlifter would differ in how they see themselves and behave. The three athletes' starkly different national contexts, upbringings, sport-specific training demands, coaching traditions, and career pathways will significantly have shaped their sense of who they are, their understanding of how they can act, and their visions as to what they can do and learn.

Despite rules and enduring social forces that normalise people, learning cultures are in flux because multiple external and internal factors change over time. Externally, the (changing) factors of other learning cultures interpenetrate and affect their adjacent learning cultures. A change in government or governmental policy may affect the financial resources a learning culture receives; as national populations evolve because of declining birth rates, migration, and ageing, the needs of learning cultures change and drive new trends and regulations. Internally, changes to context-specific rules, emerging loopholes, and new problems demand changes to the practices of learning cultures. As these changes take place, individuals must manage this instability and adapt. At a micro level, the learning this entails represents a concrete mechanism through which individuals' sense of who they are, how they can act, and what they can do and learn is shaped. At a macro level, the learning and development individuals experience act as further internal factors that affect learning cultures. That is, as people adjust to changes through interpreting, negotiating, and performing a learning culture's changing practices, they may influence its activities. In so doing, learning cultures evolve.

However, while TLC's reflexivity between being structured and structuring grants individuals agency, it does not mean that individuals can invent culture at will. In contrast, Hodkinson, Biesta, and James (2008) acknowledge that social structures, ideologies, institutions, spaces, and material objects have history and endurance. In elite sport, the commodity orientation outlined in Chapter 1 is one such enduring characteristic. This orientation naturalises athletic competition, which is based on and normalises deep-seated inequalities between participants and groups of participants, gender ideologies, sporting spaces, material objects such as sporting equipment and clothing, and organisations such as fan clubs, media, and sponsors. Yet contemporary elite sport is not set in concrete. The demands the commodity expectations place on sport organisations and practitioners have created critical debates about the impact of elite sport on athletes' health and well-being and on their lives after sport (e.g., Côté, Lidor, & Hackfort, 2009). In some countries, hypercompetitiveness is less common (see Chapter 1 on the situation in Sweden). As research continues to demonstrate that intense competition is detrimental to children and young adults and causes them to drop out of sport (e.g., DiFiori et al., 2014; Fraser-Thomas, Côté, & Deakin, 2008), sport governing bodies and sport organisations, such as the Swedish Sport Confederation (2017) and the Swedish Floorball Federation (Persson & Bååth, 2011), are implementing strategies to reduce the focus on competition.

How do individuals *learn* as participants of this elite sport learning culture? In the following, I change my focus from the mode to the process of learning and consider how and why individuals learn through participating in learning cultures.

Cultural theory of learning

Building on TLC, Hodkinson, Biesta, and James (2008) adopt the broad assumption in CTL that learning is *embodied*. Embodying has been theorised as a process of internalisation, as does Shilling (2017), who suggests that embodying occurs through the sensory, kinaesthetic, and reflective input individuals receive from the surroundings they participate in. Individuals see, touch, taste, smell, and hear; they perform human activity; and they think, reflect, interpret, judge, and make pragmatic decisions. Through these actions, individuals '*incorporate* the "outside" world via symbolic representations but also bodily sensations' and the intelligible reactions, meaning, and emotional attachment these create (Shilling, 2017, p. 1209, emphasis in original).

While Hodkinson, Biesta, and James (2008) do not specifically discuss the process of embodying, they propose two metaphors to express the embodied nature of learning. First, they use the metaphor of 'becoming', which they argue entails social, practical, and embodied learning. A basic assumption of embodied learning is that a person, through his or her performance in learning cultures, 'is constantly learning through becoming, and becoming through learning' (Hodkinson, Biesta, & James, 2008, p. 41). This becoming develops sense of self, which constitutes who athletes see themselves to be, what they do and how they do these things, and what they see possible in the future. Second, to detail the process of becoming, Hodkinson and colleagues (Hodkinson & Hodkinson, 2004; Hodkinson, Biesta, & James, 2008; Hodkinson, Sparkes, & Hodkinson, 1996) propose the metaphors of 'horizons for action' and 'horizons of learning.' Figuratively, horizon indicates 'vision', meaning that what individuals can 'see' is who they perceive they can be and what they perceive they can do and learn at present and in the future. Specifically, *horizon for action* refers to how a learning culture and an individual's backgrounds, dispositions, and experiences constitute (potential) actions. It defines how we habitually act in certain contexts and situations. *Horizon of learning*, in contrast, refers to how individual dispositions to knowledge and learning shape a person's habitual orientation towards learning (Bloomer & Hodkinson, 2000b). A university student, for instance, may regard her business degree in utilitarian terms, perhaps as a ticket to paid employment and material items that she hopes to be able to buy with her salary. Another student may regard their university studies as personal development and have no specific professional ambitions.

Horizon of learning acknowledges that dispositions to knowledge and learning can change over time and that individuals may develop multiple dispositions in order to suit particular contexts. With regard to the above student who regards her university degree as personal development, he may, due to unforeseen circumstances (i.e., financial difficulties), come to understand her education as a means to secure employment (Bloomer & Hodkinson, 2000b). With regard to the business student, she may not only read courses with a career plan in mind but also start to visit a Mandarin language course because she has fallen in love with a Chinese citizen.

Horizons for action and horizons of learning develop from birth. Through learning about, performing, sensing and making sense of, and negotiating the activities that make learning cultures, as well as through adjusting to external and internal changes, horizons form and transform. While this entails normalisation, the multilayered incorporation of 'the outside world' through the sensory, kinaesthetic, and reflective input Shilling (2017) refers to is never an exact replication. It always allows negotiation through individuals' capacity for intelligible thought activities and pragmatic decision-making. Often, the learning that occurs through this doing is imperceptible because an individual's learning culture and her sense of self are stable. The human activities that she performs take on a routine-like character. At times, however, individuals experience novelty, opposition, conflict, and life-changing events. The habitual activities and existing horizons are challenged and become inadequate. In some cases, and particularly if an individual considers occurring changes as 'interruptive', they may cause a person to change their horizons (Hodkinson & Sparkes, 1997). Some such turning points represent predictable life transitions, such as when a child enters school or a junior athlete becomes a senior player. Ahead of such a structural turning point phase, the child or athlete and those supporting her are likely to be aware that her entrance into the new context will require time to adjust. At other times, however, turning points can occur unexpectedly. At such times, forced turning points may traumatize individuals, as they suddenly come to realise that their horizons have become unproductive or even obsolete. In elite sport, such forced turning points have been reported in relation to the death of family members or friends, surprise losses at major competitions, and serious injuries (Barker-Ruchti, Lindgren, Hofmann, Sinning, & Shelton, 2015; Barker-Ruchti, Rynne, Lee, & Barker, 2014). Individuals may also initiate a change, such as deciding to become a vegetarian, create a family, or migrate. While some such self-initiated turning points are part of normative life paths, others represent intentional (political) action. In elite sport, a normative career path may include an intra-national move to a regional or national training facility and/or international migration. A personally motivated turning point may be the inclusion of certain training exercises. Lastly, research by Barker-Ruchti and colleagues (2015) shows that turning points can entail events that create *initiating opportunities*, such as when an athlete is given the opportunity to play in a game even though she is young and still commonly benched or when a sports club invites an athlete to take on an assistant coaching position. While these opportunities may not immediately be life changing, they may lead to significant changes later on.

New or changed situations may generate (critical) reflection over culture, situation, horizons, and practices. Hodkinson and Sparkes (1997) argue, as do others (Mezirow, 1990; Shilling, 2017), that if individuals perceive turning point events and phases as being disruptive and as requiring assessment, learning becomes more conscious or has greater transformative potential. This may be particularly so for moments of crisis following forced turning points because they can act as 'wake-up calls' or for self-initiated turning points that follow frustrations and an identification that change is necessary. In either case, individuals will have spent considerable time reflecting over self, life, and future to come to decide how to change (Barker-Ruchti et al., 2014; Cope, 2003; Cope & Watts, 2000).

Research has shown that in contrast to the transformative potential of forced and self-initiated turning point experiences, athletes who are faced with tightly bound expectations of being and conduct, and who thus have few possibilities to negotiate their horizons for action and horizons of learning, only learn according to the prescribed expectations (Barker, Barker-Ruchti, Rynne, & Lee, 2014). This limit as to who athletes can be positions them as passive receivers that are expected to adopt prescribed horizons. In elite sport, sport stakeholders may not endorse athletes' negotiation of horizons to suit their individual needs. Rather, the expectation is that they adjust at any prize, which research demonstrates can foreclose athletic identity (Murphy, Petitpas, & Brewer, 1996), create athlete apathy and a desire to drop out (Denison, 2007), and significantly complicate athletes' retirement process (Barker-Ruchti & Schubring, 2016).

In summary, CTL tells us that individuals' social, practical, and embodied engagement in learning cultures shapes their sense of self, life, and learning. The metaphor of becoming, through its horizons for action and horizons of learning, expresses this continuous and reflexive process of normalisation and intelligible action. Internalisation occurs through a way of life that entails practices, intelligible action (i.e., judgement, anticipation, and purposeful political action), and a number of life events and phases that create particular experiences. These external and internal factors configure idiosyncratic horizons for action and horizons of learning and may alter dispositions of learning. Through this becoming, individuals' actions produce and reproduce, but they also challenge and possibly alter career pathways and learning cultures. This is where TLC's macro perspectives and CTL's micro perspectives articulate to offer a lens through which to envision how social and structural influences, *as well as* individual backgrounds and engagement, configure individuals' selves, conduct, and pathways. In some elite sport contexts, however, athletes' positioning and ability to negotiate expectations are limited, which constrains their learning as self-development.

Some critical reflections

Critical engagement with theoretical perspectives is important—not only to understand a theory's limitations but also to reveal one's embodied scientific practice and the valuing this entails. In this spirit, I wish in the following to critically engage with my choice of the cultural perspective, with its metaphorical and material limitations, and lay out my reasoning in continuing to argue for a cultural perspective from which to think about athlete learning. Enright and Gard's (2016) response to Hodkinson, Biesta, and James's (2008) cultural theory of learning serves as my starting point for this engagement.

I was introduced to Hodkinson and colleagues' cultural theory of learning as I was reading constructivist literature of learning in relation to a research project on elite athletes' learning and participating in a professional development course on student supervision. I remember rather clearly that when reading this literature, 'lightbulbs went on' as to how the theory could help me to think about the data I had produced in interviews with former elite athletes. I saw possibilities to outline the tightly bound commodity culture of elite sport and how its contexts allowed practices and shaped elite athletes' learning. I further found the notion of learning through human activity useful, as the athletes had recounted a multitude of problematic practices they had engaged in and yet spoke of how they had come to understand and negotiate the practices their engagement required. Lastly, I liked the longitudinal potential because I saw how over time elite athletes dealt with a myriad of serious events and conflicts, which interrupted and even dislocated their athletic careers.

My introduction to the cultural perspective of learning, as my 'seeing' connections between cultural learning theory and empirical data, illustrates how 'theorising about the world is an inescapably embodied and grounded action' (Enright & Gard, 2016, p. 42). While I would like to regard coming across ideas as opportunities, I am aware that a lack of critical engagement with one's theorising can heighten theoretical bias. I am thus grateful for Enright and Gard's critical response to Hodkinson, Biesta, and James's (2008, p. 30) cultural theory of learning, as it allows me to pinpoint theoretical shortcomings and to reflect on my own embodied theorising. In terms of shortcomings, Enright and Gard (2016) are particularly critical of Hodkinson, Biesta, and James's (2008, p. 30) claim that by placing 'the individual learner squarely within a cultural theory of learning', they remedy existing theories' hierarchizing of context and individual. Enright and Gard (2016) argue that this 'scaling' to move between context and individual does not actually prevent their polarising. I am cognisant of this criticism and have paid particular attention to levelling the mode and process of learning by highlighting how learning occurs through *doing* elite sport. I do still, however, present TLC and CTL consecutively and thus maintain the distinction between contextually and individually driven learning.

A second criticism Enright and Gard (2016) raise relates to Hodkinson and colleagues' claim that their overcoming of mind-body dualism, which they argue prevents individual-social and structure-agency divisions, creates a successful holistic theory of learning. What Enright and Gard question is whether a theory can be holistic, and they argue that society and individuals are only some elements that affect learning. Artefacts, (digital) technology, and social media are also important and influence learning (Casey, Goodyear, & Armour, 2016; Kerr, 2016). I have taken this limitation to heart and have paid at least some attention to how material objects relate to learning. I am not claiming, however, to have collated a 'theory of everything' (Enright & Gard, 2016, p. 49). Rather, the cultural perspective of athlete learning in elite sport has provided me with *a way to think about* and create a situated understanding of learning.

Conclusion

The cultural perspective of learning conceptualises culture as ways of life. These ways of life entail human activities that individuals perform in particular contexts, at particular times, and because they are meaningful. The human activities that ways of life entail create learning cultures. Learning occurs as individuals perform the activities of a learning culture. This learning instils knowledge and competencies but also creates horizons for action and horizons of learning that reflect a learning culture's way of life, which represent dispositional learning. The horizons construct individuals' sense of self. As contexts change and selves evolve, so do practices, requiring individuals to adjust their horizons for action and horizons of learning. Thus, learning is a continuous social, practical, and embodying process.

Note

1. Hodkinson led the research project Transforming Learning Cultures in Further Education from 2001 to 2005. From this research, Hodkinson and colleagues published extensively, including Hodkinson, 2010; Hodkinson, 2005; Hodkinson, Ford, Hawthorn, & Hodkinson, 2007; Hodkinson, Ford, Hodkinson, & Hawthorn, 2008; and Hodkinson & Macleod, 2009.

References

Barker, D., Barker-Ruchti, N., Rynne, S. B., & Lee, J. (2014). 'Just do a little more': Examining expertise in high performance sport from a sociocultural learning perspective. *Reflective Practice*, *15*(1), 92–105.

Barker-Ruchti, N., Lindgren, E.-C., Hofmann, A., Sinning, S., & Shelton, C. (2015). Tracing the career paths of top-level women football coaches: Turning points to understand and develop sport coaching careers. *Sports Coaching Review*, *4*(1), 117–131.

Barker-Ruchti, N., Rynne, S. B., Lee, J., & Barker, D. M. (2014). Athlete learning in Olympic sport: A cultural analysis. *Sports Coaching Review*, *3*(2), 162–178.

Barker-Ruchti, N., & Schubring, A. (2016). Moving into and out of high-performance sport: The cultural learning of one women's artistic gymnast. *Physical Education and Sport Pedagogy*, *21*(1), 55–68.

Bloomer, M., & Hodkinson, P. (2000a). The complexity and unpredictability of young people's learning careers. *Education + Training*, *42*(2), 68–74.

Bloomer, M., & Hodkinson, P. (2000b). Learning careers: Continuity and change in young people's dispositions to learning. *British Educational Research Journal*, *26*(5), 583–597.

Bourdieu, P. (1977). *Outline of a theory of practice*. Cambridge: Cambridge University Press.

Bourdieu, P. (1985). The forms of capital. In J. G. Richardson (Ed.), *Handbook of theory and research for the sociology of education* (pp. 241–258). New York: Greenwood Press.

Casey, A., Goodyear, V. A., & Armour, K. M. (2016). *Digital technologies and learning in physical education: Pedagogical cases*. London: Taylor & Francis.

Cope, J. (2003). Entrepreneurial learning and critical reflection: Discontinuous events as triggers for 'higher-level' learning. *Management Learning*, *34*(4), 429–450.

Cope, J., & Watts, G. (2000). Learning by doing—An exploration of experience, critical incidents and reflection in entrepreneurial learning. *International Journal of Entrepreneurial Behaviour and Research*, 6(3), 104–124.

Côté, J., Lidor, R., & Hackfort, D. (2009). ISSP position stand: To sample or to specialize? Seven postulates about youth sport activities that lead to continued participation and elite performance. *International Journal of Sport and Exercise Psychology*, *7*(1), 7–17.

Denison, J. (2007). Social theory for coaches: A Foucauldian reading of one athlete's poor performance. *International Journal of Sports Science and Coaching*, *2*(4), 369–383.

Dewey, J. (2002). *Human nature and conduct*. North Chelmsford, MA: Courier Corporation.

Dewey, J. (2007). *Experience and education*. New York: Simon and Schuster.

DiFiori, J. P., Benjamin, H. J., Brenner, J. S., Gregory, A., Jayanthi, N., Landry, G. L., & Luke, A. (2014). Overuse injuries and burnout in youth sports: A position statement from the American Medical Society for Sports Medicine. *British Journal of Sports Medicine*, *48*, 287–288.

Enright, E., & Gard, M. (2016). Media, digital technology and learning in sport: A critical response to Hodkinson, Biesta and James. *Physical Education and Sport Pedagogy*, *21*(1), 40–54.

Fraser-Thomas, J., Côté, J., & Deakin, J. (2008). Understanding dropout and prolonged engagement in adolescent competitive sport. *Psychology of Sport and Exercise*, 9, 645–662.

Goodson, I. F., Hodkinson, P., Field, J., Biesta, G., & Macleod, F. J. (2011). *Improving learning through the lifecourse: Learning lives*. London: Routledge.

Hodkinson, H. (2010). Learning to work no longer: Exploring 'retirement'. *Journal of Workplace Learning*, *22*(1/2), 94–103.

Hodkinson, H., & Hodkinson, P. (2004). Rethinking the concept of community of practice in relation to schoolteachers' workplace learning. *International Journal of Training and Development*, 8(1), 21–31.

Hodkinson, P. (2005). Learning as cultural and relational: Moving past some troubling dualisms. *Cambridge Journal of Education*, *35*(1), 107–119.

Hodkinson, P. (2008). *Understanding career decision-making and progression: Careership revisited*. Retrieved from https://secure.toolkitfiles.co.uk/clients/29820/sitedata/Journal_Archive_Secure/nicec-journal-issue-21-winter-2009.pdf#page=4. Paper presented at the John Killeen Memorial Lecture, London.

Hodkinson, P., Biesta, G., & James, D. (2008). Understanding learning culturally: Overcoming the dualism between social and individual views of learning. *Vocations and Learning*, *1*, 27–47.

Hodkinson, P., Ford, G., Hawthorn, R., & Hodkinson, H. (2007). *Learning as being*. Retrieved from http://www.leeds.ac.uk/educol/documents/163314.pdf.

Hodkinson, P., Ford, G., Hodkinson, H., & Hawthorn, R. (2008). Retirement as a learning process. *Educational Gerontology, 34*(3), 167–184.
Hodkinson, P., & James, D. (2003). Transforming learning cultures in further education. *Journal of Vocational Education and Training, 55*(4), 389–406.
Hodkinson, P., & Macleod, F. (2009). Contrasting concepts of learning and contrasting research methodologies: Affinities and bias. *British Educational Research Journal, 36*(2), 173–189.
Hodkinson, P., & Sparkes, A. C. (1997). Careership: A sociological theory of career decision making. *British Journal of Sociology of Education, 18*(1), 29–44.
Hodkinson, P., Sparkes, A., & Hodkinson, H. (1996). *Triumphs and tears: Young people, markets and the transition from school to work.* London: David Fulton.
Kerr, R. (2016). *Sport and technology: An actor-network theory perspective*: Oxford: Oxford University Press.
Kerr, R., Barker-Ruchti, N., Schubring, A., Cervin, G., & Nunomura, M. (2017). Coming of age: Coaches transforming the pixie-style model of coaching in women's artistic gymnastics. *Sports Coaching Review*, 1–18.
Larsson, H., & Quennerstedt, M. (2012). Understanding movement: A sociocultural approach to exploring moving humans. *Quest, 64*(4), 283–298.
Mezirow, J. (1990). How critical reflection triggers transformative learning. In J. Mezirow and Associates (Eds.), *Fostering critical reflection in adulthood: A guide to transformative and emancipatory learning.* San Francisco: Jossey-Bass.
Murphy, G. M., Petitpas, A. J., & Brewer, B. W. (1996). Identity foreclosure, athletic identity, and career maturity in intercollegiate athletes. *Sport Psychologist, 10*(3), 239–246.
Overbye, M. (2018). An (un) desirable trade of harms? How elite athletes might react to medically supervised 'doping' and their considerations of side-effects in this situation. *International Journal of Drug Policy*, 55, 14–30.
Persson, E., & Bååth, J. (2011). *Svensk Innebandys Utvecklingsmodell.* Retrieved from http://www.innebandy.se/Global/SDF/Norrbotten/1617/Svensk_Innebandys_Utvecklingsmodell.pdf.
Shilling, C. (2017). Body pedagogics: Embodiment, cognition and cultural transmission. *Sociology, 51*, 1205–1221.
Swedish Sport Confederation. (2017). *Strategi 2025—Svensk idrott—Världens bästa! Arbetsunderlag Strategisk Plan 2025.* Retrieved from http://www.strategi2025.se/globalassets/riksidrottsforbundet-2025/dokument/strategi 2025-svensk_idrott_varldensbasta-utskriftsversion.pdf.
Säljö, R. (2003). From transfer to boundary-crossing. In T. Tuomi-Gröhn & Y. Engeström (Eds.), *Between school and work: New perspectives on transfer and boundary-crossing* (pp. 311–321). Amsterdam: Elsevier.
Williams, R. (1983). *Keywords.* London: Fontana.

Part II

Showcasing athletes' learning in elite sport

The following chapters present nine case studies of elite athletes and their learning as self-development. The cases represent five current and four former athletes who participate(d) in basketball, biathlon, boxing, ice hockey, rugby, and women's artistic gymnastics. The basketballer, the biathlete, one boxer, the ice hockey player, and one rugby player identified as men; one boxer, the gymnast, and one rugby player identified as women; and one boxer identified as gender non-binary. They represent countries around the globe, including Canada, Germany, Eastern Europe, England, Germany, Japan, New Zealand, Norway, Scotland, and Somalia. Two athletes had migrated from one country to another—but each for very different reasons.

All nine athletes had invested countless hours into training for their sports, and train(ed) and compete(d) at the professional or highest amateur levels. All of them stated that they recounted to have experienced significant athletic success, which included Olympic, international, national, and professional sport success. The (former) athletes, however, also reported events and phases that they had found difficulty to deal with, including issues relating to ageing, authoritative coaching practices, billeting/boarding, cultural norms, cultural and religious conflict, de-selection/non-drafting, gender, illness, injury, migration, and sexuality. The case study authors have paid particular attention to these challenges and the learning as self-development this generated.

Each of the case studies presented in the following nine chapters is structured in a similar way. The first section of each case study introduces the athlete, his/her/their national and local sport contexts, and the specific career events and phases that characterise his/her/their learning and career development. In a middle part, the authors present the athlete's case materials. The athlete's biography structures this part of the chapter, and author interpretations are provided throughout or following the case study materials. These interpretations are made using the cultural perspective of learning presented in Chapter 3. In a third section, the authors close the case study with a summary.

Chapter 4

Maintaining a dual career horizon in women's artistic gymnastics: A case of a female gymnast

Astrid Schubring, Natalie Barker-Ruchti, Roslyn Kerr, Georgia Cervin, and Myrian Nunomura

Gymnastics is not everything.

Learning focus and case material

In this case study, we present the 'becoming' (Hodkinson, Ford, Hodkinson, & Hawthorn, 2008) of an elite gymnast—Moa[1]—as she developed her career from youth to junior and senior gymnast. We particularly focus on how Moa maintained a dual career horizon in elite sport and how her decision to study and a subsequent unexpected injury became turning points that engendered learning and transformation of her self and career.

To reconstruct Moa's career progression, we draw on data generated through an in-depth career interview that the first author conducted with Moa as a 24-year-old top-level gymnast. The interview is part of the study *Coming of Age: Towards Best Practice in Women's Artistic Gymnastics*, in which an international team of researchers aimed to understand reasons for career prolongation in women's artistic gymnastics (WAG) (Kerr, Barker-Ruchti, Schubring, Cervin, & Nunomura, 2015; Kerr & Moore, 2015). In order to understand Moa's 'learning as becoming' (Hodkinson, Biesta, & James, 2008), the first author analysed the interview transcript and re-created the gymnast's career in chronological order. Drawing on the vocabulary of sociological learning scholars (Hodkinson, Biesta, & James, 2008; Hodkinson, Ford et al., 2008; Hodkinson & Sparkes, 1997), which this book adopts for the context of elite sport (see Chapter 3 for details), particular focus was given to Moa's *dispositions*, *horizons for action*, and *horizons of learning*, as well as to *turning points* that Moa experienced (e.g., non-selection for the Olympic Games, starting to study, major injury) to understand Moa's *becoming*. During the writing process, the first author invited Moa to read and comment on the career description and the interpretations from her experiential point of view. Moa responded positively and agreed to the publication of the case study. The analytical findings were further audited in the author group, which refined and strengthened the interpretations (Creswell & Miller, 2000). In the following, we present Moa's learning as becoming in three chronological phases. Using the gymnast's own words, we have called them (a) 'Practicing pretty hard': From initiation into gymnastics to age 13; (b) 'There are international competitions, one after the other': From entry into the national team to age 19; and (c) 'Gymnastics is not everything': From entry into university to age 22.

'Practicing pretty hard': From initiation into gymnastics to age 13

Moa was unsure whether she was three or four years old when her parents enrolled her into kinder gymnastics in a club because she 'rollicked about the house a lot'. From kinder gymnastics, Moa's engagement in artistic gymnastics developed into what she sees as 'just the way it is':

> You do gymnastics and then a bit more and at some point, there is a talent scouting. It seems like you are not all that bad at what you do and then it just took its course.

Once scouted at the age of six, Moa started training at the regional training centre and participating in what she referred to as 'smaller competitions'. From there on, her career developed steadily: 'I just kept getting better'. At the age of 10, her country's national gymnastics federation selected Moa into the national youth squad. The next year, the regional training centre expanded, and together with her coach, who had been training her since she had started at her home club, the training group moved to a new, 'big training centre' where Moa still trains today.[2] Together with the improved training structure, Moa remembers training intensively: 'We were all practicing pretty hard here.'

Only shortly after the relocation and the improvement in training facility, Moa experienced another change in her training environment, which she retrospectively described as an initial spark in her career:

> Then we acquired this new Russian coach, who is still my coach today. I switched to her when I was 11 or 12, I can't really remember. It was a bit of a privilege for people to have allowance to be trained by her, because she is Russian. And you could see how fast one was making progress with her as coach. It was pretty cool that I was able to get trained by her. That was the time when I started to participate in smaller international competitions.

The reputation of success that East European coaches often enjoy in elite WAG culture (Girginov & Sandanski, 2004; Kerr & Moore, 2015) inspired and motivated Moa. In the following two years, Moa adapted to her Russian coach's (Lena's) working style, which Moa characterized as follows:

> We work by Russian standards. Russia was always known to work with large volumes [in terms of repetition of skills]. So you do and do and do and do again, until you get it right eventually. It will probably be alright, it will look

> good eventually or so. That is the track I was led onto and the training mentality I have developed.

Lena's emphasis on repetition and large volumes marries well with the hard-working 'learning culture' (Hodkinson, Biesta, & James, 2008) Moa was already familiar with through her years at the training centre. The fact that Lena started coaching Moa in early adolescence, a phase of extensive learning and skill development in WAG (age 11 to 14), further facilitated the gymnast's adaption to the Russian learning culture Lena embodied.

> In your young days, you still learn a lot of new things. A lot is done with the volume. You learn new things. Now, I don't learn many new things. I don't learn five new elements to incorporate them. But at a young age you try everything, you have to try everything to be able to see whether the element is in your line or is not in your line.

Contrasting her training as a young gymnast with her training today, Moa remembered constantly learning new elements and working on the perfection of fit between her own bodily dispositions and the skills she learnt. The coach-athlete relationship that Moa and Lena developed through these adolescent years of learning was characterized by 'mutual trust in each other', and Lena became not only 'the most important person for me [Moa] in the gym' but also the coach who 'escorted me to my successes and to the point where I'm at right now'.

Moa is aware of the formative impact that both the centre's 'working hard' learning culture and Lena's 'learning through repetition' culture had not only on her career but also on her becoming the gymnast she is today:

> Talent alone doesn't do it. Sure, I have some talent, yes; otherwise I probably wouldn't have made it this far. But I'm someone who really worked hard. Lilly [Moa's coach at the time of the interview] says that, too. I do everything with diligence.

Analytical summary of Moa's first career development phase and learning

Moa's early gymnastics career developed steadily from recreational gymnastics to smaller international competitions. Although Moa encountered three significant 'turning points' (Hodkinson & Sparkes, 1997), all resulted in supporting her continuous performance and career development: (a) The structural turning point of talent scouting, as well as (b) the enforced relocation to a 'big training centre', gave Moa access to enhanced training volumes and higher-quality coaching and facilities. While these changes also involved increased demands, Moa was able to adapt to them and to develop a 'horizon of learning' (Hodkinson, Biesta, & James, 2008) based on the extension and perfection of gymnastics skills. Her personal dispositions, such as passion for movement and talent, facilitated Moa's learning career.

Further, Moa incorporated the learning culture at the gym and developed an ability to 'practice hard'. The third and most significant turning point in Moa's early career phase was (c) the arrival of a Russian coach, which resembles the 'initiating opportunity' described by Barker-Ruchti and colleagues (2014). The coach Lena and the learning culture she embodied led Moa to perfect her ability to practice extensively to the degree that diligence became her 'second nature' (Bourdieu, 1984). In addition, Moa's trust in Lena enabled her to experience a further leap in her learning. Her athletic development and the status rise she experienced through the reputation of her coach endorsed her adoption of a 'horizon for elite gymnastics'.

'There are international competitions, one after the other': From entry into the national team to age 19

In order to facilitate the combination of an educational career with gymnastics, Moa switched at age 14 to an elite sports school that closely cooperated with the gymnastics training centre and the elite sport support infrastructure.[3] While the latter also offers places for student athletes at a boarding home close by, Moa preferred to live with her parents 'outside on the countryside ... where it is more rural, everything there is a bit more harmonious, more personal.' Commuting, Moa still felt connected to home and the friends from her 'old school' but gradually lost touch with them. At her new school, Moa made few friends. 'I never felt like I really arrived at that school'. Beside school, most of her time was now absorbed by training, competitions, and travelling.

The hard training and extensive learning Moa experienced with the support of Lena's coaching continued to bear the promised fruits of athletic development and success. At 15, Moa participated in her first international championship as a junior national team gymnast.

> It was quite exciting for me, being part of the national team, carrying the national emblem on your chest. That was my first station at the national team. Since then I'm part of the national team and there were international competitions, one after the other.

In the following three years, Moa confirmed her position in the national team. She medalled in different apparatuses at the annual national championships and competed in World Cups, often ranking among the top eight. Each year, she also competed with the national team in continental and/or world championships.

While Moa pushed her gymnastics career forward, her parents—in contrast to others—remained somewhat distant from the competitive gymnastics learning culture Moa had become a part of.

> It would never occur to my parents to say, alright, let's go watch our daughter at a competition. Not because they weren't interested.... I was watching other parents that came together with their children and sat there watching

> the whole time and then take their kids back home. But my dad would just drop me off and told me to call him when I needed to be picked up again. That's just the way it was for me, my parents not being there.

The outsider horizon that her parents maintained did not hold Moa back. She set her sporting horizons for action ever more clearly on participation in the next Olympic Games (OG). The thought of the event filled Moa with passion: 'It's just the biggest, most beautiful, best event an athlete could experience'.

Simultaneously with her preparation for making the OG qualification, Moa pursued her last years of high school education. While her dual career ambition was put to the test with the final year exams being scheduled just a few months before the Olympic Games, Moa maintained her dual career horizon for Olympic participation *and* graduation.

The year prior, Moa's national team qualified a team of six gymnasts for the OG. At the regional training centre, Lena and Moa worked hard to prepare for the two selection events the national federation had scheduled. They knew that the first spots on the team were 'reserved' for the best all-round gymnasts and the apparatus specialists with a chance to medal. But 'it was obvious, I would compete for place five' intended for a gymnast with the greatest 'team service [stable all-around performance]'. The competition in the team was tough, and Moa knew that 'it would be a tight squeeze'. Finally, the selection decision was communicated—a moment Moa recalled in detail:

> I remember how I was sitting in the changing room. I looked at my mobile and saw the head coach is calling. She said I wasn't selected. I went out and was crying. My coach and the others were standing outside and knew what was going on immediately.

Moa was devastated about not being selected, especially as her non-selection was contested by the local association.

> When it was published that I was not on the team, a lot of people sat down and calculated everything and told me: 'No matter how we put it, Moa is always on the team.' Then the head coach presented a different calculation and told us these and these are the selection criteria. But that is not the way it is. Well, you can assume it like he did, but it doesn't say so distinctly.

The non-selection literally *tore down* the horizon for Olympic participation, which the 19-year-old gymnast had focused her sight on throughout endless hours of training. The unclearness in the calculation of the results further led her to question her belief in the formula that 'hard work will pay off'.

> After that, I knew this went terribly wrong. I didn't reach my goal. I didn't reach where I wanted to get. I didn't go to the Olympics and experience how great it can be.

Despite non-selection, the national gymnastics federation called Moa to the training camps for the Olympic team. She overcame her initial resistance and participated, tentatively re-establishing her horizon for nomination and OG participation, as most selected gymnasts 'weren't a 100% fit'. The hoped-for second chance did not become real; however:

> They told me, you're still flying with the team, as a back-up gymnast. You can go along everywhere. We pay everything. So I thought, alright, as a tourist I go along and make the most of it.

Even with the emotional roller coaster and the final non-selection, Moa passed her final exams, actualizing her horizon for graduation from high school. During the exam time, Moa also made contact with friends from her 'old school' and even celebrated 'the prom night' with them. Against the backdrop of the non-selection experience, the time with her friends at home confirmed Moa in the following conviction:

> It's important to have friendships outside, because in sports there are mostly no friendships. You see each other as a rival in a way, it's a community of purpose.

After graduation, Moa left with the national team for the Olympic Games. She tried to make the most out of it, but on-site she experienced the situation as absurd and unjust:

> The bad thing was I had to watch how the whole team was knackered. That is, they were all injured .... and I was the only one that was fit. Every day I did all four apparatuses. I did everything and the others always had to watch out for their health. That's when I thought, this is really mean.

Moa's first Olympic Games experience turned out very different from what she had hoped and prepared for. While she 'did go to the Olympics and experienced how great it can be', Moa was not allowed to participate. Moa was moved first by anger and frustration but then also by the greatness of the Olympic experience. It was the latter feeling that hung over and created an even greater desire and conviction in her: 'This, I really want to experience again'. Moa decided to maintain her horizon for participation in the Olympic Games for the next cycle and to pursue her career in elite gymnastics.

Analytical summary of Moa's second career development phase and learning

Throughout adolescence, Moa pursued the horizon for elite gymnastics she had developed through her earlier learning career. In this horizon, the change to an elite sports school that facilitated student athletes pursuing a dual career appears 'pragmatically rational' (Hodkinson & Sparkes, 1997). The choice to move to the school at the same time as entering senior gymnastics further reflects the elite-level learning culture Moa was socialized in, which recommends that hopeful gymnasts move into elite sport infrastructures to economize time for training (Barker-Ruchti & Schubring, 2015). However, Moa only partly aligned, as she chose to continue to live at home. It is possible that her parents' resistance to playing 'the part of the athlete parent' (McMahon & Penney, 2015) by not getting overly involved with their child's competitive youth sport endeavours played a role in Moa maintaining a horizon for a 'life outside the gym', which included high school graduation.

Besides the change of school, Moa's integration into the senior national team constituted another structural turning point. This event was followed by a time of 'confirmatory routines' (Hodkinson & Sparkes, 1997) during which Moa participated in national and international competitions, consolidating her spot in the team and her rankings. The routines further 'reinforce(d) career decisions already made' (Hodkinson & Sparkes 1997, p. 40) and led Moa to develop an horizon of becoming an Olympic gymnast. Moa's disposition to practice extensively, remain injury-free, and learn continuously supported this career horizon. The loss of the hoped-for turning point through not being selected into the Olympic team disrupted Moa's steady career progression for the first time. The ambiguity of the selection procedure further challenged the cultural premise that hard work 'will look good eventually', which she had embodied. Although Moa was forced out of the envisaged career pathway and limited to 'observing' the OG, the greatness of the event (Jensen, Christiansen, & Henriksen, 2014) and possibly also her superior bodily condition (compared to the injured team members) contributed to Moa re-embracing her dream of becoming an Olympic gymnast. In so doing, Moa did not let a sporting failure shake her Olympic horizon (for similar findings, see Sarkar, Fletcher, & Brown, 2015). While gymnastics-wise the Olympic year became a roller coaster, Moa managed to maintain her long-lived dual career horizon. Supported by her family, friends, and the elite sports school, the gymnast realized her educational goals. The successful graduation in turn corroborated Moa's horizon for a life beyond gymnastics.

'Gymnastics is not everything': From entry into university to age 22

In the post-Olympic year, Moa confirmed her potential in different international competitions and became all-around national WAG champion. During this time, she undertook an internship at the local federation, which allowed her to train and travel to camps and competitions. Although she enjoyed the sporting success, Moa was aware that 'four years are a very long time' and that she would need a fallback option to her horizon of Olympic participation. Moa remembered all too well the emotional roller coaster, the pressures, and the unpredictability of the selection procedure involved in her first Olympic preparation.

> After it [OG] though, I said, okay, gymnastics is not everything. I am starting to study. Because you need something beside it. You cannot just do that. Also, my father kept pushing…you should start doing something for your vocational future. So I started to study. And that showed me as well, gymnastics is not everything.

One year after the Olympics, the 20-year-old started studying at the local university. She continued to live at home to keep her study costs low[4] and to avoid taking on a part-time job. Although her university schedule was 'really school-like', 'the study load was new'. In order to meet the demands, Moa capitalized on 'what [she] had learnt in sports, discipline and to work with a high degree of concentration'. The hard-working mentality she had embodied as a gymnast shaped the horizons of learning and for action she adopted in her university studies.

> Studies are exhausting. And I really dedicated myself to it, because once I get into something, I do it right. Somehow, I believe, that was all too much for me. My body just said I need a break now. I don't want anymore, I cannot do anymore.

By the end of the first university term, Moa incurred a serious injury at a training camp that abruptly forced her career progression and sporting life to halt. The injury required an operation and lengthy rehabilitation.

> The physician told me back then: 'I would love to diagnose a broken bone that heals within six weeks, but a [name of injury] does take six months, maybe even longer'.

The injury interrupted the training and competition routine the 21-year-old gymnast had pursued over more than 15 years. While the injury displaced Moa from the gym and competition life, it did not dissolve her horizon for the Olympic Games scheduled two years later. Further, and in contrast to the disruptive and identity-threatening effect many injured athletes experience (Howe, 2004; Madrigal & Gill, 2014; Schubring & Thiel, 2014), for Moa the elite sport injury 'is not necessarily a bad thing'; rather, it provided her with a time-off period that opened the door to new learning experiences:

> That was a very imprinting time, because it brought new experiences with it. Sure, it was a challenge to be injured. I don't even know for how long I haven't been in a gym and didn't do any gymnastics. But it was okay to do rehab. To grow fit again. And maybe my mind just needed that, and my body just demanded that time. And so I had to learn how to be patient, which paid off in the end.

Aiming for a full recovery, the gymnast spent 'a lot, a lot of time' with rehabilitation. For the rehabilitation, she chose centres with expertise in the recovery of injured elite athletes even though it demanded her staying several hundreds of kilometres away from home. Moa dedicated herself to rehabilitation but felt 'somewhat insecure' about how far she could load the injured limb.

> Well, it was the first injury I had. I didn't know how to handle that and so he [treating physician] told me, most people he treated made more progress than me.... So I said, well, whatever. Well, I cannot do more than... I had the feeling, I just can't. And he was always like come on, dare it, do it.

Moa withstood the pressure regarding the speed of her healing process and established what could be termed an 'interim horizon for rehabilitation'. As the rehabilitation progressed, she became ever more confident in maintaining her own pace, despite the fact that 'some smiled at me and said, well your healing is taking quite a long time'. Although Moa at the time had a clear horizon for elite gymnastics and participation in another OG, her focus on rehabilitation was closely connected to her dual career horizon:

> I don't just need that [limb] for gymnastics, you know... I still need this [limb] until I grow old. That is more important to me.

During rehabilitation, Moa experienced a lot of support from her parents, friends, and the people at the rehab centre. She cherished having a 'life outside the gym' and the fact that her friends at home 'don't necessarily see me as a gymnast'. While at the gym, 'it is always about success ... in my circle of friends, they couldn't care less'; even 'if I should stop with gymnastics, I'm still somebody to them.' Further, the injury allowed her 'some time to come down a bit' and to dedicate herself to her studies.

After the summer, Moa gradually increased her training. She focused on the one apparatus that required the least loading of her injured limb. Moa felt that the injury and the rehabilitation training had made her more patient and taught her to practice with greater consciousness and not to 'just do something airy-fairy', given the risk for injury in training for gymnastics with this attitude. This becoming led Moa to establish a safety regime for herself as she trained to qualify for an international championship that was a stepping stone for qualification in the Olympic team:

> I always tried to listen to my body. Listening to my inner voice, what is possible and what is not. If I wasn't 120% sure that I could do it, that I would land on my feet again, then I wouldn't do it.

Throughout the winter and spring seasons, Moa practiced hard on the apparatus: 'I practiced it till I dropped. I practiced a lot, a lot during that time.' She felt her performance improve even if her body had not regained its full strength. At the international championship, the 22-year-old gymnast succeeded in qualifying for, competing in, and medalling in that one apparatus final she had trained hard for. Moa was overjoyed and described this international championship as one of two career highlights: 'The finals, that was crazy. To receive a medal in the end, after all that had happened, satisfied me a lot'.

Looking back on the injury experience and the learning it had engendered, Moa concluded:

> I do believe an injury like that was implanting for me, for the whole process… I did get something new out of this…problem…finding ways to get in shape again. Of course, it is a challenge, too. Well, I was injured and I thought to myself, no, I want to come back, maybe even better than before.

Analytical summary of Moa's third career development phase and learning

In this third career phase, Moa continued to pursue and overtly commit to the dual career horizon she had maintained during her school years. In gymnastics, Moa held onto her horizon for Olympic participation. Capitalizing on her embodied dispositions of practicing with diligence, she dedicated herself to the 'confirmatory routines' (Hodkinson & Sparkes, 1997) of training and competition. In doing so, she successfully progressed in her career even in the 'post games transition' (McArdle, Moore, & Lyons, 2014), reaffirming her identity in the elite WAG learning culture.

In her life 'outside of the gym', she decided after an initial search phase to study–a pragmatically rational career decision that allowed her to prepare for a vocational future while pursuing an elite sport career. From a cultural theory of learning perspective (Hodkinson, Biesta, & James, 2008), individual, contextual, and career-specific factors informed Moa's choice. These include Moa's proven academic abilities, a horizon for a life beyond gymnastics, her parents' campaigning for the importance of preparing for her vocational future, and her failed OG selection. The last, an 'adversity-related experience' (Sarkar et al., 2015), taught Moa the frailty of career progression and the dependency of success on so many more factors than 'hard work'. Her choice to study and the becoming she experienced in the university context further consolidated her horizon for a life beyond gymnastics. Moa's engagement in academic studies followed another, injury-induced turning point. While the injury occurred unexpectedly, Moa saw its origin in fatigue accumulated through years of intense training, competition, and qualification pressures topped by the new first-year study load (Giacobbi et al., 2004). Further, the way Moa approached learning demands at university reflected the mode of learning she had been subjected to in gymnastics and had gradually embodied as a part of her: to work hard, with uncompromising dedication and great diligence. While this disposition allowed her in the long run to master and succeed in her dual career horizon, at that point in time it contributed to her pushing beyond her bodily need for recovery.

The forced time-out from her gymnastics life triggered important learning in Moa. It opened the door to the learning culture at the rehabilitation centres and allowed her to integrate further into the university program and her circle of friends. Through rehabilitation, Moa learnt other ways to strengthen, exercise, and build up her body. Although the horizon for action of some therapists appeared compromised by an elite sport learning culture focused on fast performance outcomes (Howe, 2004; Roderick & Waddington, 2000), Moa met people with a more holistic horizon for healing. Further, Moa's already established horizon for a life beyond gymnastics enabled her to develop a horizon for sustainable healing. Even her lack of experience with major injuries contributed to Moa's effort to care for her injured body with patience. Both components led Moa to develop increased consciousness for her bodily needs, abilities, and limits. As her body recovered and increasingly tolerated loading, Moa felt confirmed in her decision to resist the pressures to speed up recovery—also from inside elite gymnastics—and to prioritize full recovery. Through the rehabilitation process, Moa gradually developed an ability 'to listen to her body', which she maintained when reintegrating into the gym to pursue her horizon of participation in the next OG. The individual medal that Moa achieved a year after her injury not only became another important career turning point but also confirmed the 22-year-old gymnast's full recovery. The medal, her greatest athletic success at that point, further testified that it was possible not only to combine a dual career horizon with a horizon for elite gymnastics but also to integrate a horizon of care into a horizon of hard work. Finally, the medal also became a milestone in Moa's qualification for the Olympic team and her participation in the OG the year thereafter.

At the time of writing this case study, Moa continues to pursue her dual career horizon. She has completed a bachelor's degree and is now studying at the advanced level. She cultivates her friendships outside of gymnastics and allows herself 'real' vacations. In gymnastics, Moa maintains her spot in the national team and competes at the highest international level. Despite further injuries, her disposition to listen to and care for her bodily needs and her ability to capitalize on a life outside of gymnastics seem to be important complements to her hard-working training mentality.

Summary of learning

In this case study, we have described the learning career Moa developed inside and outside of elite gymnastics. Covering a time span of 20 years, Moa's case evidences that learning careers in elite sport, like learning careers in other vocational contexts, do not develop in a linear fashion (Bloomer & Hodkinson, 2000). As described in the analytical summaries, Moa's career intersected with various structural, self-initiated, and forced turning points, which affected her horizon for action and horizon of learning. Some turning points, such as the change to a Russian coach and the entry into the senior national team, confirmed Moa's previously developed horizon of hard work. Other turning points, such as her non-qualification for the Olympic Games and the injury she incurred in her early 20s, triggered learning, leading Moa to choose new career directions (e.g., to study) and/or to develop new dispositions (e.g., greater consciousness of her bodily needs, abilities, and limits). However, turning points alone cannot explain Moa's learning career.

Individual dispositions, such as Moa's bodily ability to withstand injuries and her academic abilities, as well as the elite sport system's dual career support and her family's learning culture, played an important role in Moa's becoming. While research outlines how parents of youth elite athletes can be socialized in and take part in their children's competitive endeavour (Elliott & Drummond, 2017; McMahon & Penney, 2015), Moa's parents exemplify a much more distant relationship, repeatedly encouraging Moa to maintain a dual career horizon. Calling for her investment in education, Moa's parents further reflected what Bourdieu (1984) described as a class-specific 'preference' for 'cultural capital', which led them to question the potential transformation of the 'physical capital' that Moa developed into 'economic capital' and future security.

Overlooking Moa's career development, the horizon for life beyond gymnastics that Moa maintained and increasingly enacted developed as a virtue for the elite gymnast. It empowered her to (a) resist the hyperinclusion and identity foreclosure that many elite gymnasts have been found to be prone to (e.g., Barker-Ruchti & Schubring, 2015; Kerr & Dacyshyn, 2000); (b) prepare early for a vocational career after elite gymnastics, which can support athlete well-being and facilitate transition out of elite sport (e.g., Park, Lavallee, & Tod, 2013; Vilanova & Puig, 2014); and (c) attend to her injury with care, resisting the pressure to return early to training and risk repeated injuring (Howe, 2004; Roderick & Waddington, 2000; Schubring & Thiel, 2016).

Viewed as a whole, Moa's learning career is unique for several reasons: First, it provides a positive example of how an adult WAG gymnast developed and successfully pursued a dual career in elite sport. Such examples are rare, especially in a sport where early peaking and extensive training have long been considered indispensable (Barker-Ruchti, Kerr, Schubring, Cervin, & Nunomura, 2017; Cervin, Kerr, Barker-Ruchti, Schubring, & Nunomura, 2017) and where dropping out after injury or missed qualification seems common. Second, Moa's learning career indicates the importance familial learning culture and supportive non-athletic relationships can have for sustainable career development in elite sport. Third, Moa's injury experience draws attention to the learning potential setbacks and time-outs from elite sport can have, if properly cared for.

Notes

1. In order to safeguard confidentiality, we use pseudonyms throughout the text and limit the details we provide on the sport context and the national elite sport system.
2. The gymnastics training centre is one of a handful of its kind spread over the country. The centre has produced top-level male and female gymnasts and attracted gymnasts from other centres. The centre is well connected to regional and national elite sport infrastructures and support services to which gymnasts have access to the federation, the region, and the national governing body of sport.
3. The elite sport infrastructure is a national sport-unspecific support centre for federations in the region. Services for youth and senior elite athletes and their coaches range from performance diagnostics to medical check-ups, nutrition counselling, dual career services, and training facilities.
4. University education in Moa's country is state funded, and study fees are minimal. However, students still have to finance their living expenses.

References

Barker-Ruchti, N., Kerr, R., Schubring, A., Cervin, G., & Nunomura, M. (2017). 'Gymnasts are like wine, they get better with age': Becoming and developing adult women's artistic gymnasts. *Quest*, 69(3), 348–365.

Barker-Ruchti, N., Lindgren, E.-C., Hofmann, A., Sinning, S., & Shelton, C. (2014). Tracing the career paths of top-level women football coaches: Turning points to understand and develop sport coaching careers. *Sports Coaching Review*, 3(2), 117–131.

Barker-Ruchti, N., & Schubring, A. (2015). Moving into and out of high-performance sport: The cultural learning of an artistic gymnast. *Physical Education and Sport Pedagogy*, *21*(1), 69–80.

Bloomer, M., & Hodkinson, P. (2000). Learning careers: Continuity and change in young people's dispositions to learning. *British Educational Research Journal*, 26(5), 583–597.

Bourdieu, P. (1984). *Distinction: A social critique of the judgement of taste* (7th edition) (R. Nice, Trans.). Cambridge, MA: Harvard University Press.

Cervin, G., Kerr, R., Barker-Ruchti, N., Schubring, A., & Nunomura, M. (2017). Growing up and speaking out: Female gymnasts' rights in an ageing sport. *Annals of Leisure Research*, 20(3), 317–330.

Creswell, J. W., & Miller, D. L. (2000). Determining validity in qualitative inquiry. *Theory into Practice*, 39(3), 124–130.

Elliott, S. K., & Drummond, M. J. N. (2017). Parents in youth sport: What happens after the game? *Sport, Education and Society*, 22(3), 391–406.

Giacobbi, P. R., Lynn, T. K., Wetherington, J. M., Jenkins, J., Bodendorf, M., & Langley, B. (2004). Stress and coping during the transition to university for first-year female athletes. *Sport Psychologist*, *18*(1), 1–20.

Girginov, V., & Sandanski, I. (2004). From participants to competitors: The transformation of British gymnastics and the role of the Eastern European model of sport. *International Journal of the History of Sport*, *21*(5), 815–832.

Hodkinson, P., Biesta, G., & James, D. (2008). Understanding learning culturally: Overcoming the dualism between social and individual views of learning. *Vocations and Learning*, *1*(1), 27–47.

Hodkinson, P., Ford, G., Hodkinson, H., & Hawthorn, R. (2008). Retirement as a learning process. *Educational Gerontology*, 34(3), 167–184.

Hodkinson, P., & Sparkes, A. C. (1997). Careership: A sociological theory of career decision making. *British Journal of Sociology of Education, 18*(1), 29–44.
Howe, P. D. (2004). *Sport, professionalism and pain: Ethnographies of injury and risk*. London: Routledge.
Jensen, R. D., Christiansen, A. V., & Henriksen, K. (2014). The Olympic Games: The experience of a lifetime or simply the most important competition of an athletic career? *Physical Culture & Sport: Studies & Research, 64*(1), 41–52.
Kerr, G., & Dacyshyn, A. (2000). The retirement experiences of elite, female gymnasts. *Journal of Applied Sport Psychology, 12*(2), 115–133.
Kerr, R., Barker-Ruchti, N., Schubring, A., Cervin, G., & Nunomura, M. (2015). *Coming of age: Towards best practice in women's artistic gymnastics*. Canterbury, NZ: Lincoln University. Retrieved from https://hdl.handle.net/10182/6515.
Kerr, R., & Moore, K. (2015). Hard work or child's play? Migrant coaches' reflections on coaching gymnastics in New Zealand. *World Leisure Journal, 57*(3), 185–195.
Madrigal, L., & Gill, D. L. (2014). Psychological responses of division I female athletes throughout injury recovery: A case study approach. *Journal of Clinical Sport Psychology*, 8(3), 276–298.
McArdle, S., Moore, P., & Lyons, D. (2014). Olympic athletes' experiences of a post games career transition program. *Sport Psychologist, 28*(3), 269–278.
McMahon, J. A., & Penney, D. (2015). Sporting parents on the pool deck: Living out a sporting culture? *Qualitative Research in Sport, Exercise and Health, 7*(2), 153–169.
Park, S., Lavallee, D., & Tod, D. (2013). Athletes' career transition out of sport: A systematic review. *International Review of Sport and Exercise Psychology*, 6(1), 22–53.
Roderick, M., & Waddington, I. (2000). Playing hurt: Managing injuries in English professional football. *International Review for the Sociology of Sport, 35*(2), 165–180.
Sarkar, M., Fletcher, D., & Brown, D. J. (2015). What doesn't kill me…: Adversity-related experiences are vital in the development of superior Olympic performance. *Journal of Science and Medicine in Sport, 18*(4), 475–479.
Schubring, A., & Thiel, A. (2014). Coping with growth in adolescent elite sport. *Sociology of Sport Journal, 31*(3), 304–326.
Schubring, A., & Thiel, A. (2016). Health-related gender boundary crossing in youth elite sport. *Sport in Society, 19*(5), 695–710.
Vilanova, A., & Puig, N. (2014). Personal strategies for managing a second career: The experiences of Spanish Olympians. *International Review for the Sociology of Sport, 51*(5), 529–546.

Chapter 5

Learning through boxing: A case of a male boxer

Christopher R. Matthews

Becoming a 'decent man'

Introduction—Possibilities for becoming in boxing

During the 10 or so years that I've been involved in boxing, I've seen countless people change their bodies, behaviours, and performances of self. For many, this has been neatly understood as a simple process of becoming a boxer. In large part, such 'becoming' involves moving from pugilistic newcomer towards a relatively comfortable embodiment of the physical and emotional grammars that are commonplace within boxing subcultures. While this is perhaps most clear within the relative disparities between the physical literacy of novices in comparison to that of advanced boxers, it can also be understood and explored by considering the manner in which people come to 'naturally' perform other cultural hallmarks associated with boxing.

In Matthews (2018), I detail my own experience of (not) becoming a boxer and how that process links to immersive research methodologies. This personal journey has plotted a fantastically challenging and sometimes damaging pathway through various gyms and types of engagement. I have encountered a series of experiences from which I have changed and developed in a number of significant ways, not always positively. This process has given me a relatively unique insight into the place the sport can occupy in the lives of those who learn the 'art' of pugilism and the ways in which they develop as both athletes and people.

Throughout the multiple projects I have worked on, I have been fortunate to interview over 250 people, including athletes of all levels, coaches, parents, retired competitors, medical officials, and those working within the governance of the sport. These formal opportunities to collect data and the multitude of less formal chats, observations, and relationships I have formed have provided a variety of insights into boxing (Matthews, 2014, 2015, 2016, 2018) and the academic study of sport more broadly (Channon & Matthews, 2015a, 2015b, 2018; Matthews & Channon, 2016a, 2016b, forthcoming). A relatively stable narrative that I have heard across all these research sites has focused on the possibilities embedded in boxing that enable young people to develop in various positive ways. Such an understanding of what young people might become through their engagement in boxing is often a strong influence that draws parents to accept and encourage their children's involvement with the sport.

One of the most consistent stories repeated to me has been the passionate belief from cultural 'insiders' that participation in boxing stands apart from most sports in its ability to help transform the lives of young people, especially boys from lower socio-economic groups. While such discourses pervade a variety of sports to some degree (see Matthews & Channon, 2016a, for a partial example from ice hockey), there is often an overtly uncritical acceptance of such simplistic ideas within boxing gyms.[1] I have always been suspicious of claims about the transformative potential of boxing, especially due to the pervasive confirmation bias that usually clouds athletes' and coaches' understandings of their sport. As a result, at various times, whether as researcher, fighter, coach, or volunteer, I have found myself encouraging people to reflect upon the realities of pain, injury, embarrassment, brain damage, self and social sacrifice, abuse, exploitation, failure, and burnout that often lie, thinly veiled, beneath ideas about boxing's power to positively affect lives.

Building on this, much of my more impactful academic work has explored such experiences as they relate to the unequal landscapes of gendered power that are still very much a feature of boxing (Matthews, 2014, 2016). However, during this time, I have also collected a wealth of data, which evidences some of the positive transformations and transitions that people have experienced, in part, through their involvement with the sport. It is towards this side of my data that I focus within this case study. Specifically, I use extracts from two different interviews, the first conducted in 2010 and the second in 2017, with Nick,[2] a 30-year-old former boxer who, alongside running his own joinery business, currently works as a part-time boxing coach.

I have known Nick since my first forays into the field of boxing during my PhD research. We have shared many chats and training sessions, so while I draw on two discrete data sets, these interviews are built on a number of years of getting to know each other as friends.[3] In what follows, I explore in detail the manner in which Nick understands boxing as a part of his personal development. My attention is focused on his experience of 'becoming' *through* the sport—specifically, in his words, becoming a 'decent man'. In so doing, I highlight the utility of cultural understandings of learning as a means to frame this process.

Learning cultures and boxing

As Natalie neatly outlines in Chapter 3, learning cultures shape and frame the behaviours of the people who inhabit them. Such spaces are 'constituted by the actions, dispositions and interpretations of participants' (Hodkinson, Biesta, & James, 2008, p. 34), and as Lave and Wenger (1991, p. 35) have it, 'learning is an integral part of generative social practice in the lived-in world'. Learning can then be understood as a process whereby individuals are more or less successfully socialised into pre-existing notions about the social world and, in this way, become the means by which that world is re-created, renewed, recast, and reinvented. It is part of the daily and part of all interactions, and it is, as such, part of the reification and potential subversion of taken-for-granted cultural expectations, standards, and assumptions about what constitutes 'normal' social life.

Learning cultures enable but also frame, inhibit, and limit that which might readily be learned. Within this process, individuals develop dispositions to learning; ways of considering what is appropriate, important, and essential to learn; and an understanding of how and in what ways one could, should, and should not learn. It is here that an individual's 'horizon of learning'—the potential learning pathways and destinations that one might consider are broadly achievable—is developed. Such conceptual maps act to shape and limit the 'horizons for action' that an individual can see as possible, permissible, and probable (Bloomer & Hodkinson, 2000; Hodkinson, Sparkes, & Hodkinson, 1996).

It is important, then, to avoid considering learning cultures as inherently, or even predominantly, 'good' in that they enable 'learners to learn'. Such a simplistic understanding strips away an essential focus directed towards the dynamics of social power that underpin cultural theories of learning—for as Foucault (1980, 1984) describes, individuals and groups can gain and maintain significant influence and power if they have the ability to shape what is considered normal, natural, and moral. Clearly, learning and education are central strands within such a process.

'Common sense' understandings of what one might find within particular learning cultures 'exist as ways of doing and ways of being that are considered to be normal. This means that learning cultures are governed by values and ideals, by normative expectations about good learning, good teaching, good leadership, and so forth' (Hodkinson et al., 2008, p. 34). For Hodkinson and colleagues (2008), learning cultures have an enduring history, and while social change is possible and probable, such shifts often occur slowly. The relative stability of such knowledge becomes engrained and embodied in the thoughts, movements, and actions of those who are drawn to enter and stay within learning cultures.

When taken together, these points help us to appreciate the manner in which learning cultures shape and frame social life. This is the same in boxing gyms as it is in other spaces. Here, culturally learned dispositions shape the ways of doing, seeing, feeling, and succeeding, which are considered 'normal' by boxers, coaches, and others associated with the sport. For example, in Matthews (2016), I explore how myths and legends about boxing intertwine with routine performance within the gym to become a largely unquestioned means by which men come to understand their time inside and around the ring. Woodward (2006) details similar findings by weaving together discussions about boxers' identities with heroic, valorised, and (in)famous spectacles of the sport.

In both these cases, the cultural heritage of boxing as a 'hard man's sport' precedes and acts to cast a conceptual shadow over the nuanced and often paradoxical realities of life inside most gyms (Matthews, 2014, 2016; Woodward, 2006). And in this regard, those that do 'step up' by stepping through the doorway into a boxing gym for the first time often have a well-developed, if mythologised, idea about what to expect in such spaces. They are then primed to expect a certain patterning of culture and, with it, a certain form of learning. It is here that stories of boxing's transformative potential draw people into pugilistic spaces and *can* become reified through the lives of gym denizens (Matthews, 2016; Woodward, 2006).

A developing body of research does much to detail the cultural landscapes within which boxers might find themselves (Boddy, 2009; Chandler, 1996; de Garis, 2000; Fulton, 2011; Hargreaves, 1997; Heiskanen, 2012; Jennings, 2015; Jump, 2015; Lafferty & McKay, 2004; Matthews, 2014, 2016, 2018; McGannon, Schinke, Ge, & Blodgett, 2018; Mennesson, 2000; Paradis, 2012; Sheard, 1997; Sugden, 1999; van Ingen, 2011; Wacquant, 2004; Woodward, 2006, 2014). Rich data, which details learning cultures, is often a central feature of most accounts from 'inside' boxing subcultures. Indeed, seldom does research on boxing (especially the ethnographic) not describe, and perhaps in some cases fetishize, the gruelling process of 'learning the ropes', which novice boxers must endure to become somewhat accepted as 'pugs'. Yet seldom does such work situate these findings within critical pedagogical literature. Furthermore, these snapshots, temporary windows into social life, often do little to detail the specifics of how such developmental learning processes might unfold away from the gym or after a boxing career has come to an end. It is on such a process that I am afforded the space to focus in this case study—specifically through a discussion of Nick's process of learning and becoming through boxing.

Becoming a 'decent man' through boxing

When I first met Nick, he had already become an accomplished boxer. At 23, he had enjoyed a successful apprenticeship in amateur boxing, winning a range of local competitions and competing successfully at a national level, and he was now taking significant steps to build a career in the professional code of the sport. We sparred a few times; I always enjoyed the strange feeling of safety that comes when you are in the ring with someone who is so much better than you. Yes, he could K.O. me in a second, but his elite level of ability also came with a confident poise and accuracy that meant he could make me work while not doing any serious damage. During our first interview in September 2010, I asked Nick about this, and he told me the following:

> I learned that control in the ring. Before I started boxing I was wild, now I'm a sharpshooter and I know it [laughs], it's been drilled into me that the skills I've learned are dangerous, really dangerous, and I've seen it, I've seen what happens when you catch someone just right and it's not pretty. So I've calmed down, I've calmed down because you 'ave to in boxing, but as well 'cause I've seen what can 'appen when you do stupid stuff outside the ring.

These comments came against a backdrop of Nick's chequered history of exclusion from school, street fights, and run-ins with local police, teachers, and other authority figures. They highlight the process of becoming that this relatively young man had already experienced as he moved from 'unruly youth' into adulthood.

Like many boys, Nick had been drawn to boxing from an early age. Eventually, despite holding fears as to the safety of the sport, his parents encouraged him to focus much of his spare time on developing his abilities. I remember speaking with Nick's dad about the change his family saw in him once he started taking boxing seriously. When I asked Nick about this, he had the following to say:

NICK: Ha, yeah, I hated school most of the time. All my mates did, we were just classic lads off of the estate you know, none of us was into [school], I was a terror, I've seen some of my teachers since and apologised 'cus they was just doing their jobs and at the time I just saw them like I saw coppers. [Pause] What was I saying?

CHRISTOPHER: I asked about boxing and school…

NICK: Yeah, basically it started with me dad using boxing as a way of making me behave, I loved it right, so much that when there was any hint of them not letting me go down the [boxing] club 'cus o' muckin' around in school or whatever, I'd actually listen to my dad. That's how it started.

CHRISTOPHER: Then what?

NICK: Erm, well it wasn't really school but after school. So, I got some OK grades 'cus when I started to get to the last couple of years when exams was coming up I started to think about jobs or college and all that. Up until then boxing just helped like I said [earlier] but when I started thinking about the future, I started thinking about school a bit like I thought about training, and [my coach] always used to ask about school and in the end he helped me with thinking about it like that.

CHRISTOPHER: What do you mean?

NICK: It's 'ard to explain, but, like, I learned very early in boxing that I had to put the graft in during the week so that I could spar on Saturdays and then I learned that I 'ad to train 'ard and put the time in throughout the year to actually do well at comps. Once my coach got me to see school like that I started to understand that if I wanted to do well [in my exams] then I had to concentrate and work 'ard, 'cus I was just never bothered about school. I couldn't see the point in it like, day-to-day, but once I started seeing it like stuff in training that you don't want to do but that's still important to actually do like core work or sprints, then I started to see the point. (September 2010)

It appears, then, that boxing provided Nick with more than simply a means of rewarding or punishing his engagement with school. It also gave him a powerful means of experiencing success and, with it, an analogical map that he could use to plot a course in other areas of his life. This disposition towards learning included a 'horizon to action' (Bloomer & Hodkinson, 2000; Hodkinson et al., 1996) that was a means by which Nick could reconsider how he understood and interacted with more formal educational settings.

With colleagues (Channon, Matthews, & Khomutova, 2018), I have drawn on a similar process to develop 'physical metaphors' when teaching. In class, we have used various physical activities—or as we have it, 'moving lessons'—to engage students' kinaesthetic sense of themselves and others, rather than depending solely on auditory and visual teaching methods. This uses students' own bodies as metaphorical or literal examples for illustrating conceptual ideas, thereby grounding and personalising abstract academic material in physical experiences. Echoing Nick's comments, we have found them to be important pedagogical tools that can enable young people to think more reflexively about their social worlds.

So while Nick was relatively disinterested in formal school-based learning cultures, he was able to develop a positive disposition to learning via boxing. Nick largely articulated this as helping develop and shape his ability to 'work hard'. When I asked him about the most important thing he thought he had learned in boxing, he told me the following:

NICK: [After a pause] If you're involved in boxing for long enough you have to learn about two things, one is 'ard work. No one stays in boxing unless eventually they either start to enjoy working 'ard or they realise [working hard] it's part of doing well, I enjoyed working 'ard and seeing the results that came from it. The second is how to lose, no matter how good you are, you lose eventually, and that's *even* if you work super 'ard. Those two things are the most important, because if you don't understand how they fit together, you might get the 'ard work bit, but what happens if you put all that time and effort in and then lose? Well, you quit, or realise [losing is] part of the game and get back to work. *That's* what's been the most important.

CHRISTOPHER: That sounds like a line from *Rocky*, ya'know, the 'it ain't how hard you hit, it's how many times you can get hit and keep moving forward'.

NICK: Yeah it is, that's it, those sort o'lines are daft in the movies, but actually, that one works quite well for most people in boxing. (September 2017)

Clearly, according to Nick, this often-mythologised idea regarding boxing's ability to instil a grinding and persistent work ethic was locked down in the realities of the lives of boxers. Here, narratives around boxing's historical and continuing connection to working-class men takes centre stage. As both Woodward (2006) and I (Matthews, 2016) have shown, such stories are experienced and engrained and become 'real' within the routine performances that are commonplace inside and around the ring. And while it is challenging to prise apart the manner in which such narratives are learned and then embodied within the performances of boxers or are already present to some degree in those who are drawn to the sport, Nick's case demonstrates how such ideas can be usefully employed by boxers in life away from the ring.

It is clear from the previous quote that Nick developed a mature relationship with losing, yet this rather philosophical understanding did little to help him negotiate the harsh economic realities of attempting to develop a career in professional boxing:

CHRISTOPHER: Earlier you said something about learning to lose, what was it like when that first happened?

NICK: I lost in amateur boxing early and I was a kid so I cried and whatever, but it was pretty easy 'cus in amateurs you're often back out [fighting] again in a few weeks. That's one of the big things, you train 'ard, you compete, if you win it's great, but you get back to training, if you lose you learn from it and then [pauses for effect], you get back to training [laughs]. Know what I mean? I don't know where else you learn that as a kid. But it was different when I lost as a pro, fucking hell, that was a nightmare 'cus that means money. No one wants to lose, especially in front of their mates and family, but as an adult, that's OK, you know, you're over stuff like that, really, and I'd learned to handle that, but in pro-boxing if you start losing regularly you ain't gonna be successful and I was in it to make bank [money] and enough to get me set up. So that was 'ard 'cus as a kid you lose and it's just your pride at the time, but as a pro it was about my future. (September 2017)

So while Nick had experienced his early losses in this positive light, providing a mature and productive acceptance of setbacks, the relatively unforgiving nature of professional boxing resulted in a different set of outcomes that accompanied losing.

While all competitive boxing has some risk attached to it, the magnification of damaging consequences that are associated with an extended career in the ring is something experienced and elite boxers are often forced to consider in a more prescient manner. When I asked Nick about what finally got him to 'throw in the towel', he told me the following:

NICK: I just lost a few times, and eventually got hurt pretty bad.

CHRISTOPHER: So what made you stop, the losses or the injury?

NICK: Both, together, but I just realised I probably wasn't gonna make it any further without really risking my health long-term. Thing is, you look at these lads that nail it in the amateurs and then get managed at the start of their pro-careers. The risk is worth taking for them 'cus it's managed and the rewards can be massive, but unless you're up there [at the elite level], you 'ave to take bigger risks to get smaller rewards, I started getting some paydays, but I just had to accept in the end that it wasn't gonna happen.

CHRISTOPHER: Then what?

NICK: It got a bit dark for a bit. [Pause] I didn't know this at the time, but I was a bit broken. I think my heart was broken or something. I was depressed, boxing was my life an' that for so long and it was gonna be my future as

> well. Coming to terms with that was the 'ardest thing I've ever had to do. I still miss it na, that's why I still come down, just to get a bit out me system. But the problem is I'm still in shape and I feel strong, so every now and then I think about getting back in [the ring] again, it's not even like I have any control over it, the thought just pops in me head even though I know I can't. (September 2017)

The infamous nature of boxing as a dangerous and potentially disabling sport means that such 'turning points' (Hodkinson & Sparkes, 1997) are usually foreseen to some degree by most boxers and, as such, *can* be prepared for. However, they also might have a 'forced' component, which can result in a more challenging and potentially traumatising set of outcomes (Barker-Ruchti, Lindgren, Hofmann, Sinning, & Shelton, 2015; Barker-Ruchti, Rynne, Lee, & Barker, 2014).

For Nick, this process was a mixture of the two; while he had given some thought to what he might do post-boxing, his career, which was supposed to provide him with a financial basis for life after the sport, was drawn somewhat short. He experienced (and still experiences) some emotional pain associated with not reaching his goals in the sport, and he didn't have a clear plan in place as to the next stage of his life; yet he had developed an orientation to learning that he knew could be deployed in other areas. Such dramatic shifts in the way that one's life is organised provide many opportunities and potential pitfalls. For Nick, it was the lessons that he had experienced via boxing that helped him through this time. He continued:

> Yeah, you know what, I eventually picked myself up and got on with it. I didn't know this at the time but I applied those lessons I'd learned in boxing to my life. I'd had a setback but there's only one way forward and that's to start working towards another goal with the same focus as I'd put into boxing. You know, embracing the graft as a necessary part of achieving what I wanted to do, like I did in the end with school. I had some money [to live off] so I went back to college. The difference was that now I wanted to do it, and I knew I wanted to be successful in whatever it was that was gonna replace boxing, so even though I felt thick as fuck at times, I just worked like a dog, thing is, though, it was boxing that learned me that work ethic, so even though I wasn't boxing properly anymore it was all still down to boxing. (September 2017)

Nick interpreted his success as a direct outcome of the lessons he had learned through boxing. He had developed a horizon of learning and a connected horizon for action (Bloomer & Hodkinson, 2000; Hodkinson et al., 1996) that prioritised application, effort, and work ethic, which appeared to stand him in good stead despite his career in boxing not providing the success or financial rewards he had strived for. Or as Archer (2007) would consider it, Nick drew on these ideas to help him make his 'way through the world'.

What is more, Nick also believed that his engagement with the sport had helped him in a broad existential way to become a better person. He largely understood this as part of the process of growing up and developing a positive appreciation for 'respect':

> When I think back and look at myself na, the main thing is, I grew up in boxing, it made me grow up, the sport does that to lads like me 'cus you 'ave to take it seriously, so for the first time in my life I had to take something seriously, and it made me start to grow up. It's nothing overnight or whatever, just the start of a process and in the end I don't know how much it was boxing or it would 'ave been something else and I would have grown up anyway, but whatever, boxing's made me a better person, it's made me respectful, and it's made me get respect from other people, not 'cus they think I'm 'ard, that means nothing in the end, but boxing taught me that in order to get respect you've got to be respectful. In the end, I look at when I started boxing and I was a terror, I was a kid like other kids, but lots of my mates didn't learn them lessons and they're still the same, they didn't grow up, I grew up, could be 'cus of losing, could be 'aving positive role models, but in the end, I think boxing taught me to be a decent man, not perfect, no-one's perfect, but there's plenty o'lads that I came up with that ain't decent. (September 2017)

Boxing provided Nick with a way of understanding the process of becoming a 'decent man'. It gave him a series of lessons that underpinned how he could conceptualise a future self whereby he would be respected and respectful. This can be understood as a horizon for action (Bloomer & Hodkinson, 2000; Hodkinson et al., 1996) largely framed by narratives of adulthood that prioritised maturity, empathy, and responsibility. And while he astutely points out that it wasn't necessarily his engagement in boxing that determined this process, his story highlights a possible manner in which his process of 'becoming' could have been positively influenced by the sport.

It is important that these claims are considered and understood in relation to the strengths and weaknesses of such data. Nick's reflections on the process of 'becoming' and growing up through his involvement in boxing are shaped by his relatively positive disposition to the sport. While he is certainly not a pugilistic zealot believing that boxing could cure all of life's ills, he had enjoyed a largely positive career inside the ring that undoubtedly shaped his reading of the sport. As such, we must consider this as he reflects back upon his process of 'becoming':

CHRISTOPHER: When did you realise that you'd got that way of working from boxing?

NICK: It's only when I've thought back you know, 'cus I've never been much for thinking about stuff like that. I just mainly fell into things, I never really decided I'd try to make it in boxing, it just happened and I guess I just knew that I 'ad to work 'ard to get better, it was the same wi' college, I never sat

> there and starting thinkin' 'right you've got to work 'ard na', that was just the way I was 'cus it 'ad been driven into me while I was down the [boxing] club. I just needed to get a new goal after boxing was done, once I decided I had to go back to college that was that, I just got my grind on 'cus I was focused and that's just what I do. (September 2017)

In this extract, Nick reconfirms his statements about boxing instilling a productive work ethic—but not before telling me that it is largely with hindsight that he now understands this. As such, we must acknowledge that these pervasive narratives about boxing might be shaping the manner in which he now reflects about his experiences.

Furthermore, embedded in Nick's answer here is an acknowledgement that what he now reads as important personal development through boxing was largely an unthinking and unconscious process. This certainly does not fundamentally undermine the data as ideologically shaped contemporary bias; rather, it highlights the manner in which such lessons and processes of becoming might be embedded into the unreflective actions of young people. And, furthermore, it highlights how discursive interpretations of the sport shape not only the ways people consciously consider boxing but also the routine actions, behaviours, and performance of boxers inside and away from boxing gyms (Matthews, 2016; Woodward, 2006).

Concluding remarks

Embedded within Nick's story of becoming a 'decent man' is a detailed case study of how participation in boxing *can* lead some people to experience important life lessons and develop a positive disposition toward learning. In many ways, these examples represent the sort of transformations that many in boxing take for granted as an inherent outcome of participation in the sport. They are certainly not presented here as such; rather, they are offered to provide *one* empirical grounding for narratives about boxing and personal development. It is then important that readers appreciate this, without essentialising the possibilities that are embedded in such participation. In so doing, it is possible to remain cognisant of the countless untold stories where boxing (and other sports) have played a damaging and deleterious role in people's development. With such a balanced view of boxing (and other sports), scholars and practitioners alike are able to reconsider the manner in which they engage with the sport to enhance potential positive outcomes while also partially managing the associated negative effects.

It is within an understanding and appreciation of the importance of the learning cultures and personal processes of becoming that occur within them that we can usefully explore such phenomena. Rather than a fetishised and uncritical reading of sport's transformative potential, the work presented in this case study, and across this book, highlights what *can* transpire within sport if young people are given a supportive and encouraging environment. And it is the important contribution that a critical understanding of social power, which lies at the foundation of the theoretical framework of this book, in large part enables this process. Here, through scholars' critical reading of sport's developmental potential and nuanced accounts of the positive process of 'becoming' in and through sport, the potentially damaging, destructive, and divisive outcomes of social relationships of power can still be foregrounded.

Notes

1. In Channon and Matthews (2018), Alex and I discuss this as it relates to the manner in which we developed the philosophical underpinnings to the Love Fighting Hate Violence campaign. This is a useful case study that can help illuminate these ideas further.
2. A pseudonym is used here and throughout the chapter.
3. Space does not permit me to detail the specifics of my methodological reflections upon this work. Such considerations are important, and I encourage colleagues with particular interests in this side of my work to see Matthews (2015, 2018) for further details.

References

Archer, M. (2007). *Making our way through the world: Human reflexivity and social mobility*. Cambridge: Cambridge University Press.

Barker-Ruchti, N., Lindgren, E.-C., Hofmann, A., Sinning, S., & Shelton, C. (2015). Tracing the career paths of top-level women football coaches: Turning points to understand and develop sport coaching careers. *Sports Coaching Review*, *3*(2), 117–131.

Barker-Ruchti, N., Rynne, S. B., Lee, J., & Barker, D. (2014). Athlete learning in Olympic sport: A cultural analysis. *Sports Coaching Review*, *3*(2), 162–178.

Bloomer, M., & Hodkinson, P. (2000). Learning careers: Continuity and change in young people's dispositions to learning. *British Educational Research Journal*, *26*(5), 583–597.

Boddy, K. (2009). *Boxing: A cultural history*. London: Reaktion Books.

Chandler, D. (1996). *Boxer: An anthology of writings on boxing and visual culture*. Cambridge, MA: MIT Press.

Channon, A., & Matthews, C. R. (Eds.). (2015a). *Global perspectives on women in combat sports: Women warriors around the world*. London: Palgrave Macmillan.

Channon, A., & Matthews, C. R. (2015b). 'It is what it is': Masculinity, homosexuality and inclusive discourse in mixed martial arts. *Journal of Homosexuality*, *62*(7), 936–956.

Channon, A., & Matthews, C. R. (2018). Love Fighting Hate Violence: An anti-violence program for martial arts and combat sports. In T. F. Carter, D. Burdsey, & M. Doidge (Eds.), *Transforming sport: Knowledges, practices, structures*. London: Routledge.

Channon, A. G., Matthews, C. R., & Khomutova, A. (2018). Moving lessons: Teaching sociology through embodied learning in the HE classroom. In C. R. Matthews, U. Edgington, & A. Channon (Eds.), *Teaching with sociological imagination in higher and further education: Contexts, pedagogies, reflections*. Singapore: Springer Nature.

de Garis, L. (2000). 'Be a buddy to your buddy'. In J. McKay, M. Messner, & D. Sabo (Eds.), *Masculinities, gender relations and sport*. London: Sage.

Foucault, Michel. (1980). *Power/knowledge: Selected interviews and other writings, 1972–1977* (C. Gordon, Trans.). New York: Pantheon.

Foucault, Michel. (1984). Space, knowledge, and power. In P. Rabinow (Ed.), *The Foucault reader*. New York: Pantheon.

Fulton, J. (2011). 'What's your capital worth?'—The development of capital in British boxing. *European Journal for Sport and Society*, 8(3), 193–218.

Hargreaves, J. (1997). Women's boxing and related activities: Introducing images and meanings. *Body and Society*, 3(4): 33–49.

Heiskanen, B. (2012). *The urban geography of boxing: Race, class, and gender in the ring*. London: Routledge.

Hodkinson, P., Biesta, G. J. J., & James, D. (2008). Understanding learning culturally: Overcoming the dualism between social and individual views of learning, *Vocations and Learning*, *1*(1), 27–47.

Hodkinson, P., & Sparkes, A. C. (1997). Careership: A sociological theory of career decision making. *British Journal of Sociology of Education*, *18*(1), 29–44.

Hodkinson, P., Sparkes, A. C., & Hodkinson, H. (1996). *Triumphs and tears: Young people, markets and the transition from school to work*. London: David Fulton.

Jennings, L. A. (2015). *She's a knockout! A history of women's fighting sports*. London: Rowman & Littlefield.

Jump, D. L. (2015). *Fighting for change: Narrative accounts on the appeal and desistance potential of boxing*. Doctoral thesis. Available at https://www.escholar.manchester.ac.uk/uk-ac-man-scw:253851. Accessed 1 July 2017.

Lafferty, Y., & McKay, J. (2004). 'Suffragettes in satin shorts'? Gender and competitive boxing. *Qualitative Sociology*, *27*(3), 249–276.

Lave, J., & Wenger, E. (1991). *Situated learning: Legitimate peripheral participation* (Vol. 521423740). Cambridge: Cambridge university press.

Matthews, C. R. (2014). Biology ideology and pastiche hegemony. *Men and masculinities*, *17*(2), 99–119.

Matthews, C. R. (2016). The tyranny of the male preserve. *Gender and Society*, *30*(2), 312–333.

Matthews, C. R. (2017). *We need to talk about the worst bits of the 'best fights'*. Love Fighting Hate Violence blog, lfhv.org. Accessed 5 March 2018.

Matthews, C. R. (2018). On (not) becoming: Involved-detachment and sports 'violence'. In D. Malcolm & P. Velija (Eds.), *Figurational research in sport, leisure and health*. London: Taylor & Francis.

Matthews, C. R., & Channon, A. (2016a). 'Its only sport'—The symbolic neutralisation of 'violence'. *Symbolic Interaction*, *39*(4), 557–576.

Matthews, C. R., & Channon, A. (2016b). Understanding sports violence: Revisiting foundational explorations. *Sport in Society*, *20*(7), 751–767.

Matthews, C. R., & Channon, A. (Forthcoming). Men, masculinities, and sport: The 'male preserve' thesis and masculine domination in/through physical culture. In L. Gottzen, U. Mellstrom, & T. Shefer (Eds.), *International handbook on masculinity studies*. London: Routledge.

McGannon, K. R., Schinke, R. J., Ge, Y., & Blodgett, A. T. (2018). Negotiating gender and sexuality: A qualitative study of elite women boxer intersecting identities and sport psychology implications. *Journal of Applied Sports Psychology*. DOI: 10.1080/10413200.2017.1421593

Mennesson, C. (2000). 'Hard' women and 'soft' women: The social construction of identities among female boxers. *International Review for the Sociology of Sport*, 35(1): 21–33.

Paradis, E. (2012). Boxers, briefs or bras? Bodies, gender and change in the boxing gym. *Body and Society*, 8(2): 82–109.

Sheard, K. G. (1997). Aspects of boxing in the Western 'civilizing process'. *International Review for the Sociology of Sport*, *32*(1): 31–57.

Sugden, J. (1996). *Boxing and society—An international analysis*. Manchester: Manchester University Press.

van Ingen, C. (2011). Spatialities of anger: Emotional geographies in a boxing program for survivors of violence. *Sociology of Sport Journal*, 28, 171–188.

Wacquant, L. (2004). *Body and soul: Notebooks of an apprentice boxer*. Oxford: Oxford University Press.

Woodward, K. (2006). *Boxing, masculinity and identity: The 'I' of the tiger*. London: Routledge.

Woodward, K. (2014). Legacies of 2012: Putting women's boxing into discourse. *Contemporary Social Science: Journal of the Academy of Social Sciences*, 9(2): 242–252.

Chapter 6

Learning through a semi-professional career and deselection: A case of a male ice hockey player

Gretchen Kerr

> I was devastated and completely lost… and felt like such a failure.

This case study addresses the cultural learning of a Canadian male ice hockey player. The athlete who engaged in this study chose the name Nathan as his pseudonym to be used throughout this case study. Nathan was 22 years of age and in his second year of university studies at the time of the interviews. Nathan's story begins as a child learning to skate and continues through the process of becoming a semi-professional player. When Nathan was not selected for a professional team, his story focuses on wrestling with his sense of self and redefining future aspirations. The data was collected through three life history interviews across the period of two months: the first addressed the early years of hockey involvement, the second focused on Nathan's experiences as a semi-professional player, and the third concentrated on the process of becoming after deselection. Each phase represented different contexts, supports, and challenges, which arguably provided opportunities for Nathan's learning.

Ice hockey in Canadian society

Winters in Canada are characterized by cold temperatures, lots of snow, and pastimes such as skating and ice hockey. The sport of ice hockey is often referred to as Canada's national sport and pastime, playing a significant role in Canadian society. Families can be found hovering around the television on a Saturday night watching professional hockey games, and when Canadians play in the Olympics or World Championships, all other activities of daily life seem to stop. When Canadians are playing in Olympic gold medal games, it is not uncommon for schools to pause classes so the children can gather in the school gyms dressed in jerseys labelled with their favourite player's name to watch the game together on a big screen. In unison, cheers erupt when the Canadians score a goal. The quote below exemplifies the significance of ice hockey for Canadian culture.

> Hockey's place in Canadian culture is closer to religion than a simple sporting pastime, a unifying force in a country of 33 million people that is often

> split by politics and language. The sport is part of the national identity, a rite of passage between fathers and sons and more recently mothers and daughters as the game has evolved beyond its traditional gender boundaries. (Keating, 2010, p. 1)

For many Canadian children, their introduction to ice skating and hockey occurs in neighbourhood community or home-made backyard ice rinks. For the latter, parents can be found late at night, when the temperatures are particularly cold, flooding the rink with water to even out the ice. It is not uncommon for neighbourhood children to congregate at backyard rinks or frozen ponds to create makeshift goalie nets and their own rules for the game. As Stephen Leacock wrote, "In a land so inescapably and inhospitably cold, hockey is the chance of life, and an affirmation that despite the deathly chill of winter we are alive" (quoted in Kidd & Macfarlane, 1972, p. 43).

Falling in love with hockey

Nathan was five years old when his father introduced him to skating in their home-made backyard ice hockey rink. With brand new skates received as a Christmas gift, Nathan ventured onto the ice with great enthusiasm, his father's hands to hold onto. After numerous falls, Nathan eventually learned to skate efficiently. He mastered the basic physical literacy skills associated with skating, including the ability to fall safely and pick himself up again. Nathan loved to skate. During the weekdays, he put on his skates right after school to catch what remained of daylight, and during the weekends, he prodded his father again and again to skate with him. Nathan described his love for hockey and his apparent absorption in the activity with the following:

> I couldn't wait to get home from school to get onto the ice. I'd play with my friends until my parents called me in for dinner. I ate my dinner as fast as I could and when the last morsel of food was gone, I got right back onto the ice until I was called in at bedtime. This was my routine day-in and day-out.

Given his love for skating and the challenges his parents experienced meeting Nathan's need and love for movement, Nathan's parents enrolled him in an introductory hockey programme. This beginner "Learn to Skate" programme was designed to teach the basic skills of skating. In hockey, competency in skating is required before one can then learn to skate with and maneuver a hockey stick. Given the previous skating experience Nathan gained in his backyard, he excelled in this programme. His skills were far more advanced than those of his peers in the programme, and as a result, he received many accolades from the coaches, the other kids, and their parents.

Nathan's coaches at this introductory level were volunteer parents who knew little about the game technically and strategically but seemed to understand the role of fun and enjoyment for young children being introduced to a new sport. Nathan's coaches treated all of the participants in the programme with respect and kindness regardless of ability and emphasized fun and basic skill development. Nathan made friends in this initial programme, and together they collected and "traded" cards of their favourite players and talked about the most recent or upcoming professional game. Their conversations were dominated by topics related to hockey. At this stage, the coaches set up pretend games by dividing the boys into two teams who played each other; the games were fun, and no one really kept score. Given Nathan's exceptional hockey skills, he was always a preferred teammate when the teams were selected. His father did the driving to and from practices and typically stayed to watch. Nathan recalled his father never applying pressure to perform well; instead, he recounted the story of his father asking "Did you have fun?" when they got in the car after every practice. In addition to two hours per week in this programme, Nathan continued to practice his skating and hockey skills in his backyard rink. Nathan's love for the entire initial experience in ice hockey is reflected in the following:

> When I think of my early childhood, it's full of fantastic hockey memories. Hockey was pure fun at this stage. I loved playing with my friends, the coaches were kind, and I got lots of positives from the experience as I was always the best player on the team. I didn't want to try any other sports… when I wasn't playing hockey, I was watching it on TV, talking about it with my friends, and doing school projects on it.

In many ways, Nathan's early experiences reflected the learning cultures advocated by researchers on youth involvement in sport. The importance of parental engagement in introducing children to sport and supporting their participation in the early years of sport involvement (Côté, 1999) was reflected by Nathan's parents and by his father in particular, who built him a backyard rink and attended his practices. Consistent with the literature on ideal conditions for youth engagement in sport, Nathan's coaches established a sport culture that emphasized informal games, shifting team members, and enjoyment (Keegan, Harwood, Spray, & Lavallee, 2009). And, importantly, Nathan brought to his first organized hockey experience a love for the activity and advanced skills for his age—developed, in part, from the opportunity to play and practice in his backyard. Consistent with the relative age effect often seen in hockey (Helsen, van Winckel, & Williams, 2007), Nathan was at an advantage in terms of size and psychomotor development as a result of being born in the first few months of the year. Contrary to the recommendations posed by child development researchers in sport that advocate for the sampling of various sports in early childhood (Côté, 1999), Nathan focused exclusively on the sport of ice hockey. However, horizons of learning were created for Nathan through parental support and engagement, kind and supportive coaches, a sport environment characterized by play and enjoyment, Nathan's love for the activity, and his advanced skills, which garnered him praise from others. Nathan clearly developed a horizon for hockey practice in this early stage, characterized by a love for hockey and a "need" to engage in hockey all the time in an unstructured and playful way; there appeared to be no greater purpose than to "play" through hockey.

Talent development

Hockey programmes in Canada are structured according to the Long-Term Athlete Development Model (Balyi, Way, & Higgs, 2013), with various programmes categorized by age of participant, focus, and purpose. Gradually, Nathan progressed through the "Learn to Play", "Learn to Train", "Train to Train", "Train to Compete", and "Train to Win" programmes. Nathan's horizon of learning as he entered more formalized and structured hockey programmes was a vision to continue to play hockey and to reach the professional level of this sport.

Nathan continued to enjoy and experience success as a player as he progressed through the various levels of the developmental programme. He experienced a number of varied coaching styles as he moved into more advanced competitive levels. His parents continued to support his development as a hockey player and to make the necessary family sacrifices to do so. Nathan's father continued to watch most of the practices, and both parents ensured they were present during games. Nathan described his parents as extremely supportive and never negative. "They always thought that whatever I did in hockey was great. I never worried about their reactions to poor performances or lost games."

Eventually, Nathan progressed to the top tier of junior hockey in Canada, called Major Junior. Major Junior hockey is governed by the Canadian Hockey League (CHL), which is considered one of the most elite amateur hockey leagues in the world, as it is a key feeder programme of new players into professional hockey leagues. The CHL drafts players as young as 15 years old, with an interest in developing these athletes into professional hockey players. The players are trained and introduced to the lifestyle of a professional player, including upwards of 70 games during the regular season, while still completing their high school diploma (Chard, 2013). For athletes who are focused on their hockey development and who have aspirations to reach the professional level, the CHL is viewed as the league of choice (Bianchi, 2010; Chard, 2013).

The CHL attracts players to the league by "selling the dream" of a professional hockey career in the National Hockey League (NHL) with a six-figure salary, prestige, and glorification. As Campbell and Parcels (2013) stated, "Major junior hockey operators in this country [Canada] sell the dream, perhaps more than anyone else involved in the game, because they sell it to the teenagers they employ, tell them it's the quickest and most important route to the NHL" (p. 223). In reality however, there is less than a 1% chance of these boys and young men advancing to the NHL (Campbell & Parcels, 2013). The CHL aggressively recruits talented hockey players in Canada in part to keep them in the country and dissuade them from going to the United States. To pursue this objective, the CHL provides the players with a small weekly allowance to support basic expenses such as travel, food, and school supplies (Bianchi, 2010); however, this small financial contribution disqualifies these athletes from transferring to the National Collegiate Athletic Association in the United States. Further, to keep athletes in Canada, the CHL commits to providing the players with an education package to cover tuition and books once they begin post-secondary studies at the end of their eligibility with the CHL (Bianchi, 2010; Ontario Hockey League, n.d.). The number of years of tuition coverage matches the number of years played in the CHL; for example, if an athlete uses his full five years of Major Junior hockey eligibility, then he could have five years of full-time post-secondary studies fully covered by the league. Importantly, this educational package is most relevant to players who do not sign a professional contract, enabling them to "fall back" onto post-secondary studies once they are no longer eligible for junior hockey.

As a result of the educational package offered, Nathan and his parents decided it was best for Nathan to stay in Canada and play for the CHL. They made this decision even though they were aware of the competitiveness of the CHL and thus the possibility that Nathan may be drafted to a team located far from home. Indeed, Nathan was drafted at the age of 16 years to a team located a four-hour drive away from his family home. As a result, he moved in with a billet family (Campbell & Parcels, 2013). Billet families are volunteers from the community who offer to take athletes into their homes. They are selected by the team and are intended to be supportive homes for the athletes. While Nathan liked his billet family and the living arrangement, he found the transition to a new school and being away from his parents, with whom he was very close, difficult. As Nathan recalled:

> I felt really conflicted at the time. There was nothing more that I wanted than to get to play pro hockey and I knew this meant living and training away from home. But I wasn't ready to leave my family and friends at school... the first year was so lonely...I called home every day and had trouble sleeping. I would have never told anyone at the time but I often cried myself to sleep.

Being in the CHL involved Nathan playing close to 70 games in a season, requiring him to travel to games on weekends and often during the school week. The implications of this demanding schedule were that Nathan often needed to leave classes early or miss them entirely. While progressing through the secondary school degree programme, Nathan maintained a lifestyle similar to a professional athlete (Bianchi, 2010). The team's game and practice schedule also restricted, if not made impossible, Nathan's ability to engage in other school-related activities such as intramurals, inter-school competitions, clubs, or student councils. The busy hockey schedule also restricted time available for family and friends. With such a restricted focus on time and energy, Nathan developed a narrow sense of self based primarily upon being a hockey player. Implications also included the development of a social circle that existed almost entirely of other hockey players given the lack of time to develop friendships outside of sport. Interestingly, these restrictions came during adolescence—a time in one's development when the experimentation with various roles, activities, and relationships is so important for healthy psychological and social development (Erikson, 1980). Further, researchers cite the risks to academic engagement and performance when students miss coursework and have low participation in school-related activities (Astin, 1984; Tinto, 1987). Academic success remained a high priority for Nathan, but he found it difficult to keep up with his schoolwork given his hockey schedule, and he was disappointed in his grades, which he perceived to be incongruent with his academic abilities and potential. He expressed feeling pressure to earn sufficient grades to ensure he was competitive enough to be accepted into university.

Nathan also expressed challenges in adjusting to more autocratic coaching styles, which often involved excessive yelling and criticisms, threats, and the use of punishments. Although he accepted these practices, he had a confident sense that they were not constructive ways to achieve the competitive goals of the junior league. Nathan expressed this disconnect in the following quote:

> I get that junior hockey is extremely competitive and that coaches need to push players. But where did they [coaches] get the idea that we want to work harder when we're punished or threatened? I'm no expert but it should be common sense that people perform better when they are praised and guided and not when they are criticized and punished.

A year later, at the age of 17, Nathan was traded to another team a few hours away. This required another move to a different billet family and to another school. While he did not want to move again, he was aware of the need to comply if he wanted to pursue his hockey career, in which he continued to experience performance success. His coaches provided accolades for his abilities and encouraged him to maintain aspirations of playing hockey professionally. Nathan now had a smaller window of opportunity—less than three years in which he may be drafted to a professional league—and he did not want to jeopardize his chances in any way, so he moved. Nathan continued to participate in the CHL and was moved a third time until his eligibility expired at the age of 20 years.

During these talent identification years, between the ages of 8 and 20 years, Nathan experienced numerous transitions that set the path for different horizons for action. The horizon for play, playfulness, and practice of the early phase did not apply as the context changed to include more structured, formalized, and demanding training and game schedules. In this second phase, the CHL prescribed, in a top-down manner, a horizon for hockey that prohibited any alternatives. The athletes were denied agency and autonomy and could not negotiate their experiences. In response, Nathan developed horizons for serious training and competition. The increase in competitiveness brought with it the introduction of more autocratic coaching styles, to which Nathan had difficulty adjusting and was philosophically opposed. In a way, Nathan kept his horizon for fun/enjoyment-based coaching, which he had developed when younger, but "put it aside" during the talent development time because he knew that his horizon clashed with the CHL expectations. One wonders whether Nathan's horizon for play and unconditional love for hockey that characterized the early phase made the adjustment to the CHL more difficult.

The three trades required moves to different teams and billet families, and although Nathan felt welcomed and supported by all of these families, he was terribly homesick and clearly struggled to cope with these new circumstances. The demanding practice and game schedule compromised such needs as performing well academically and spending time with family, both of which he valued highly. Despite these changes in horizons for action, Nathan's horizon of learning did not change, as he maintained his aspiration to reach the professional level of hockey.

Of great disappointment, at the age of 20, was the fact that he had not been drafted by a professional team by this time.

A consolation prize

Those CHL hockey players who are not signed by a professional team by the age of 20 tend to shift paths, start their university education, and play hockey for a university team. Although Nathan had always intended to earn a university degree at some point, he viewed the transition from the CHL to university as a sign of failure, as his chances of pursuing a professional hockey career were gone. Not being drafted into the professional hockey league was a forced and unexpected turning point for Nathan. University studies and playing hockey for the university were consolation prizes in his perspective, as indicated below:

> All of my life—or at least as I remember it—was devoted to my love for hockey and my hopes of making it into the NHL. And along the way, I was never discouraged from pursuing that hope…my parents were supportive as long as I kept up in school…my coaches praised my hockey ability and encouraged me to keep going. And then I waited and waited for the call about being drafted [to a professional team] and it never came. I couldn't believe it…I never gave that option serious consideration. I felt like I got hit in the head…I was devastated and completely lost…and felt like such a failure. I should have been happy about being accepted to university but instead I felt like it was a consolation prize.

This sentiment was also reflected in the work of Chard (2013) who, after interviewing junior and NCAA hockey players about how they view Canadian university hockey, concluded that these players saw the transition to university hockey as a sign of failure in achieving their professional dreams.

Initially, Nathan was lost because his horizons for action and of learning were still as he had developed them during the talent development phase. He embodied them because he had grown into them and they had been reinforced over the period of many years. In fact, his previous horizons led him to a particular choice of university. Specifically, in spite of aggressive recruitment efforts from various universities, Nathan made his decision based upon the quality of the hockey programme and its coach and the level of support given to athletes at that particular school. Nathan's experience is supported by Miller and Kerr's (2002) findings that student-athletes in Canada were selecting universities with their athletic experience and aspirations as the primary focus. Additionally, these athletes claimed they were not concerned about their abilities to meet the academic demands or to successfully engage in university coursework and athletics at the same time. Being able to continue in their sport at a high performance level gives many students a reason to continue their education, but issues arise if athletic performance is their sole reason for entry (Gaston-Gayles, 2005).

Nathan was 21 when he began university studies, four years older than most first-year students. In fact, the CHL precludes the possibility of hockey players assuming the traditional path of initiating post-secondary education directly from secondary school at the age of 17, and recent data indicate that close to 90% of the incoming university hockey players are 21 years of age or older (Internet Hockey Database, 2016). Developmentally, this age difference can have significant implications for a hockey player's ability to relate to and connect with classmates. Further, some authors (e.g., Chard, 2013) have questioned the extent to which hockey players entering university have abandoned their hockey aspirations and are prepared to transition to making a primary commitment to academics. Criticisms have been lodged against the CHL for inappropriately keeping the dream of a professional hockey career alive instead of preparing athletes for education (Campbell & Parcels, 2013). It is in the best interests of the CHL to keep the dream alive even when it is not realistic, as the league receives a development payment for each athlete who goes on to play professional hockey (Bianchi, 2010). On the other hand, if an athlete chooses to cash in his education package, the CHL team must cover the cost of his education. As a result, a financial incentive exists for teams to focus resources and attention on encouraging hockey development rather than educational and personal development.

During Nathan's first year at university, he struggled to manage his time between academic and athletic demands. Although he had successfully balanced these pursuits during high school, he was finding the academic demands of university to far exceed those experienced previously. Further, he was missing numerous classes due to travel to games and, unlike in high school, found it difficult to understand the material without being present in class. Similarly, Ayers, Pazmino-Cavalles, and Dobose (2012) claimed that student-athletes miss over 20 classes a year and spend more time on athletic-related activities than academic-based activities. Although student-athletes enter university with the belief that they can manage academic demands (Adler & Adler, 1987; Gaston-Gayles, 2015), research from American and Canadian university settings indicates that student-athletes often feel they do not have the time to focus fully on both academics and athletics and, as a result, prioritize their athletic endeavours (Ayers et al., 2012). In addition to student-athletes having a greater sense of confidence in athletics and receiving more immediate gratification and positive feedback and recognition from sport, attendance and performance at training are heavily policed, unlike attendance in class (Althouse, 2007).

One way student-athletes may balance the demands of academics, athletics, and social involvements is to restrict their social spheres to the athletic roles, thus restricting their social engagements to those that take place with teammates. In fact, Weiss and Robinson (2013) report that student-athletes did not feel they were missing out on any aspects of college experiences; these perspectives may be attributed to the narrow athlete identities developed and the finding that student-athletes' primary peer group tends to be teammates and other athletes, making the athlete experience also a social one. Weiss and Robinson (2013) reported that student-athletes "spend disproportionate amounts of time with their teammates" (p. 98), which can be facilitative if the athletic team members are academically committed (Miller & Kerr, 2002) but debilitative if they are academically disengaged (Adler & Adler, 1991).

Nathan experienced significant psychological and social difficulties in transitioning to university. Giving up the horizon of professional hockey career aspirations brought with it a sense of loss, confusion, and turmoil. For as long as he could remember, he defined himself as a hockey player and engaged in horizons for a career in hockey. Without time or reasons to contemplate other identities, aspirations, and interests, Nathan was unclear about his identity, alternative interests, or new directions he wished to pursue.

While Nathan was impressed with the high calibre of hockey at the university level, he found himself less motivated to train and commit his time and energy to hockey. He was disappointed that the attention and recognition players received were substantially less than what he had become accustomed to in junior hockey. Nathan's horizons also changed because the university context did not reinforce the previous horizons. He received ideas, impressions, and thoughts from different contexts, and to cope with these, his horizons needed to transform. This was, of course, not easy after many years of hockey horizons.

He also had to devote far more time and attention to schoolwork than he had previously in junior hockey, which had the effect of pulling him away from his sport-related identity. Over time, his narrowly defined athletic identity was challenged by a growing identity as a student. And of significant influence was Nathan's loss of a hockey-related goal to which to aspire. For so many years, Nathan was motivated by the pursuit of a professional hockey career, and without that goal in sight anymore, he wondered why he was continuing to play. Somewhere along the process of talent identification throughout childhood and adolescence, the initial feelings of intrinsic joy of playing the game were lost. While he still enjoyed playing, this enjoyment was not sufficient to keep him happy devoting so much time and energy to the team. These sentiments are reflected below:

> I couldn't explain why I lost my desire to play on the team. If you asked me whether I still liked to play hockey, I would say "yes, for sure", but for

> some reason, I couldn't muster the motivation to devote the time and energy required to play on the university team. Maybe my love for playing slowly diminished after all those years of training, changing teams and homes, or maybe I needed a better reason to play...like without the goal of professional hockey anymore, I didn't have a good enough goal to work towards...or maybe I just got to the stage of wanting to do other things. I don't know ...but I do know that I lost my drive to play for the university team.

After his first year in university, Nathan decided not to return to the university hockey team. Despite encouragement from his coaches and teammates to return for another year, he could not be swayed.

This final phase of Nathan's story was characterized by a major event—not being selected for a professional team—which marked a significant turning point and a new horizon for Nathan. Over the 16-year period of talent development, Nathan developed a narrow or tunnel identity defined by being a hockey player. Not only did his love for the game and motivation to advance his skills contribute to this narrow sense of self, but also the social structures of talent development in hockey were conducive to a rather exclusive athletic identity. More specifically, the experiences of being a CHL player, including the competitive environment, demanding schedules, move from one's home, and numerous transitions to different teams and homes, precluded the development of any other identities. Additionally, given the financial incentives provided to the CHL when a player is drafted to the NHL, it is no wonder that the CHL encourages players to remain in hockey. Further, the structure of the educational package provided to players, which provides post-secondary tuition for each year that they compete in the CHL, sends players and their families the message that players should remain in the CHL as long as possible, earning credit towards university tuition while they wait to be drafted to the professional leagues. For the vast majority of CHL players who are not drafted, the structural setup of the CHL not only keeps the dream of professional hockey alive—perhaps unrealistically—but also delays entrance to university, thus demarcating differences between former CHL players and their peers, and precludes the experiences required for diverse identity development during adolescence and early adulthood. The promotion and reinforcement of horizons for professional hockey within the CHL context preclude other horizons, potentially leaving hockey players feeling lost without hockey.

Towards the end of the life history interviews, I got the sense that Nathan was dancing on the edges of new horizons, particularly in terms of moving towards becoming a more dedicated student. He expressed enjoyment and what seemed genuine interest in the pursuit of new knowledge through his university courses, providing new horizons of learning. As Nathan said, "I'm not sure what else I'll be good at besides hockey or what will pique my interests but I'm enjoying the time to explore those questions." It appeared that the uncertainty about his future direction did not cause distress and that he was quite comfortable with having time to explore avenues that were not possible while playing hockey.

The remaining challenge for Nathan in this latter phase was establishing friendships outside of hockey. According to Nathan, the age difference between himself at age 22 and other second-year students, who tended to be closer to 18 and 19, had significant repercussions for him, as stated below:

> You wouldn't think that three years' difference in age would make a big difference but it seems to. Many of my classmates are 18 and 19 years old and still interested in partying all the time and doing stupid stuff. I feel like I skipped that stage with the commitments of hockey and now have replaced my focus on hockey with a focus on school. I can't really relate to my classmates so it's pretty lonely. I don't fit in with my friends who are still playing hockey and I don't fit in with my classmates…I'm sure they'll catch up in terms of maturity but for now, I spend a lot of time alone.

Conclusion

Nathan's story illustrates the various horizons that typify the process of becoming a highly competitive ice hockey player in Canada. Nathan's childhood experiences in hockey were characterized by horizons for fun, play, enjoyment, and interactions with friends through hockey. The process of learning about hockey and about himself was enhanced through the support and encouragement provided by his parents, including their attendance at practices and games. Nathan's early learning was also influenced by coaches who could be described as having child-centred coaching practices, which included fun, praise, and the inclusion of play and informal games.

As Nathan navigated the talent development process in hockey, horizons changed. His initial horizon for love of the game, advanced skill development, and parental support was challenged by a more competitive and demanding sport structure. Participating in the Major Junior League presented several significant turning points for Nathan's learning, including autocratic coaches, moving away from his home and parents, and three moves between teams and billet families, creating unstable living arrangements. The competitiveness of the league and the associated training and game schedules led to struggles to maintain his desired academic standards, prompting Nathan to learn ways to balance both effectively. The role of the sport system—the CHL in Nathan's case—cannot be ignored. By virtue of the CHL's policies and procedures and its financial incentives, young players like Nathan are encouraged to defer post-secondary education in favour of playing hockey and pursuing a professional career. The social conditions for a talented young hockey player encourage a narrow sense of self focused almost exclusively on being a hockey player. One may argue, as in Nathan's case, that the context and conditions of the talent development process in Canadian hockey set the majority of players up for significant disappointment, disillusionment, and loss when they do not make the professional league. Deselection for Nathan was an unexpected event that changed his situation, and, initially, his horizons of what he saw he could do (horizon for action) and where he saw he could go in terms of his learning (horizon of learning) were inconsistent with the changed situation. He still saw himself as a hockey player, with horizons for action that are productive in this particular context and horizons of learning that are limited to hockey performance and conduct. The unexpected event of deselection created a new horizon for action. Although the process was slow and painful, Nathan started to reflect on and question his hockey horizons, priorities, and future aspirations. Although it was a difficult process, deselection was also an opportunity to learn more about himself and to think deeply about where he wished to devote his energies next. Nathan's horizons today represent movement towards interests, enjoyment, and commitments to university studies, although he struggles with establishing non-hockey friendships and an appropriate social circle.

References

Adler, P., & Adler, P. (1987). Role conflict and identity salience: College athletics and the academic role. *Social Science Journal, 24*, 443–455.

Adler, P. A., & Adler, P. (1991). *Backboards and blackboards: College athletics and role engulfment.* New York: Columbia University Press.

Allain, K. A. (2014). "What happens in the room stays in the room": Conducting research with young men in the Canadian Hockey League. *Qualitative Research in Sport, Exercise and Health*, 6(2), 205–219.

Althouse, J. N. (2007). *Testing a model of first-semester student-athlete academic motivation and motivational balance between academic and athletics.* Doctoral dissertation. Penn State Electronic Theses and Dissertations. Retrieved from https://etda.libraries.psu.edu/files/final_submissions/2899.

Astin, A. (1984). Student involvement: A developmental theory for higher education. *Journal of College Student Development*, 40(5), 518–519.

Ayers, K., Pazmino-Cavalles, M., & Dobose, C. (2012). The 20-hour rule: Student-athletes time commitment to athletics and academics. *VAHPERD Journal, 33*(1).

Balyi, I., Way, R., & Higgs, C. (2013). *Long-term athlete development.* Champaign, IL: Human Kinetics.

Bianchi, M. (2010). Guardian of amateurism or legal defiant? The dichotomous nature of NCAA men's ice hockey. *Seton Hall Journal of Sports and Entertainment Law*, 20(1), 165–203.

Campbell, K. (2007, November 13). *Just how tough is it to reach the NHL?* Retrieved from http://sports.espn.go.com/nhl/news/story?page=campbell1113.

Campbell, K., & Parcels, J. (2013). *Selling the dream: How hockey parents and their kids are paying the price for our national obsession.* Toronto: Penguin Group.

Canadian Interuniversity Sport. (2014). *Athlete's guide.* Retrieved from en.cis-sic.ca/information/members_info/pdfs/pdf_elig_pack/14-15/athletes_guide.pdf.

Chard, C. (2013). Understanding the brand meaning of the Canadian Interuniversity Sport hockey league: An insurance policy if all else fails. *Sport in Society*, 16(3), 327–339.

Chard, C. R., Hyatt, C., & Foster, W. M. (2013). Assets and obstacles: An analysis of OUA hockey from the coaches' perspective. *Sport, Business and Management: An International Journal*, 3(3), 246–259.

Côté, J. (1999). The influence of the family in the development of talent in sport. *Sport Psychologist*, *13*(4), 395–417.

Erikson, E. (1980). *Identity and the life cycle*. New York: W.W. Norton.

Gaston-Gayles, J. (2004). Examining academic and athletic motivation among student athletes at a division I university. *Journal of College Student Development*, *45*(1), 75–83.

Gaston-Gayles, J. (2005). The factor structure and reliability of the student athletes' motivation toward sport and academics questionnaire (SAMSAQ). *Journal of College Student Development*, *46*(3), 317–327.

Gaston-Gayles, J. (2015). Engaging student-athletes. In S. J. Quaye & S. R. Harper (Eds.), *Student engagement in higher education: Theoretical perspective and practical approaches for diverse populations* (2nd edition) (pp. 209–220). New York: Routledge.

Helsen, W., van Winckel, J., & Williams, A. (2007). The relative age effect in youth soccer across Europe. *Journal of Sport Sciences*, *23*(6), 629–636.

Internet Hockey Database. (2016). http://www.hockeydb.com.

Keating, S. (2010, January 10). Ice hockey is more than a game to Canadians. Sports News. Thomson Reuters. Retrived from https://www.reuters.com/article/us-olympics-icehockey-canada/ice-hockey-is-more-than-a-game-to-canadians-idUSTRE61913G20100210

Keegan, R., Harwood, C., Spray, C., & Lavallee, D. (2009). A qualitative investigation exploring the motivational climate in early career sports participants: Coach, parent and peer influences on sport motivation. *Psychology of Sport and Exercise*, *10*(3), 361–372.

Kidd, B., & Macfarlane, J. (1972). *The death of hockey*. Charlottesville, VA: New Press.

Miller, P., & Kerr, G. (2002). The athletic, academic and social experiences of intercollegiate student-athletes. *Journal of Sport Behavior*, *25*(4), 346–367.

Miller, P., & Kerr, G. (2003). The role experimentation of intercollegiate student athletes. *Sport Psychologist*, *17*(2), 196–219.

Ontario Hockey League. (n.d.). OHL prospective player information: Education. Retrieved March 6, 2016, from http://www.ontariohockeyleague.com/page/ohl-prospective-player-information.

Tinto, V. (1987). *Leaving college: Rethinking the causes and cures of student attrition*. Chicago: University of Chicago Press.

Tinto, V. (2012). Moving from theory to action: A model of institutional action for student success. In A. Seidman (Ed.), *College student retention: Formula for student success* (2nd edition) (pp. 251–266). Lanham, MD: Rowan & Littlefield.

Weiss, S., & Robinson, T. (2013). An investigation of factors relating to retention of student-athletes participating in NCAA division II athletics. *Interchange*, *44*(1–2), 83–104.

Chapter 7

Career learning in youth elite biathlon: A case of a male biathlete

Astrid Schubring

You realise how fast it can all be over.

Learning focus and case material

The present case study reviews the career progression of the athlete Cyril[1] from his entry into biathlon at age 8 to junior elite level at age 18. Specific focus is given to how this 10-year-long career span, changing relationships with team colleagues, and an illness experience contributed to Cyril developing a horizon for the precariousness of an elite sport career and the necessity of focusing on self-survival and care of health.

To reconstruct the athlete's career development and 'becoming' (Hodkinson, Ford, Hodkinson, & Hawthorn, 2008), I draw on an in-depth biographical mapping interview[2] I conducted with Cyril when he still was a member of the German national youth biathlon team.[3] Repeated reading of the interview transcript together with Cyril's career visualisation helped me to first reconstruct his career chronologically. Next, I used the theoretical framework introduced in Chapter 3 of this book to identify significant career events and learning that shaped and changed Cyril's self and career horizon. Before presenting Cyril's learning and career development in three phases, I will provide background on the Olympic sport of biathlon and the career context the German elite sport system offers young athletes like Cyril.

German biathlon as career context

Biathlon, a combination of cross-country skiing and rifle shooting in five-shot clips, derives from military exercise and emerged relatively late (1960 to late 1970) as an Olympic discipline with standardized rules and regulations. The female discipline became Olympic in 1992. Today, Olympic athletes compete in five events (individual, sprint, pursuit, relay, mass start), with different distances for men and women; mixed-gender events use a lightweight rifle.

In Germany, biathlon enjoys great popularity as a winter sport event. This is due to a series of successful men and women athletes who have won over 50 Olympic medals, placing Germany at the head of the medal table by 2018.[4] As one of eight winter sport disciplines, biathlon is governed by the German Ski Federation (DSV), which is a member organisation of the non-governmental German Olympic Sports Confederation (DOSB).[5] As elite sport is an integrated part of organized sport for all in Germany, children and youth typically start training for biathlon at a local club. Biathlon clubs are spread throughout the country but mainly in 5 of the 16 federal states that possess mountainous regions with suitable snow conditions and training facilities. For youth who aim to develop a career in biathlon, selection into the regional/national squad system[6] is important, as membership provides access to specialised training, a dual career, medical support, and, importantly, funding. Squad membership is performance based and needs to be confirmed anew each year. While the first selection level (in biathlon up to the age of 15) is administered and funded by the federal states, which allows a larger number of athletes to be supported, the second level is at the interface between the federal states' and the national funding system, limiting squad membership to about 20 boys and girls per age group.[7] Once selected, young biathletes either stay with a successful club or they travel/move to a regional performance centre. These centres collaborate with so-called elite sport schools[8] that offer extra flexibility, full- or part-time boarding, and learning support to allow for a dual career despite frequent absences for training camps and competitions. The transition from youth into junior and senior biathlon is critical, as it coincides with the end of upper secondary schooling in Germany and fully funded positions for elite biathletes in the army or at the customs are limited.

Starting out: From initiation into biathlon at age 8 to age 13

Cyril started biathlon at age 8. Given that none of his family was actively involved in organized sport before, Cyril's entry into biathlon happened 'by accident' when a coach of the local club visited his school to invite children to a trail-running event. With some friends, Cyril participated in the event and was subsequently invited to a trial session at the club. Cyril remembers the session being REALLY great fun 'and was hooked'.[9] A year later, when Cyril passed what the club had set up as the age demarcation for initiating children to rifle shooting, the attraction of the sport grew even further. 'I was age category TEN and was already shooting. It was very exciting.' Cyril was further motivated by doing well at the local and regional competitions he participated in with others from his club—notably Sim a same-aged boy who he had become friends with. Things 'went step-wise upwards', and Cyril recalls his first years as 'a NICE time, because we always had a pretty good TROOP back home in our club. That was always FUN, also result-wise.'

In line with his athletic development, Cyril was soon nominated for the regional squad and, together with Sim, was invited to additional training at the regional performance centre in Springton. The invitation came the same year as Cyril finished primary school education, and the choice to also visit the elite sport school in Springton was easy: 'That year I went up to Springton to attend the school and then was driven HOME every evening. As I just live some 20 miles away.' While visiting classes five and six at the elite sport school, Cyril commuted daily. Despite the geographical closeness and others commuting with him, Cyril experienced the transition from primary to secondary school, the change in training, and the travelling as taxing:

> You were DONE after training and then you had to travel HOME and before eight you came to nothing.... There were points where you were PRETTY wiped out ... it just all involved a lot of stress.

Beside the increased demands in school, Cyril experienced the training culture at the performance centre as differing sharply from that of his home club:

> The FIRST years at home, you thought it was FUN. But then at Springton with a real TRAINING group, it got straight down to the nitty-gritty and then you realized what really counted.... In the TRAINING GROUP it is tougher. Every training session turns into a battle to prove time and time again that you are actually good.

Despite the change, Cyril performed well and also in the following two years was 'sweeping the board at the regional competitions'. While Cyril gradually got more used to the increased performance pressures in school, moving to Springton as a boarder at age 13 still felt like a relief:

> At the boarding school you have a lot more LEISURE TIME in the evening. You can do more for SCHOOL because after training you are there and don't need to travel somewhere, so that was better.

While a lot of the other boarders suffered homesickness, Cyril actually enjoyed being away from home not only because of the gain in time but also 'because you could do stuff in the evening with the very same people you'd spent the day with'. Further, he always had his club-colleague Sim to talk to when things got tough.

Analytical summary of Cyril's early learning and career development

Cyril's socialization into biathlon differs from what recent literature describes as a typical pathway into (elite) sport (Côté, 1999; Wheeler, 2012): It is not through 'social capital' (Bourdieu, 1984) in the form of family members or friends that he entered biathlon but through the initiative of the local winter sport club aiming to recruit children at school. This more institutionalized talent identification approach, which resembles systematic talent screening used in former Eastern bloc countries including the former German Democratic Republic (Green & Oakley, 2001), paved Cyril's way in a sport that fascinated him and that he enjoyed even after years of training. The positive approval of his physical 'dispositions' (Hodkinson, Biesta, & James, 2008), good sporting results, and, first and foremost, a supportive training group, joyful training, and his friendship with Sim contributed to Cyril gradually developing a *horizon for biathlon to be a fun leisure-time activity*. An important factor in the development of this horizon was his excitement about learning biathlon skills and at early age being allowed to use a rifle and shoot—a symbol and body technique associated with traditional masculinity, heroism, and adulthood (Wellard, 2009). Highly motivated and spurred on by his athletic development, Cyril developed fast and, after two years, was selected in the regional squad and training centre. This performance-based selection constituted the first major career 'turning point' (Hodkinson & Sparkes, 1997), which overlapped with the age-based 'transition' (Schlossberg, 1981) from primary to secondary school. While this synchrony in timing facilitated, on the one hand, integrating into the elite sport school that cooperates with the centre, it also multiplied the 'transition work' Cyril had to do in order to adjust to the change in school and training context. The whole situation also compromised Cyril's well-being because his previously developed *horizon for biathlon as joyful* clashed with the 'learning culture' (Hodkinson et al., 2008) dominant at the centre. There, the focus was less on enjoyment, learning, and mutual support and more on competition, performance development, and constant proving of his 'athletic self' (see Brewer, Van Raalte, & Linder, 1993; Sparkes, 1998). While this type of athlete development context has been identified as risky and prone to cause overloading, self-doubt, and injury in young athletes (Bergeron et al., 2015; DiFiori et al., 2014; Schubring, 2014), Cyril withstood the pressure despite fatigue and outperformed the others in his region. He gradually adapted to and, with his move to the boarding school, fully integrated into the performance-focused learning culture.

Pushing through: From age 13 to age 16

Cyril soon felt at home at the boarding school. While he liked to spend the weekends with his family, during the week he enjoyed having all other athletes just next door to spend time with. Even though the move to the boarding school relaxed his time schedule, biathlon-wise the competition pulled tighter with new national events to travel to during the season. Cyril recalls his transition into age category 13 as a point of change: 'Well, it really kicked off from age group 13, 14, 15 when the German PUPILS cup [Deutscher Schülercup][10] was and you competed against the best in Germany'.

Despite the cup competitions being a new arena for Cyril, he was able to maintain his performance level, placing among the best nationally as both a 13- and a 14-year-old. The athletic successes led to continued membership in the regional squad and furthered Cyril's motivation and confidence. While Cyril had initially been stressed by the competitive culture at the centre, he gradually embodied a *horizon of learning through rivaling* and sought to compete against more senior athletes to sharpen his performance edge:

> It always SPURRED me on when I could run with the TOP ONES. We had one in our training group who had been in the national team and you were always looking FORWARD to train with him because you KNEW what he had ACHIEVED and if you were to train AMBITIOUSLY you actually could achieve it as well. So even among EACH OTHER with the OLDER or SAME-AGED the ambition was always to lock horns with them in training.

In line with the training culture at the centre, his own horizon of learning, and also the performance focus at the national level, Cyril acquired what can be called a *horizon for contextually limited friendships with teammates*. Switching between friendship and rivalry became natural:

> You are in fact FRIENDS but in competition there are actually no friends, all are RIVALS. After the competition you shake hands, love, peace, harmony and so. But in competition, if there is a situation you are not pulling BACK, you push THROUGH. There is no give-away.... For example in downhill runs or in slopes there is cutting in or MASS start that is the most extreme example where it gets straight down to the nitty-gritty. Someone will pull BACK but you do not want to be it.

The year Cyril entered age category 16 constituted another, enforced turning point in his career. The biathlete was required to exchange the air rifle reserved for the under-16 age groups for a small-calibre rifle. This structurally prescribed transition was challenging, as it demanded re-learning and adjusting his shooting routine. At the same time, Cyril needed to perform well throughout the season to reach a ranking that would qualify him for the national youth squad. At the first cup competitions, Cyril's performance went 'a bit DOWN'. He realized that he had become 'spoiled by success' and that 'that first year' it would actually be 'a success to feature somewhere in the top ranks'. As the season advanced, Cyril managed to stabilize his performance and to finish in the top rankings of his age group. Despite his successful qualification for the national youth team, the season left traces: Through the 'change of athletic reference group' (see Schubring & Thiel, 2014), Cyril became aware of the precariousness of an elite sport career, which forced him to readjust his previously taken-for-granted career vision:

> PREVIOUSLY at competitions you always thought well it's GOING nicely and BUSINESS as USUAL, but then when you race with the OLDER ones, you REALISE how fast it can all be OVER.

Following this season, Cyril entered grade 11. He was grateful that the elite sport school scheme allowed him to extend the last two high school years over three years. He knew that the extension would give him more time to prepare for the leap from youth to junior biathlon, having already relaxed his school schedule and liberated time to train. In addition, the school had been and would be supportive of the winter sport athletes:

> When we [athletes] have been often ABSENT or so then we went to the teachers and they sat down with us to catch up with the content so that we don't lag miles behind because somehow we also have to write the A-levels.

In contrast to the previous winter, Cyril, now age category 17, started out by winning the first competitions. 'That was of course a HIGHLight'. The season proceeded 'positive', and although he lost some ranks, he placed 'not bad', qualifying for a contested place in the national youth squad. However, in contrast to his own positive career development, Cyril had to witness former teammates dropping out and top biathletes losing ranks:

> When you travelled to the GERMAN cup and raced with absolute top ones, you could see some that would become a CHAMP and others that would come to naught and that is sometimes SAD. Especially if they are of your own troops, some you earlier on took as an example. You wanted to become like them and then you see how quickly it is all over… it's a PITY. I can see it with Sim and another one from my club who has already dropped out. You DO miss the person because they could always pull you up in training or you could joke with them. You realize someone is missing. [Pauses] And for HIM it is sad. But you know it is an INDIVIDUAL sport and you have to save your OWN ass. Either you make it or you don't make it. [Pauses]. Of course you suffer with them… but everyone is responsible for oneself.

Analytical summary of Cyril's learning and career development

Between 13 and 16 years of age, Cyril experienced an extremely dense career phase marked by multiple transitions that he had to handle. In the beginning of this phase, Cyril was still in the transition process of having moved out from home into a boarding school. While moving early away from home has been found to compromise some youth elite athletes' well-being and careers—at least temporarily (Barker-Ruchti & Schubring, 2015; Egilsson & Dolles, 2017; Schubring, 2014)—Cyril soon felt at ease and even thrived on being a boarder. Taking a closer look, the positive transition experience seemed to be facilitated by a number of personal, social, and organisational factors. These facilitators include individual dispositions such as his ease to socialize and his positive athletic development, supportive social relationships such as Cyril's friendship with Sim and the closeness to his family, and the organisational support the youth athletes received through the elite sport school scheme, at the boarding home, and at the regional performance centre.

Following the move to the boarding school, Cyril experienced three turning points, with all of them being structurally induced by the chronological sequencing of athlete development in German biathlon (see the introductory section): (a) starting to compete on the national youth level at age 13, (b) changing from air to small-calibre rifle at age 15, and (c) making the transition from regional to national squad system at age 16. Cyril was able to adjust to these changes and to synchronize his athletic skill development with the requirements set despite increasing competition, continuous selection pressures, and the rigid, structurally driven pacing of development. The athlete's narration highlights that the 'synchronization process' was not just a bodily one but involved learning and change of self. More specifically, he developed 'a taste' (Bourdieu, 1984) for competition and a *horizon of learning through rivalry*. While his horizon for biathlon as fun faded out, the vision of becoming one of the top biathletes became part of his vision. This change in career vision also affected how he navigated friendships with teammates. To be able to prioritise winning in competition over social bonds, Cyril developed a *horizon for contextually limited friendships*. In a similar way, he learned to subordinate school education to working on his competitive edge and to rely on the elite sport school scheme to help buffer potential absences or gaps in knowledge. Maybe the most critical and painful learning process Cyril experienced in this four-year-long career phase is his becoming aware of the precariousness of an elite sport career. Both the career pathways of his local teammates and the national competitions became for him a relentless reminder of the transitory nature of the career pathway he was perusing. Driven by this disillusioning awareness, as well as the highly competitive and result-driven selection system, Cyril—not without some inner conflict—came to embody a *horizon for self-survival*, with the bottom line being 'you have to save your own ass in order to make it'.

Slowed down: From age 16 to age 18

After a break from the winter season that gave Cyril time to catch up on schoolwork and prepare for the end-of-term exams, the centre started the summer training. Cyril was motivated, and the momentum of the previous season's good results propelled him forward. Further, being invited to training camps with the national youth team still was thrilling. Cyril was at ease in the team but stayed on his guard, knowing they all would become competitors once the season started. At camps, he aimed to be concentrated and lock horns with the biathletes from other centres to test and work on his performance, knowing that it was results that counted.

Fall came, and Cyril felt fit and better trained than ever. He could see how the training hours and his pushing his body had built up his muscles and endurance. Further, his shooting had become more stable, which gave him confidence at the shooting stand and recognition from the coaches. Confirming his perception, the now 17-year-old performed extremely well at the entry event in October, taking a top ranking in his age group over three competitions. Spurred by the success, Cyril felt confident of the winter season starting in December. To prepare for it, his regional training centre travelled for camps to snow-sure ski resorts abroad. There, training was intense, and Cyril was glad each time he could return to the room he shared with Sim and two others. However, there was also a downside to it:

> We were several in a room and one got SICK and at the end of the season it came to light that he had glandular fever,[11] but he did not say anything and we all SLEPT there and actually all CAUGHT it without really KNOWING.

After the training camp, Cyril tried to recover and get ready for the winter. However, as the season got under way, Cyril struggled to regain his previous top form. Feeling strangely out of shape, Cyril began to seriously worry about 'WHAT the problem was', especially as he was dropping ranks in the overall table:

> You could see it at the RESULTS. BEFORE you were always at the lead among the first six and then you peaked at the results and you were rank TWENTY and stuff like that. You weren't USED to that at all! The shooting was GOING nicely in the season but in the RACING, there was NO WAY forward and you were starting to crack yourself up.

Cyril and his coach struggled to come to grips with the athlete's sudden drop in performance and his getting sick time and time again. As things did not improve, they decided to see a physician. Based on a blood panel, the doctor affirmed to Cyril that 'everything is in order'. Building on the positive diagnosis, Cyril and his coach agreed to first do some basic training to help him come back into the season and then to train full again. Despite all efforts and hard training, Cyril 'hit the bottom' at the next cup competition:

> I started the FIRST day, but didn't make it to the finish because it was—the coaches took me out because I looked SO bad.…Then I was really SICK and laid LOW for two WEEKS and then the season was actually all over. The last competition, I was just racing to be on the starting list, in order to make it in the squad and still collect some points.

As the season drew to an end, Cyril no longer fought for a top place but only for his reselection in the squad. At the end of season, it was only his top results from the first competitions that 'compensated for the illness' and 'saved' him a place in the national squad. However, the season had been an extreme setback that threatened not only Cyril's athletic performance but also his career continuation and athletic self. While he still pondered the 'why question', Cyril, together with some teammates, was called in for another medical check-up, which revealed that they had all been infected with glandular fever at the preseason training camp. On top of that, they learnt that their efforts to 'train over it' and compete had actually worsened their condition and even led to an impairment of the heart muscle. While Cyril recovered from the illness and its impairing effects and even was able to come back into summer training in time, thinking of the season and its disastrous consequences for some made him feel ill at ease:

> The ONE that was SICK [of his roommates] had to stop because he got cardiac irregularities. It really sat on his HEART. He was always with us at the heart specialist, but now he has to stop and they have to see how they can somehow sort it out.

Like the lesson drawn from the previous winter season, the illness experience enforced Cyril's horizon for the precariousness of an elite sport career. The following drop in performance further taught him that 'ambitious training' would not be enough 'to make it' but that it in some cases could be risky or even detrimental to his health and athletic success. Embracing the insight and drawing from his own (and his teammates') illness experience, the now 18-year-old Cyril responded by broadening his horizon for action. Previously focused on self-survival, the biathlete integrated a *vision for preventative health care*, as expressed in the following reflection:

> I have noticed this spring and summer that you can't always touch everything everywhere. You have to pay a little more attention to your health. Because it was pretty harmless how it initially happened, but then it was an extreme setback. And for me the next two years are all about the SQUAD, because I will also finish school. If you then don't make the JUMP—then it was a nice time and THAT's IT. So you DO know what it is all about and that you need to pay a little more attention to sustain your health.

Analytical summary of Cyril's learning and career development

Albeit the above-reported third career phase was relatively short, it was an intensive time that challenged Cyril existentially. During the approximately 18 months, the youth athlete went through a number of 'normative', age-based transitions (Schlossberg, 1981). These included him moving from grade 11 to grades 12 and 13 in school, moving into older biathlon age groups, and meeting the annual qualification norm to remain in the national squad. While these transitions were important steps in Cyril's athletic and educational careers, they were overshadowed by the unforeseen and lengthy illness that 'disrupted' (Bury, 1982) the athlete's so far rather consistent, positive career pathway. According to Bury (1982), chronic illness experiences become disruptive, as they (a) breach taken-for-granted assumptions and behaviours when bodily states and remedying them require all attention, (b) call forth rethinking of one's biography and self-concept, and (c) necessitate mobilising resources to alter the situation. In Cyril's case, the disruptiveness of the months-long infection can be clearly sensed, as the illness set its own agenda and changed the course of Cyril's season into a downward slide, which neither he nor his coach knew the cause or how to alter it. As for other elite athletes, the illness became an existential crisis, threatening not only the youths' physical health and well-being but also their athletic self and biographical continuity (e.g., Smith & Sparkes, 2005; Sparkes, 1998).

The chronological reconstruction of Cyril's illness experience further sheds light on how personal dispositions, social relations, cultural norms, organizational conditions, and timing worked together in shaping the career crisis. With regard to the latter, the timing of the illness in competition season and during a critical qualification phase in Cyril's career complicated early, adequate treatment (including rest) and encouraged training and competing sick. With regard to organizational conditions, the result-based qualification norms for squad membership, as well as flaws in the health care management, facilitated the spreading of the infection in the team and its going undiagnosed for so long. The performance-focused learning culture Cyril was a part of, his *horizons for self-survival and learning through rivalry*, and his success journey also made it difficult for the athlete (and the coach) to acknowledge, make sense of, and nurse the illness early. However, Cyril could talk to his coach, who intervened and supported Cyril in searching out medical care and deciding to take Cyril out of competition—actions that possibly prevented further harm but that are not a natural matter of course in elite sport (for counterexamples, see Cavallerio, Wadey, & Wagstaff, 2016; DiFiori et al., 2014; Roderick & Waddington, 2000; Schubring, Bub, & Thiel, 2014).

The learning Cyril gained from the crisis partly confirmed his *horizon for the precariousness of an elite sport career.* While this horizon had emerged from observing the career pathways of less successful teammates and top athletes, the illness had taught Cyril firsthand the precariousness of pursuing an elite career. Recovering from mononucleosis and its health consequences, the 18-year-old athlete embraced the gained experiential knowledge. Cyril adopted a *horizon for preventive health care*, which he considered key to mastering the career transition from youth to senior, which awaits him together with the end of school education.

Cyril pursued his career vision after having graduated from the elite sport school at 19-years of age. However, the following years, he was not able to make the 'JUMP' from youth/junior to senior level and to gain a place in the German top biathlon team. Today, Cyril is no longer envisaging a career in biathlon, but still lives and works in the region, where he has grown up and started out with biathlon.

Summary of learning career in sport

In this athlete learning case, I have focused on the career path of a German biathlete from entry into local club training at age 8 to becoming an 18-year-old national youth team member about to finish high school education. Building on the athlete's biographical narration, the case provides an in-depth insight into the 'lived' (Merleau-Ponty, 1974) career development experiences and learning of a young biathlete.

Reviewing the 10-year-long career span, two career turning points (Hodkinson & Sparkes, 1997) stand out: first, Cyril's selection for the regional squad and training centre, which occurred at the time of his integration in the elite sport school, and, second, the infection with mononucleosis, which endangered his health and career continuation. While his entry into biathlon, the change to the elite sport school, and the move to the boarding home were self-initiated, the illness represents a forced and unexpected turning point. However, structural turning points appear omnipresent in Cyril's career, such as changes in age grouping for training and competition, the change from air gun to small-calibre rifle, the transition between regional and national squads, and the annual selection for the squad. Considering the 'learning culture' (Hodkinson et al., 2008) of the local and national athlete development system the biathlete grew up in, this spread of changes, transitions and turning points during his career may be paradigmatic for a well-developed, but rather rigid, age- and performance-based support system that risks leaving youth athletes with a limited number of alternative (less institutionalized) career pathways to choose from.

Despite the rigidity and fast sequencing of transitions, Cyril showed great ability to adapt to changes in learning cultures, master transitions, and sustain a horizon for becoming an elite biathlete. To do so, Cyril engaged in learning that allowed him to both draw on and develop (a) personal dispositions, such as athletic ability, fascination for the sport, and lack of injury; (b) social relationships with his family and other athletes; and (c) an athletic environment that provided specialised training and dual career support. By learning to adjust, biathlon shaped Cyril's becoming: Cyril gradually disregarded his early *horizon for biathlon as joyful leisure-time activity* to embrace *a horizon of self-survival*, which better suited the competitive squad culture. The unexpected illness experience brought about another change and led Cyril to integrate *a vision of care of health*. Taken together, this athlete's horizontal changes demonstrate adjusting to the elite sport learning culture and change events, as well as coping with them. While this process is necessary for athletes' 'survival' in a system based on competition, it places them on edge and at risk of serious ill health, as was demonstrated by the athlete who concealed his initial infection and others who trained and competed sick. Even if the question remains open why Cyril's first check-up resulted in dire misdiagnoses, the athlete's story stresses the importance of taking infections and young athletes' reporting of symptoms seriously. Further, it suggests that a more holistic understanding of athletes' individual dispositions, biographies, current career situations, and training protocols may facilitate early recognition and prevention of health hazards in athletes.

To conclude, Cyril's career path illustrates how learning is both a result and an essential ingredient of how individuals navigate their career paths through changing contexts (Hodkinson et al., 2008; Hodkinson & Sparkes, 1997). For the sport of biathlon, Cyril's case is important because research on (elite) biathletes' career, health, and illness experiences is yet missing. The close analysis of Cyril's lived career development experience may provide a starting point for coaches and support staff (even beyond biathlon) to identify critical transitions, such as the change from air gun to small-calibre rifle, but also health risks in youth or flaws in the athletic career development or medical support system. Notably, the detailed reconstruction of Cyril's illness and the handling thereof can allow stakeholders to identify points for early intervention and strategies to increase knowledge in youth athletes, coaches, and medical personnel to prevent, diagnose, and treat mononucleosis among elite athletes.

Notes

1. For confidentiality reasons, pseudonyms are used for persons and places.
2. For details on the interview method, which involved the drawing of thematic career development lines to facilitate recall, see Schubring, Mayer, & Thiel (in press).
3. The interview was part of a larger study of German youth elite sport (Thiel et al., 2011).
4. Information on Olympic medal tables in biathlon derives from https://en.wikipedia.org/wiki/ List_of_Olympic_medalists_in_biathlon.
5. The DOSB is a merger of the former German Sports Confederation (DSB) and the National Olympic Committee (NOK), which since 2006 governs both sports for all and elite sport (DOSB, 2018b; Petry & Hallmann, 2013).
6. The hierarchically structured squad system is a key feature of German elite sport and talent development. Based on performance and age, talented and successful athletes are grouped in different squad levels, with the first level being purely federal and the top level including athletes placed top-10 in the world (for details, see DOSB, 2017).
7. Up to the junior level, youth are trained in mixed-gender groups.
8. Currently, 43 elite sport school structures exist in Germany, offering schooling to about 11.500 youth athletes at over 100 different schools. Seven elite sport schools focus on winter sports (DOSB, 2018a).
9. Quotations are adjusted for readability, and capitalization is used to display emphasis.
10. The cup, like the national and international cups, consists of a series of about 10 to 15 biathlon competitions held between September and March at different event locations in Germany and bordering Alpine countries. Competition results are closely monitored by coaches and athletes alike, and there is competition among the regions for the best placement of 'their' athletes.
11. 'Glandular fever', medically termed 'infectious mononucleosis' (IM), is a viral infection caused by the Epstein-Barr virus, a member of the herpes virus group. IM commonly occurs in adolescents and young adults with 30-50 days' incubation time, which complicates prevention. There is a risk of misdiagnosis, as symptoms and course of illness vary individually but typically involve fatigue, fever, and sore throat. There is also a risk of chronic symptoms—notably fatigue but also neurologic, hematologic, cardiac, and respiratory complications. Athletes with acute IM should avoid contact sports and vigorous activities to recover without harm. It is recommended to be symptom-free before return to play (see for details Becker & Smith, 2014).

References

Barker-Ruchti, N., & Schubring, A. (2015). Moving into and out of high-performance sport: The cultural learning of an artistic gymnast. *Physical Education and Sport Pedagogy*, *21*(1), 69–80.

Becker, J. A., & Smith, J. A. (2014). Return to play after infectious mononucleosis. *Sports Health*, 6(3), 232–238.

Bergeron, M. F., Mountjoy, M., Armstrong, N., Chia, M., Côté, J., Emery, C. A., … Engebretsen, L. (2015). International Olympic Committee consensus statement on youth athletic development. *British Journal of Sports Medicine*, 49(13), 843.

Bourdieu, P. (1984). *Distinction: A social critique of the judgement of taste* (7th edition) (R. Nice, Trans.). Cambridge, MA: Harvard University Press.

Brewer, B. W., Van Raalte, J. L., & Linder, D. E. (1993). Athletic identity: Hercules' muscles or Achilles heel? *International Journal of Sport Psychology*, 24(2), 237–254.

Bury, M. (1982). Chronic illness as biographical disruption. *Sociology of Health and Illness*, 4(2), 167–182.

Cavallerio, F., Wadey, R., & Wagstaff, C. R. D. (2016). Understanding overuse injuries in rhythmic gymnastics: A 12-month ethnographic study. *Psychology of Sport and Exercise*, 25, 100–109.

Côté, J. (1999). The influence of the family in the development of talent in sport. *Sport Psychologist*, *13*(4), 395.

DiFiori, J. P., Benjamin, H. J., Brenner, J., Gregory, A., Jayanthi, N., Landry, G. L., & Luke, A. (2014). Overuse injuries and burnout in youth sports: A position statement from the American Medical Society for Sports Medicine. *Clinical Journal of Sport Medicine*, 24(1), 3–20.

DOSB. (2017). *Anpassung der Kaderstrukturen/Kaderdefinitionen im Olympischen Sommer- und Wintersport zum 01.01.2018* [Adaption of the squad structure in Olympic summer and winter sport from 01.01.2018.]. Frankfurt a.M.: DOSB. Retrieved from https://cdn.dosb.de/user_upload/www.dosb.de/Leistungssport/Olympische_Spiele_Downloads/2017_12-07_Kaderdefinitionen-Olympischer_Sommer-Wintersport-EF_FINAL.pdf.

DOSB. (2018a). Eliteschule des Sports [Elite sport school]. Retrieved from https://eliteschulen.dosb.de/.

DOSB. (2018b). Leistungssport [Elite sport]. Retrieved from https://www.dosb.de/leistungssport/.

Egilsson, B., & Dolles, H. (2017). 'From heroes to zeroes'—Self-initiated expatriation of talented young footballers. *Journal of Global Mobility: The Home of Expatriate Management Research*, 5(2), 174–193.

Green, M., & Oakley, B. (2001). Elite sport development systems and playing to win: Uniformity and diversity in international approaches. *Leisure Studies*, 20(4), 247–267.

Hodkinson, P., Biesta, G., & James, D. (2008). Understanding learning culturally: Overcoming the dualism between social and individual views of learning. *Vocations and Learning*, *1*(1), 27–47.

Hodkinson, P., Ford, G., Hawthorn, R., & Hodkinson, H. (2007). *Learning as being*. Retrieved from http://www.leeds.ac.uk/educol/documents/163314.pdf.

Hodkinson, P., & Sparkes, A. C. (1997). Careership: A sociological theory of career decision making. *British Journal of Sociology of Education*, 18(1), 29–44.

Merleau-Ponty, M. (1974). *Phänomenologie der Wahrnehmung*. Berlin: Walter de Gruyter.

Petry, K., & Hallmann, K. (2013). Germany. In H. Kirstin& P. Karen (Eds.), *Comparative sport development: Systems, participation and public policy* (vol. 8, pp. 75–86). New York: Springer.

Roderick, M., & Waddington, I. (2000). Playing hurt: Managing injuries in English professional football. *International Review for the Sociology of Sport*, *35*(2), 165–180.

Schlossberg, N. K. (1981). A model for analyzing human adaptation to transition. *Counseling Psychologist*, 9(2), 2–18.

Schubring, A. (2014). *Wachstum als Herausforderung. Soziologische Analysen des Wachstumsmanagements jugendlicher Spitzenathleten und Nachwuchstrainer* [Growth as a challenge: A sociological analysis of the growth management of youth elite athletes and their coaches]. PhD dissertation. University of Tübingen, Tübingen.

Schubring, A., Bub, E.-M., & Thiel, A. (2014). 'How much is too much?' The social construction of elite youth athlete exercise tolerances from the coaches' perspective. *Journal of Sport and Social Issues*, 39(4), 308–331.

Schubring, A., Mayer, J., & Thiel, A. (2018). Drawing careers: The value of a biographical mapping method in qualitative health research. *International Journal of Qualitative Methods*, Volume 17: 1–12. DOI: 10.1177/1609406918809303

Schubring, A., & Thiel, A. (2014). Growth problems in youth elite sports: Social conditions, athletes' experiences and sustainability consequences. *Reflective Practice*, *15*(1), 78–91.

Smith, B., & Sparkes, A. C. (2005). Men, sport, spinal cord injury, and narratives of hope. *Social Science and Medicine*, *61*(5), 1095–1105.

Sparkes, A. C. (1998). Athletic identity: An achilles' heel to the survival of self. *Qualitative Health Research*, 8(5), 644–664.

Thiel, A., Diehl, K., Giel, K. E., Schnell, A., Schubring, A., Mayer, J., … Schneider, S. (2011). The German Young Olympic Athletes' lifestyle and health management study (GOAL study): Design of a mixed-method study. *BMC Public Health*, *11*, 410.

Wellard, I. (2009). *Sport, masculinities and the body*. New York: Routledge.

Wheeler, S. (2012). The significance of family culture for sports participation. *International Review for the Sociology of Sport*, 47(3), 235–252.

Chapter 8

Learning through rugby, migration, and a professional career: A case of a male rugby player

Roslyn Kerr and Koji Kobayashi

People always ask me 'am I Japanese or Kiwi?'

This case study considers one rugby player's cultural learning through his career from a beginner in New Zealand to a member of the Japanese national team and a professional club. The data was collected through a life story interview with the athlete, hereafter referred to as Taro, who shared considerable detail about his experiences as a rugby player.

Taro's story is an unusual one. While there have been other studies examining the migration of foreign-born athletes to Japan (see Chiba, Ebihara, & Morino, 2001), including those focusing on New Zealand players specifically (see Chiba & Jackson, 2006; Sakata, 2004), Taro's story contrasts with these because he was a child of Japanese parents who grew up in New Zealand. It is this tension between his New Zealand upbringing and Japanese cultural heritage that we focus on in order to shed light on the ways in which learning can be affected by international migration and the transition to a professional career.

New Zealand and Japan have very different rugby systems and cultures. In New Zealand, rugby is the traditionally dominant sport for men (Chiba & Jackson, 2006; Pringle, 2004) and is supported by a competitive club and school system that produces numerous successful athletes for the Super Rugby competition and the World Cup–winning All Blacks. By contrast, rugby is a minor sport in Japan, and elite players are more likely to develop at an older age, through high schools, universities and clubs owned by corporations (Chiba & Jackson, 2006; Sakata, 2004). It is Taro's journey from a New Zealand schoolboy rugby player to a Japanese national team member that we explore in this case study.

Migration and cultural difference

The cultural theory of learning perspective (as outlined in Chapter 3) stems from a basis of practice, emphasising that it is through practices that individual learning occurs. One practice that has been identified as having a particularly strong impact on learning is that of migration. Studies of migration and learning have traditionally focused on the transfer of skills, particularly in relation to job acquisition. However, more recently, the work of Hodkinson and related scholars has been applied to the migration context in an acknowledgement that the process of acculturation is far more complex than focusing only on job skills (Morrice, 2014). As Morrice (2014, p. 152) described:

> The process of migration disrupts inherited frames of meaning and the accumulated biographical repertoire of knowledge and understanding; migrants are required to learn new behaviours, quite probably a new language, understand new rules and to adapt to new values and another type of social space. It is difficult to imagine any other life event in which learning becomes so wholly part of daily life experience, with few, if any, aspects of life left untouched by the need to learn.

In this quotation, Morrice focused on the enormity of the 'newness' faced by the migrant that therefore requires a significant amount of learning in every aspect of the migrant's life. Jarvis (2006) posited that we can understand the difficulties faced by migrants through examining the connections or disconnections between biography and experience. Specifically, Jarvis (2006) suggested that our biography provides us with a particular set of expectations and understandings about the world, which affects how we behave. Therefore, in a situation where our current experiences are similar to those in our biography, we feel comfortable, since we know how to behave and what the expectations are. However, in the context of migration, he argued that 'our biographical repertoire is no longer sufficient to cope automatically with our situation, so that our unthinking harmony with our world is disturbed and we feel unease' (Jarvis, 2006, p. 16). He used this to explain feelings of culture shock and to understand the immense learning that must occur for a migrant to acculturate to a new place.

Morrice (2014) likens Jarvis's (2006) argument to that of Bourdieu, who coined the term *habitus* to describe one's embodied understanding of the world that develops through life experience. Bourdieu (1984) conceptualised the world as made up of distinct cultural fields, each consisting of sites of struggle where one's place in the field is determined by one's habitus and levels of capital. He described individuals as like 'fish in water' when their habitus matches the values of the field, which resembles Jarvis's (2006) notion of 'unthinking harmony with our world', both of which are disturbed through migration.

Another aspect of migration is that the capitals accumulated by individuals may not be exchangeable in their new environment they have emigrated to (Morrice, 2014). Bourdieu (1999, p. 511) described a potential outcome of a mismatch among habitus, capital, and field as 'a habitus divided against itself, in constant negotiation with itself and its ambivalence, and therefore doomed to a kind of duplication, to a double perception of self, to successive allegiances and multiple identities'. Morrice (2014, p. 154) argued that such changes lead to 'intense reflection and learning', and it is these learnings that we are interested in examining in this case study.

The above presupposes a significant difference in national and cultural norms between an athlete's former and new countries, and there are several studies that confirm these differences in the sporting context. Stambulova, Alfermann, Statler, and Côté (2009) argued that studies examining different sport development systems show a marked difference between the Western sporting traditions, including those of North America, Western Europe, and Australia, and those that stemmed from a Soviet bloc model. Collins and Bailey (2013) also observed the Western vs Eastern bloc comparison while focusing on the way that ideas from the Eastern bloc have been adopted in many Western nations through factors such as migration. In terms of differences between the New Zealand and Japanese systems, Chiba and Jackson (2006) identified that in the sport of rugby, Japan was characterised by an emphasis on hard work, which played out through long training sessions, a running game, and a more authoritarian relationship between coaches and athletes, while in New Zealand there is an emphasis on quality of training, a physical game, and more open communication between coaches and athletes. The uniqueness of the Japanese sport system has also been highlighted by previous studies in terms of its focus on the centrality of school and corporations in providing sports, as well as cultural underpinnings deriving from Confucianism[1] (Kobayashi, 2012; Light, 2008; McDonald & Hallinan, 2005). Given these differences and the likely disorientation caused by migration, it is no surprise that studies have found that so-called borderless athletes face considerable issues with, for instance, multiple national identities, sport-specific eligibility rules, and nation-specific naturalisation processes (Chiba et al., 2001).

In what follows, we present Taro's learning journey. The first section focuses on Taro's early years as a school rugby player in New Zealand. Next, we examine his migration to Japan to take up a professional contract and an opportunity to represent a Japanese national team. Finally, we discuss the maturing stage of his professional career and life as a husband and father. We argue that each of these periods included very different learning environments for Taro and, in being so different, acted as turning points where Taro experienced significant growth and deep learning.

Childhood in New Zealand: Becoming a kiwi

Taro was born in Japan and moved to New Zealand as a preschooler after his parents decided to migrate. Taro's parents were both Japanese, and after years of hard work, they were able to obtain the status of permanent residency in New Zealand. Taro recalled that his engagement with rugby was influenced not so much by his parents but by his friends:

> ...my friend's dad just invited me to go play rugby down with his team when I was about six or seven..., so I just went down there and started playing and have done it since. ...all I remember is playing and enjoying it and all of a sudden I signed up.

From the time of his introduction, rugby became his main interest and activity and also served as a dominant component of his identity. Taro's rugby progress was impressive, as he ended up playing in the First Fifteen for one of the most prestigious high schools for rugby in New Zealand. Taro appreciated the environment that he was in, which facilitated a gradual progression of interest and skills:

> I think the great thing about New Zealand is that you play touch rugby and then you play 10-a-side rugby and then you play tackle, and it evolves into a full adult game. So, not all the rules are the same when you're a kid. You play with 10 people and you don't lift in the lineouts. You don't push in the scrums. And then you get to 13, you start pushing. And you get to 14, you start lifting in lineouts. I don't know the specifics, but they gradually introduce all the rules into rugby because it is a dangerous sport. So, you sort of want to learn the skills slowly....

When growing up, Taro also appreciated the choice of sports and seasonality of sports in New Zealand, which allowed children to try out other sports:

> ...I think that's why people gain different skills from different sports, interacting with different people and also just getting a different perspective, and not doing the same thing all year round. So, you actually look forward to the next season as well.

Taro reasoned that he was able to continue playing rugby because 'I just did what I enjoyed really, so I went to high school and didn't study much, didn't study at all really, just played rugby.' During adolescence, Taro found that playing rugby provided him not just with enjoyment but also with a sense of identity with, or belonging to, a wider New Zealand culture. In other words, rugby provided a platform through which he became a 'Kiwi' (a common nickname for people from New Zealand), as his self was strongly associated with the national culture. This also reflects his experience of being isolated and racialised as an 'Asian kid' in the white-dominant schools that he attended:

> ...I think [the place], when I came..., was a very much European city... I think there were just over 400 kids at the primary school that I started at and I was the only Asian kid, so that was difficult in itself. Looking back, there was a little bit of bullying as I obviously looked different. It just took time to get used to, I was really oblivious to it and didn't really know. But now I look back and I sort of see what happened back then, but it was all part and parcel. I did identify myself with the Kiwi rugby players more as I got older... I just wanted to hang out with the rugby guys, and thinking back now, it's probably more of an identity thing.

In a way, he used rugby to form his closer associations with the 'rugby guys', which then enabled him to align himself with the dominant culture of New Zealand.

As such, anything Japanese was something to avoid, de-emphasise, and disassociate with in order to purify his Kiwi identity:

> …I sort of did purposely separate myself from [Japanese friends] just to hang out with the rugby guys and just to be seen as one of them as opposed to, um. It's hard to explain, but I find now that I didn't really integrate as well with the Japanese family friends as much. So, my way of… being a Kiwi was by not studying Japanese. I didn't study Japanese. I did everything that a Kiwi would do.

When asked whether he would be a different person if he did not play rugby, Taro answered, 'I 100% would be yes'. In short, rugby for Taro in his adolescence was not just about playing sport but also about learning, engaging, and embodying values and norms of New Zealand through the institution of rugby as a cultural practice.

Analysis

The learning culture during his school years was one shaped by fun and enjoyment. Indeed, Taro's description of his early learning environment was almost identical to that advocated by various Western talent development frameworks that emphasise the importance of enjoyment and learning through play (see, for example, Baker & Côté, 2006; Balyi & Williams, 2010). Even in high school, where training may have become more intensive, Taro did not experience it as such. Consequently, in his early years, Taro developed a confidence and sense of self related to his rugby abilities that contributed to him establishing an almost limitless horizon of learning in the field of rugby.

However, as Hodkinson, Biesta and James (2008) point out, an individual's horizon of learning is not established only through the learning culture. Following Bourdieu, they argue that an individual's disposition (habitus) and capitals are also significant. For Taro, what was also important during this phase was his identity as the only Asian child in school. Rugby was (and arguably remains) the quintessential sport for New Zealand boys, with those playing the sport well often receiving the adulation of their peers and wider authority figures (Pringle, 2004). Taro's skill in rugby acted as a form of capital that meant that he was able to access the rewards that rugby success produced and thus allowed him to identify himself as a Kiwi and feel he fitted in with his peers. He described himself as not very academic, with rugby instead being the area where he excelled. In Hodkinson and colleagues' (2008) terms, Taro was able to access the opportunity to learn to become an excellent rugby player because his disposition (or habitus) and his capitals fit together with the learning culture of rugby.

Representing Japan and becoming a professional

Although young Taro enjoyed playing rugby and appreciated the cultural learning associated with it, his horizon of learning was limited to the context of

New Zealand until he returned to Japan around the age of 20. While Taro in his adolescence resisted being associated with anything Japanese, the offer to play for the Japanese national rugby team was irresistible. Taro described:

> …the national coach at the time rang me up when I was playing club rugby here [in New Zealand] and said 'do you want to come and join us and try and make the World Cup?' I didn't actually plan to. From about 15, I've had a manager that's helped me out—that is a rugby agent over there—and [the manager] said 'do you want to go to high school over there?' and I said 'no, I want to stay here'. He said 'do you want to go to uni over there to play rugby?' and I said 'no, I'll stay here'. I planned to finish my PE [Physical Education] degree, so I could obviously become a teacher because that's what I enjoyed as well, but obviously an opportunity to go to a World Cup doesn't come around very often, so I said I might as well have a go and ended up making it.

For Taro, representing a nation was significant because 'it's obviously the highest honour you can play for'. As he prepared for his first Rugby World Cup, he withdrew from tertiary education in New Zealand and joined one of the clubs in the Top League (the professional rugby league in Japan). Thus, the chance to play for the Japanese national team also paved his way into a professional rugby career in Japan. However, moving back to Japan brought many challenges for Taro. One of the hardest challenges was the language barrier. Since Taro did not study Japanese and spoke little Japanese when growing up in New Zealand, he found it difficult to master the language and understand the culture underpinning the ways in which the language was used. One of the distinguishable characteristics of the Japanese language is *keigo* (honorific speech), through which juniors are expected to use a different set of vocabulary and grammar to show respect and politeness when speaking to seniors. The prevalence of *keigo* in everyday conversation reinforces the importance of the seniority-based social hierarchy across a variety of domains in Japanese society (see Light, 2008). Coming from New Zealand, Taro was not aware of the difference in social systems and therefore rather shocked by it:

> …the hierarchy system in Japan I struggle with because I've never learnt. I didn't know about it, and I was the youngest player by a few years as well. So, that was always difficult, and obviously *keigo* or the language speaking to the elders was always difficult, but everyone knows that you're there to play rugby as well. So, people were really patient with me now that I look back. That was probably the hard thing. So, it took me good two to three years to get fully used to it….

The language learning was not just a matter of daily communication off the field but actually had a direct impact on his on-field performance because:

> …whether it be in English or Japanese over in Japan, it's how you communicate when you play your best in sport. So, I think I had to communicate

> well with the rugby players over there, and then when I went to Japan, I had to basically relearn Japanese as well.... So, I ended up being a translator.... On field, you sort of have to communicate on the spot and make decisions really quickly. So, I think it's probably my biggest asset on the field....

Taro's improved bilingual ability was highly regarded by his Top League clubs and Japanese national teams, as they often had several English-speaking (and non-Japanese-speaking) players, coaches, and staff. Through the experience of living in Japan and interacting with both Japanese and non-Japanese, Taro had a chance to reflect on his old and new selves: 'If you get to travel and you get to live in a different place, you learn a bit more about yourself, a bit more about a different culture and things'. Consequently, Taro was able to reassess his self in association with Japan and recognise the fluidity of cultural identifications:

> People always ask me 'am I Japanese or Kiwi?' but I'm Japanese and I grew up in New Zealand. I'm not Japanese sometimes, and I'm not Kiwi sometimes. It's just an identity thing. I knew I was Japanese as I've always had a Japanese passport.... So, I've always had the opportunity at the back of my mind that I could represent Japan one day. For me, I've always wanted to play at the highest level. I've always wanted to play well for who I played for as well. Whether it be a [high school] jersey or a [amateur club] jersey or a [professional club] jersey, I just wanted to play well and then one thing has always led to another which through a little bit of hard work and aspiring to be the next level, I've ended up in the Japanese jersey....

It was also this stage of his life and career when Taro was able to apply his learning from the PE degree to understanding the cultural differences underpinning the styles of coaching in New Zealand and Japan:

> ...while I was learning teaching, obviously there's skill based learning and then there's game sense learning. I find it here [New Zealand] they teach a lot of the game sense learning. For example, the game is soccer, in Japan all you'd do is practice the pass. So, you get really good at passing, but when it becomes a game..., they don't actually execute the skill very well.... In New Zealand, I find they teach a lot of game sense where they won't specifically teach the pass, but they'll put five guys in a square in a big area, and they'll have two guys that try and get the ball off them. So, it's all about guys trying to get into space and passing the ball to a person in space, and then understanding that, trying to get the ball off the opposition or holding onto the ball as opposed to just isolating a skill. I find it here—because you're only learning the game sense and you want to get better, you learn the skill yourself, so you go away and learn the skill and then you come back to the game. And then you get better at the game and then you'll want to get better at the skill. So, it's a continuous learning here... whereas in Japan it's so isolated and it's all about repetition....

In line with the findings by Chiba and Jackson (2006), Taro confirmed that the Japanese environment tends to demand longer hours and a higher frequency of training, whereas in New Zealand there are fewer training sessions with a greater emphasis on practicing to play games than on practicing just for the sake of training.

However, Taro was not entirely dismissive of skill-based learning and the emphasis on it in Japan:

> It's not saying one way is right or the other.... For me, I think that's the reason why I've continued for so long and why I enjoy it and even going back to Japan and I do a lot of skill based learning. I can still find fun in it now, but if I just grew up on skill based learning, I don't think I would have lasted or have wanted to continue... Japanese players are a lot more skilful in terms of catching and passing. Their skill level is really high, but the game sense side and coaching side is completely different....

In sum, the move to Japan clearly provided Taro with many challenges as well as learning opportunities both on and off the field. While it took more than a few years, he eventually found ways to adapt himself to the different social system and to develop his rugby skills and bilingual communication. Thus, learning through cultural adaptation played a key role in his progressing to a successful professional career.

Analysis

Taro's move to Japan to play professional rugby consisted of a significant turn in his learning about both rugby and his cultural heritage. His move was a turning point in the sense that Hodkinson and Sparkes (1997) and Hodkinson, Sparkes, and Hodkinson (1996) describe it: as a transition point that initiated a new horizon of learning. Though in reflection of Hodkinson and Sparkes's (1996) and Bourdieu's (1984) argument about the relationship between structure and agency, this turning point came about owing to a structural opportunity appearing and Taro using his agency to accept it.

In terms of rugby skills, Taro described how, in contrast to his life in New Zealand, the Japanese system entailed countless repetitions of movements such as passes in order to learn to execute them perfectly. He perceived this to be the opposite of the game sense style he had experienced in New Zealand, where learning was perceived to take place through playing the game. To some extent, this transition is similar to that experienced by the gymnast in Barker-Ruchti and Schubring's (2016) study, which described the move from a fun-orientated to task-based environment. However, unlike the gymnast, Taro considered this transition as a positive learning experience through which he learnt how to 'find fun in' the task-based environment. Furthermore, Taro already possessed rugby/cultural capital from New Zealand that he could transfer to Japan. His rugby training from New Zealand meant that his embodied habitus allowed him to learn the technical skills easily in Japan and adapt to the new style of coaching despite it being very different from his previous experience. Consequently, in contrast with Morrice's (2014) assertion that individuals can experience culture shock and disorientation when their experience and expectations do not match, Taro did not experience this very strongly, as he was able to manage the gap by becoming a cultural and language translator and using this competency as his 'biggest asset' on the rugby field.

However, outside of the field of rugby, Taro's learning was very different. In the context of Japan more broadly, Taro felt a strong sense of disorientation, as he found his previous horizon for action to be obsolete. As someone of Japanese appearance, he was easily perceived, or stereotyped, as having mastery of Japanese language and cultural competence. However, having grown up in New Zealand speaking English rather than Japanese and having developed a strong New Zealand habitus, he was significantly challenged for his level of 'Japaneseness'. Such challenges were commonly experienced by naturalised foreign-born players in Japan, as noted by Chiba and colleagues (2001). For example, his lack of competency in *keigo* would have been instantly perceived as 'rude' or 'impolite' by those who did not know he grew up in New Zealand. Here, he experienced Morrice's (2014) sense of disorientation where his horizons for action, as developed through his New Zealand experiences, did not match with an expected level of language skills and cultural understanding in Japan, and especially in the business context where the use of formal language is a norm.

At the same time, this turning point proved significant for Taro to reflect upon the process of 'becoming' Japanese through 'learning' Japan and 'representing' a Japanese national team. As noted by Hodkinson and Sparkes (1997), interruptive turning points can have significant transformative potential, and such was the case here, with Taro's migration triggering an intense learning phase where he not only transitioned to a professional career but also 'became Japanese' through adapting to both language and behaviour. After this learning phase, Taro developed a new horizon for action within the field of Japanese rugby in being one of the few players acting as a cultural translator who could speak both English and Japanese fluently. Consequently, his horizon of learning broadened beyond merely rugby skill. His New Zealand knowledge and language coupled with his recently acquired Japanese knowledge and language provided him with bilingual/bicultural capability, which he was able to transfer into rugby.

Maturing as a professional and becoming a husband/father

At the time of the interview, Taro had spent about 10 years as a professional rugby player in the Top League. Becoming and being a professional rugby player for Taro was an undoubtedly fundamental part of who he was given this provided a sense of transcendence from such categories as 'Japanese', 'Asian', and 'Kiwi'.

As a mature and senior player in both his club and the national team, Taro had developed a personal philosophy of professionalism:

> …being a professional, you're actually paid to play and perform, you're not just paid to act like a professional or pretend you're a professional. You have to actually win games and perform well, so I think that's the realisation as opposed to doing it for fun…. Your mindset has to change that, have to do everything for you to perform on a Saturday. All your preparation has to be geared towards that…. Some jobs, you get an annual report once a year, rugby players get an annual report every week. That's basically your performance, your annual report is on every Saturday in the game.

For Taro then, his playing career goal was achieved when his professionalism—doing everything to perform to one's best—produced the result of winning at the highest level. Indeed, Taro mentioned his last World Cup as the career highlight so far and reasoned that this produced the best outcome at the highest level that he ever played:

> Because you always try and play at the highest level especially now that I'm a professional player, you try and perform at the highest level and you're under pressure and you want to play your best. I think as a team, we performed our best at the most important time…. Sometimes rugby is a funny game where you put so much effort into it, you might have the best practice or best training leading into a game, and then you might have a terrible game. Or you might have the worst preparation, and then have best results. But, I think we prepared the best and played the best which is really pleasing that we were able to do it at the highest level at the World Cup, so that's probably my personal highlight.

As part of the process to achieve this personal and collective highlight, one of the key learnings for Taro was to adapt to a particular style of coaching, which would be best described as authoritarian and, from his point of view, was prevalent in Japan. As Taro puts it, '[w]hether you agree with it or don't agree with it, the Japanese seem to respond better to authoritarian coaching'. Adaptation to an extremely authoritarian style of coaching was assisted by a sports psychologist working for the national team. Taro described this learning process as follows:

> It was sometimes very hard to understand where [the coach] was coming from, but she [the sports psychologist] brought it to the senior player group and said 'look, at the end of the day you can't change your boss', so you need to change the way you're thinking and how you react to it because if you react to it in a negative way, then it just spirals whereas if you take him for what he just said, understand where he's coming from and then just let it go…. So, it's just basically understanding firstly the coach and who he is and then understanding yourself and interpreting it differently, which was the best advice

> or mental process that we had been given from her to deal with him. I could probably deal with anyone now.

Given Taro's profound engagement with rugby environments in both New Zealand and Japan, he was able to critically and reflexively assess the pros and cons of the authoritarian style of coaching. When asked whether he liked the coaching style, Taro responded:

> I don't like it. Do I agree with it? In some respects, I do, but he's the best at what he does.... What he does is that he creates pressure at training. So, he's always putting you under pressure..., he's always having a go at you, always questioning you to the point where he questions if you put too much mayonnaise on your food, you're going to get fat. It's draining, it's tiring, but a test match at the highest level is all of that. So, it took me forever to understand him and understand why he does things.... Whether you agree with him or not, he gets the result, so you can't question it really.

When asked how his coaching style contrasted with that in New Zealand, Taro explained:

> He would be completely different to a New Zealand coach. He creates an environment where you figure out problems on your own, but he's in control of that. A New Zealand coach would create an environment where there's five leaders in the team, and the coach gives you a blank piece of paper and goes 'ok, you guys come up with how you want to play' and then we'll manage that and try and emulate that on the training paddock, so you can play like that in the game whereas [the Japanese coach] would give you a piece of paper that would have four bubbles in it and you have to work within those four bubbles. So, he's in control of those bubbles. Then, you put your ideas in, but whether he listens to those ideas, I don't know. (Laughter)

From his experience then, the Japanese style of authoritarian coaching may work when there are players who need to be constantly pressured to perform one's best and coaches who want to exert strong control and leadership to follow their game plans.

It was also around the time of this World Cup when Taro's private life was changed dramatically with marriage and the birth of a child. The growing sense of responsibility as a husband and a father caused him to consider that it may be time to settle down and start a post-playing career in New Zealand. Taro pointed out a common problem with a transition from a professional rugby career to a post-playing career: 'A lot of Kiwi rugby players generally go [to Japan] as a professional, so they get paid a lot of money to go. When they do finish, they struggle with post-career choices if they haven't prepared very well...'. In particular, Taro envisioned that the rugby network and cultural learning that he acquired through his early life would help building his post-playing career: '…the one thing I do want to do is to combine my Japanese and English and my rugby experiences in both countries and getting into player representation or player welfare sort of thing'.

Taro also insisted that his family would come first and therefore it may affect choices for a post-playing career:

> I don't think it'll be coaching either because I don't think that's a career that I really want to get into. Good coaches these days only last five years in one place and bad coaches get fired after six months. …I don't think after taking [my wife] to Japan for over 10 years whether travelling around the globe with small kids is an ideal career option. So, I'd like to be settled down somewhere, and if I have to travel, I have to travel from a base.… Just for family reasons, I wouldn't become a coach.…

Consequently, Taro felt that his transition from one of the 'rugby guys' in New Zealand to a professional rugby player in Japan extended not just the horizon of learning but also a range of opportunities, or horizons for action, for a post-playing career through engagement with rugby, culture, and language in both countries.

Analysis

Taro's previous experience of rugby as fun, with a recently acquired and growing understanding of Japanese customs, was challenged by the extremely authoritarian style of the coach of the Japanese national team. Prior to this point, he was aware of and familiar with this type of coaching through his involvement with Top League clubs—which Chiba and Jackson (2006) reported to be normal in Japan; yet the level of control and pressure exerted by the coach required him to approach it differently. It was the sports psychologist who facilitated his learning and provided a coping mechanism by which Taro was able to understand the coach's motives for behaving in the way that he did. He was consequently able to rationally understand and appreciate the positive value of the coaching approach, which from his understanding prepared the team to perform best under tremendous pressure at the highest level.

He also understood his ability to cope with the pressure as a part of his competency and identity as a professional player. This aspect of his competency and identity had taken time to develop through his longevity in professional teams, but he had come to realise the utmost necessity of performing well on a weekly basis and making this a priority in response to the pressure from his employers, the fans, and the media. Given his history of focus on rugby, this was not a difficult shift for Taro to make, but it was still a significant learning curve in that it required him to sacrifice many aspects of life for rugby and therefore established a new professional identity in his habitus.

Beyond his identity as a mature professional player, during this later stage of his career, a significant change was the extension of Taro's learning horizon

(Bloomer & Hodkinson, 2000) to prepare for life beyond rugby. Where previously his learning had been focused primarily on the rugby context, his learning now expanded to include the roles of husband and father. In essence, he began making a transition from an athlete-focused identity, which had been his habitus up until this point, to a post-playing career and father-orientated identity. Despite the fact that Taro spent about 10 years in Japan as a professional rugby player, his desire to settle down in New Zealand for a post-playing career indicates that his horizons of learning and for action were firmly informed and shaped by his New Zealand experience and identity.

Conclusion

Taro's rugby career brought with it a constant broadening of learning horizons through the different stages. Initially, his experience was characterised by a love of the game, and rugby provided him with a 'Kiwi' identity. Once he moved back to Japan, however, he gained higher levels of Japanese language and cultural competency but was also challenged in terms of his level of 'Japaneseness', as he struggled with *keigo* during the first few years of migration. Interestingly, his New Zealand upbringing provided him with, on the one hand, highly competent rugby knowledge and skills—which were transferable cultural capital between the nations—and, on the other hand, obstacles in understanding Japanese customs and language—which were nation-specific cultural capital. Thus, his horizon of learning significantly extended during this early time in Japan. Another turning point occurred when he had to adapt to the extremely authoritarian style of the national team's coach, a coaching style that required substantial adaptation in how to manage coach-player relationships. Finally, in becoming a husband and father, his horizon extended beyond rugby to prepare for a future non-player career and identity that would allow him to provide more time and security for his family.

This case study shows how the different phases of Taro's life/career, including migration, national/professional team involvement, and marriage and fatherhood, acted as significant turning points for deep learning to occur. All three triggered a sense of uncertainty, posed tremendous challenges, and resulted in a change in his identity, competency, and values. Where he began playing rugby purely for enjoyment, he then used rugby to embrace his Japanese cultural heritage upon migration, develop into a professional career, and plan his transition to post-player life to support the next generations of international rugby players.

Note

1. Confucianism is the philosophy developed by Chinese philosopher Confucius in the fifth and sixth centuries B.C. It is commonly understood in relation to its emphasis on values of family, loyalty, hard work, integrity, and seniority. Confucianism was spread over centuries across East Asia and in particular Japan in the fifth or sixth century A.D.

References

Baker, J., & Côté, J. (2006). Shifting training requirements during athlete development: Deliberate practice, deliberate play and other sport involvement in the acquisition of sport expertise. In D. Hackfort & G. Tenenbaum (Eds.), *Essential processes for attaining peak performance* (pp. 92–109). Oxford: Meyer & Meyer Sport.

Balyi, I., & Williams, C. (2010). *Coaching the young developing performer*. Leeds: Coachwise.

Barker-Ruchti, N., & Schubring, A. (2016). Moving into and out of high-performance sport: The cultural learning of one women's artistic gymnast. *Physical Education & Sport Pedagogy*, *21*(1), 69–80.

Bloomer, M., & Hodkinson, P. (2000b). Learning careers: Continuity and change in young people's dispositions to learning. *British Educational Research Journal*, *26*(5), 583–597.

Bourdieu, P. (1984). *Distinction: A social critique of the judgement of taste*. Cambridge, MA: Harvard University Press.

Bourdieu, P. (1999). The contradictions of inheritance. In P. Bourdieu (Ed.), *Weight of the world: Social suffering in contemporary society* (pp. 507–513). Cambridge: Polity Press.

Chiba, N., Ebihara, O., & Morino, S. (2001). Globalization, naturalization and identity: *The case of borderless elite athletes in Japan*. *International Review for the Sociology of Sport*, *36*(2), 203–221.

Chiba, N., & Jackson, S. (2006). Rugby player migration from New Zealand to Japan. *Football Studies*, *9*(2), 67–82.

Collins, D., & Bailey, R. (2013). 'Scienciness' and the allure of second-hand strategy in talent identification and development. *International Journal of Sport Policy and Politics*, *5*(2), 183–191.

Hodkinson, P., Biesta, G., & James, D. (2008). Understanding learning culturally: Overcoming the dualism between social and individual views of learning. *Vocations and Learning*, *1*, 27–47.

Hodkinson, P., & Sparkes, A. C. (1997). Careership: A sociological theory of career decision making. *British Journal of Sociology of Education*, *18*(1), 29–44.

Hodkinson, P., Sparkes, A., & Hodkinson, H. (1996). *Triumphs and tears: Young people, markets and the transition from school to work*. London: David Fulton.

Jarvis, P. (2006). *Towards a comprehensive theory of human learning*. Oxon: Routledge.

Kobayashi, K. (2012). Globalization, corporate nationalism and Japanese cultural intermediaries: Representation of *bukatsu* through Nike advertising at the global-local nexus. *International Review for the Sociology of Sport*, *47*(6), 724–742.

Light, R. (2008). Learning masculinities in a Japanese high school rugby club. *Sport, Education and Society*, *13*(2), 163–179.

McDonald, B., & Hallinan, C. (2005). *Seishin* habitus: Spiritual capital and Japanese rowing. *International Review for the Sociology of Sport*, *40*(2), 187–200.

Morrice, L. (2014). The learning migration nexus: Towards a conceptual understanding. *European Journal for Research on the Education and Learning of Adults*, *5*(2), 149–159.

Pringle, R. (2004). A social-history of the articulations between rugby union and masculinities within Aotearoa/New Zealand. *New Zealand Sociology*, *19*(1), 102–128.

Sakata, H. (2004). *The influence of foreign players on the transformation of Japanese rugby over the last three decades*. Unpublished master's thesis. University of Canterbury, Christchurch, New Zealand.

Stambulova, N., Alfermann, D., Statler, T., & Côté, J. (2009). ISSP position stand: Career development and transitions of athletes. *International Journal of Sport and Exercise Psychology*, *7*(4), 395–412.

Chapter 9

Ageing in professional sport: A case of a professional male basketball player

Laura G. Purdy, Geoff Kohe, and Rūtenis Paulauskas

It doesn't matter how old you are, what matters is the condition you're in.

This case study focuses on Tomas Kovak, a male professional basketball player who has played in the highest leagues (e.g., EuroLeague) in several European nations. With over 20 years of professional experience, he has represented his home nation in the Olympics, World Championships, and EuroBasket. This player, a symbolic character, was developed from an amalgamation of interview data with three 'ageing' male professional basketball players working in European clubs. To protect the identities of these players, this data was consolidated to create a fictional athlete character. As such, the resultant narrative has been (co)constructed by the authors and arranged to story a common experience of 'ageing' players in this particular context. In addition to problematizing ageing in sport, the case study coheres with wider research projects that aim to understand player welfare, identity, and experiences in the professional sport settings within and beyond Europe (Kohe & Purdy, 2016; Purdy, Kohe, & Paulauskas, 2017; Purdy, Kohe, & Paulauskas, in press). This narrative highlights ways in which ageing is embodied and the learning processes that occur vis-à-vis ageing in a particular learning culture (in this case, elite sport). In addition, the narrative is intended to evidence the dialectic relationship between the athlete's ageing processes and the wider sociocultural complex of professional sport of which their experiences are a part.

Professional sport is a context characterised by normalised assumptions about the body, the limits of the performing body, the inherent degeneration of the body over time, and the disjuncture between 'weakened' bodies and the sustainability of 'peak' performance (Allen & Hopkins, 2015). Consequently, some organisations and individuals within the professional sport industry may have ideas regarding the appropriate chronological age (or 'best before' date) at which an athlete may be advised to retire or begin transition toward retirement. Here, scholars have drawn attention to the variations in the physical maturation of elite athletes and the related implications of their longevity for peak performance (Faulkner, Davis, & Mendias, 2009). While there may be exceptions where 'gifted' athletes might outperform their younger counterparts up to a certain age (in some research demarcated as 40 years; Faulkner et al., 2009), some stakeholders may perceive an 'optimum zone', in which athlete ageing is viewed as positive (i.e., when an athlete is perceived to be 'experienced'), and a later period when one is considered to be past their 'best before' date. This varies across sports.

In basketball, not unlike many other professional sports, threats to the careers of professional players largely relate to physicality and/or performative aspects of the game. Consequently, players' priorities with regard to the performative relate to the protection and increase of their playing minutes (and consequently their statistics). These statistics become a valuable part of their strategy to remain, and move (horizontally and vertically), within the profession.

The professional basketball system in Europe is comprised of four tiers. Currently, the top tier is the Turkish Airlines EuroLeague (comprised of 16 teams). This is followed by the EuroCup (45 teams) and then the Champions League (32 teams). The fourth tier is comprised of domestic leagues (e.g., Spanish ACP, Lithuanian LKL, Russian VTB). The scope of the regional and domestic leagues thus makes basketball in Europe an attractive career. Given the advantageous nature of employment within elite levels of the game, it makes sense that players may wish to potentially prolong careers and may be adverse to accepting ageing discourses within the industry that may curtail continuation in the sport and/or further learning opportunities.

Introduction of the specific focus within learning/career development

Current research on ageing and the work undertaken in sport is useful to demonstrate how effects of ageing impact upon particular individuals and populations. There is substantial literature, for example, that has focused on the physical consequences of ageing and performance in sport (e.g., Brander, Egan, & Yeung, 2014; Fried & Tauer, 2011; Hollings, Hopkins, & Hume, 2014). Recognition of ageing is important within high-performance sporting environments—particularly in scenarios where an athlete's biological development and the consequences of ageing have implications for athlete selection, funding, and resource allocation decisions and for projection planning for individual or team success (Allen & Hopkins, 2015). The concern is that current ageing discussions within sport shape discourses that reinforce normalised ideas of ageing as a process of bodily decline and perpetuate a culture that stereotypes how the process of ageing occurs and should be managed. In the first instance, there is the need to consider the complexities of ageing as a social phenomenon and the consequences of ageing that extend beyond the level of individual embodiment. As Laz (1998) argues, ageing is both a social and a collective practice that is given meaning and discourse in everyday interactions and performances. Moreover, ageing is not, and cannot be, easily bound by institutional and structural mechanisms that treat the process as purely linear, generic, and prescriptive. Within sport, for example, discussions of an athlete's ageing narratives should be broadened to recognise the external contextual forces within sport that craft the ways in which ageing is experienced and also the related effects that the individual's ageing may have on their wider social networks and structures (e.g., on the coach, team, organisation, family, agents, or the media).

Age is not, we recognise, always invisible; occasionally, it comes to the forefront of our consciousness, and we must deliberately make sense of age, often in the context of particular events or milestones, changes in our physical appearance or physical condition, or social roles and norms (Laz, 2003). In this case study, we move beyond notions of age being biological and given and consider that ageing is negotiable and learned. Our approach follows the prevailing literature that has drawn attention to instances whereby individual athletes' participation and transitions through sport have demonstrated a resistance to a linear progression narrative (e.g., one in which participation changes concomitantly with age-related body concerns) (Phoenix & Smith, 2011; Tulle, 2008). Recognising the predominance of narratives that reaffirm ageing stereotypes, these studies also highlight the need to provide new considerations of ageing that challenge stereotypes and associations between sport and positive outlooks on ageing. In what follows, we present a narrative that explores some of the ways in which ageing discourses have been made evident within the experiences of athletes within a professional basketball context. In accord with the literature that has challenged prevalent conceptualisations of ageing in sport, the intention is to offer new renderings that acknowledge athlete agency, opportunity, and autonomy.

Prevailing scholarship has focused not only on the biophysical and psychosocial aspects of ageing but also on the implications ageing has with respect to individual competitiveness and performativity, their longevity and sustainability within their chosen careers and related transitions (Rüst, Knechtle, & Knechtle, 2012; Warriner & Lavallee, 2007). The interest in this case study is on how individuals understand ageing as it relates to their career experiences and transitions (specifically in the process of becoming a basketball player), how they make meaning out of transitional phases, and how they learn, adjust, and negotiate the consequences and effects of ageing in meaningful ways. Part of this meaning making about ageing also involves consideration of the discourses of ageing (which prompt thoughts amongst athletes and other stakeholders), how they respond, and if alternative discourses are possible. Knowledge of career longevity is useful, scholars contend, as it can provide essential information to inform athletes' progression plans and coaches' training programmes, as well as inform longer-term considerations about individual and team development (Allen & Hopkins, 2015; Allen, Vandenbogaerde, & Hopkins, 2014).

Case material

I'm 38 years old. I've been a professional basketball player for over 20 years. The chance to play basketball professionally was a really big thing for me. People thought because I started the sport later than most, it would be impossible for me to get to the highest level. So throughout my career, I've been motivated to prove the opposite. Also, because I had been involved in other sports, moving to basketball meant that I had to work hard to get to the level of the other players my age. But early on I saw how this work translated into results, so I put a lot of time and energy into improving. And this effort has carried on through my career. I do extra training in the off-season, I pay attention to what I eat, and I don't drink much alcohol.

I never thought about how long I'd play professional basketball. I just played. About age 30, I remember wondering how long my body could sustain the physical demands of the sport and mentally, how long I could stay at that level, but when I started, no way! While I'm under no illusion that my career will last forever, unlike some of my friends whose bodies are worn out from the sport, I can still play at the same level and same intensity as those more than 10 years younger than me!

When I started my professional career, I wanted to play in the first division, and when I reached that, my goal changed to play in the better teams and at a higher level. Finally, I wanted to play in the national team, to go to EuroBasket and the Olympic Games. While most of my career has been focused on achieving these milestones, I always knew I couldn't stay at the top level forever, but I didn't really know how to prepare for the step-down. While most of my career has been focused on achieving these milestones, I always knew I couldn't stay at the top level forever, but I didn't really know how to prepare for the step-down. I thought about what it might be like—the level of play, the intensity of training—but I hadn't thought about the little things. For example, I used to have several top teams trying to sign me, but a few years ago, my phone stopped ringing as often, and now it rings even less. Initially, it was difficult to accept that the best teams weren't interested; I really missed the top level of basketball, the communication in the team, the organisation, the coaches, the personnel, the players around me, and the quality of games and practices. When I first moved out of the top league, I felt more like a semi-professional and it was very difficult to find the motivation to get through the season. Actually, I wasn't sure I would continue playing because I couldn't adjust to that team's way of thinking. That first season out of the top league was a difficult season for me, but the next season I got signed to a team with a mentality that was more similar to my own. During that season, I didn't have any trouble motivating myself. Now that I know what conditions I like and can do well in, I won't sign with a club that doesn't match. There would be no point.

I started to become aware of 'age' when I saw how long it took me to recover. My recovery after practice and after games got slower and slower. I noticed how my speed started to change—my quickness on the court. Small injuries started to occur, but really the main issue was the time it took to recover—after games it takes me much longer before I'm ready to play again. However, through trial and error and the advice of various coaches, sports doctors, and physiotherapists, I became better able to read my body, to know what training suited me and how

I should prepare and recover. So I guess I'm one of the lucky ones who figured this out so that I can still be able to play at this age and at this level.

As a young player, I don't recall differentiating between my teammates; to me everyone was the same. The more experienced players might have explained and demonstrated some skills or showed younger players elements of how they should play and the attitude to have, but I didn't categorise teammates as 'young' or 'old'. I guess I never really thought about age, but now I experience it. Sometimes in the locker room, the younger players make jokes about my restricted movement after a game. I laugh and tell them I look forward to seeing what they are up to when they are my age. I doubt many will be physically able to play! Sure, they can joke that they might have more energy, but they don't have the experience or the understanding of the game that I have. I watch them run all over the place, while I move smarter. I know how to read the game, where I need to be and at what point. I don't need to kill myself and waste energy by running all over the place.

I think some of my younger teammates are familiar with what I've done in my career, so they respect me. At least I think they do! They seem to listen when I speak. There are times when I feel like a father figure when I'm around them. I talk to them about warming up properly and the importance of stretching—I never did much of either at the start of my professional career! They might ask questions as to why they are doing a particular drill and I explain, so I guess my coaching career has already started! It hasn't always been easy though, there have been a few moments when I've had to bite my tongue to stop myself from saying something to a young teammate who can't seem to do the most basic things. For the most part, however, I've had the privilege of playing with good players who help push me to perform.

Looking at my career now, although it was really difficult at the time, the transition out of the top teams has not been terrible. When I was trying to make it to, and stay at, the highest level, I put 100% energy into my work. Now, while I still train and play with intensity, moving from the top league has opened up time for me to concentrate on other things, develop new interests. A couple of years ago, I thought that eventually I might like to be a coach, so I started studying part-time at the university. I guess in the past couple of years, basketball has started to take on a different role and become another part of my life; playing basketball is no longer my whole life.

In an ideal world, if I could play for a team of a high standard, I'd like to play for another couple of years, but it isn't really up to me. I noticed when I turned 35, it became more difficult to get signed. I would only get one-year contracts because clubs tend to think that older players will have injuries and these could be chronic. Maybe one year the body is okay, and then the next it isn't. It's the same with motivation. So a one-year contract is the safest option for a club.

It's too early to know what I'm doing next season because the season isn't over. So I will stay in contact with my previous team and wait to hear their plans in a couple of months' time. Although I've decided to go for a new contract, I need to wait to see if a team wants me. I guess I'm at a crossroads in my career. I know if

I can't get a contract, I will retire. And if I retire, I'm done. It would not be possible to take two or three years off and come back. Well, it might be possible to play at a much lower level, but I cannot imagine doing that. I don't need to end my career playing for a team in a city league, for little money. So when I stop, I will stop forever. In my career, I have had great performances and have tried to do the maximum of what I could. I have given over 20 years to the sport! When it ends, I don't think I will miss anything! Okay, I may miss the life in the team, the relationships with the other players and coaches, but I won't miss the life of an athlete. For 10 months a year, my life has been crazy with practices, games, and trips. It would be nice to be a normal person, to have weekends and time to spend with family and friends. But right now I have no injuries, I'm still ready to play at a high level, so maybe a good contract will come! If not, the last three to four years have helped me prepare to leave. I'm no longer anxious to know if I've played my last season. I'm content to wait; I'm ready for whatever will come next.

Analytic block outlining the athlete's learning/career development and future learning and career development

Entrance into basketball

In order to understand the intersection of ageing and learning within Tomas's experience, it is useful to review his start in professional basketball and the ways in which he learned to 'be' within the sport. Here, Tomas perceived a space in which he saw opportunities for his development and future potential in the sport. As Hodkinson, Biesta, and James (2008) would suggest, Tomas's horizon for action, in particular, was comprised of the chance to build his identity by working in a new cultural context, playing a new sport, and learning different skills. To recall, Tomas had not specialised in basketball from a young age; rather, he entered the sport as an adolescent. Given his teammates had started the sport as children, Tomas's late entrance meant that his developmental priorities and initial learning were intensified as he brought himself up to speed with the demands of the sport and worked to improve his recognition in the team. Tomas's experiences echoed those of other athletes who have transitioned into another sport and had to negotiate the new sport and the specific culture of the club, team, and coaches (Benson, Evans, & Eys, 2016; Schinke & McGannon, 2014). While this previous sporting experience and his predilections for sport and physical activity afforded him particular physical literacy, he still needed to learn the culture—essentially, not just how to 'be' a basketball player but also how to 'be' *in* basketball. To clarify, by the time they get to the elite level, players such as Tomas have amassed considerable technical skills and prowess on the court that afford them physical capital in the sport (which effectively contributes to an identity of 'being' a basketball player). Players' experiences, however, must also extend beyond the performative to include learning about the sociocultural contours of the sport and the professional sporting context (this is what comprises 'being' in basketball) (Carless & Douglas, 2013). Eventually, Tomas realised that his hard work, dedication, motivation, and personal and professional development were affording him recognition and opportunities that had not previously been considered possible. In Tomas's case, the process of becoming a basketball player required not only understanding the game but also establishing working relationships with the coach and teammates that would enable him to progress and be successful in the sport. Although Tomas could not have envisioned how his career may have played out or what his longevity in the sport may have been, his horizon for action was, in this regard, orientated on demonstrating his strong work ethic and ability to learn new skills within his new context. Such an approach, Tomas hoped, would aid his transition and afford him recognition as a valued member of the team. Tomas's strategies also entailed a horizon of learning in which he must understand the complexities of his new work and roles, who he was becoming as an athlete from a different sport, and the processes that were required for him to perform at the level expected of him by his coach and contemporaries.

Becoming a professional basketball player: The early days

In the initial stages of his professional career, and not unlike many athletes, Tomas's story was woven with an array of learning experiences from which he draws meaning about himself. His understanding of himself and his performance of his role as a basketball player was what constituted his career identity (Meijers, 1998). Over time, his career identity developed via his continued learning experiences in the sport and his personal development (Barker, Barker-Ruchti, Rynne, & Lee, 2014). In tandem, Tomas was also learning what it meant to be an employee within a particular work setting (Kohe & Purdy, 2016; Meijers, 1998). Essentially, Tomas was developing a professional identity in response to the cultural conditions of the club and its influence on his role as a player. As described above, employment in the upper echelons of European basketball requires players to not only demonstrate physical proficiency but also become savvy individuals who possess business acumen and nous and can adeptly respond to the commercial expectations and organisational imperatives of their employment. As part of this identity work, for example, he learned how a strong work ethic, which included extra training, stretching, and close attention to diet, contributed positively to his performances and subsequent contracts with preferred teams (e.g., EuroLeague, national squad). What is important here is that this formative learning was fundamental in establishing Tomas's assumptions about the sport and its ethos, his role(s) within the context, and who he is and may be able to be as a result of further engagement and learning in the environment. He was particularly concerned with proving himself in the sport and demonstrating to sceptics that he could succeed. When he learned that his actions had positive consequences in terms of his performance, he reorientated his thinking and strategies to firmly entrench himself in the team and establish himself as an integral player (Carless & Douglas, 2013).

Becoming an ageing professional basketball player: Middle career

Notwithstanding Tomas's invariably successful progress in the sport, there were moments of reflection when he considered his tenure. What precipitated Tomas feeling his ageing was threefold. First, Tomas felt that his recovery was delayed and his on-court time decreased. Second, he became more aware of his teammates' comments about his ageing. Third, his contracts shifted to one-year appointments. However, his physical condition and his desire to continue playing quelled his concerns about career longevity. Yet, advantageously, what was helpful to Tomas is the cultural learning and subsequent knowledge acquisition over the years, which effectively provided him with an understanding of how the context operates, the relative worth of his own capacities and abilities beyond merely the performative, and what he needed to do to negotiate his situation to enact a different career outcome. These processes, concomitantly, shaped his horizon for action; that is, in this case, they afforded him an opportunity to construct and orientate a horizon for ageing in and beyond sport.

Being an ageing professional basketball player: Late career

Congruent with many other players' experiences toward the latter stages of their careers, Tomas reached a period in which a confluence of external pressures and internal reflections precipitated a step change in his identity formation, personal expectation, and professional possibilities (Cosh, Crabb, & Tully, 2015; Douglas & Carless, 2009). The most significant change was the transformational learning that occurred as Tomas realised his embodied experiences in the sport were changing (Bennett, Scarlett, Hurd Clarke, & Crocker, 2017; Waskul & Vannini, 2016). Part of this learning also entailed understanding that his performances were yielding different outcomes in terms of career possibilities (for example, less attractive playing statistics in comparison to those of his contemporaries) and that these required new horizons for action to be formed so that he could continue to experience the achievements to which he had become accustomed. What becomes apparent is that the consequences of his ageing (e.g., changes in body and employability options) necessitated both life and career decisions (Ronkainen, Ryba, & Nesti, 2013). For Tomas, a significant disruption occurred with his initial move from the top league in Europe. While the experience afforded him opportunities to maintain his sporting prestige irrespective of his age, his frustrating social interactions with some of his less experienced, immature, and, in his view, 'incapable' peers threatened what he believed 'being' in professional basketball was all about. At this point, he questioned his future in the sport. However, following a new contract with a team that shared his performative mentality and professional needs and roles, Tomas gained clarity again about his horizon and his potential future in the sport.

Echoing other research examining athletes' post-sport transitions (Cockerill, 2005; Stambulova, Alfermann, Statler, & Côté, 2009), Tomas's experience highlights that some athletes may exhibit considerable agency when deciding to exit sport (or transition to less professional levels within sport). Here, it is possible to acknowledge that there is an inherent self-control aspect to ageing within Tomas's horizons. Moreover, while athletes may have agency to determine their movements out of sport on their own terms, as Gill (2007) has suggested, there are generally 'preferred' courses of retirement action, and while these norms may clash with individuals' own expectations, athletes who understand the process may have a smoother transition. Tomas, however, still maintained a degree of agency in this process in determining what conditions and circumstances he was willing to accept.

While Tomas's future may not be certain, the way in which he understood the consequences of ageing within the context of his basketball career meant that he could create a horizon for action that included appropriate strategies for transformation. This may have involved, for example, being open to new opportunities, adjusting to different personal and professional contexts, facilitating alternative social connections and networks, and realigning personal expectations and priorities. Tomas's interest in pursuing a coaching career subsequent to his professional playing led to his enrolment in a degree programme in coaching. This decision to study could be viewed as a self-initiated turning point in which Tomas recognised his current horizon is inadequate for his particular needs and decided to create a new space and priorities for his development. Coaching possibly offered a comfortable role in a context with which Tomas was familiar and in which his identity has been heavily invested. Moreover, it provided him with a potentially less traumatic transition than might be experienced by moving into a non-sport context, as it afforded a chance to utilise existing forms of capital and knowledge to his advantage. Given his previous successes, for instance, with top teams, he might be afforded more opportunities, at least initially, to ply his trade. As Mallett, Trudel, Lyle, and Rynne (2009) noted, a successful athletic career may provide more access to coaching positions and allow a coach to get a 'foot in the door'; however, the coach's record becomes more pertinent for future employment.

Tomas's experience in professional sport demonstrates that approaches to understanding athlete learning may benefit from a more substantive recognition of the subjective and socially constructed nature of identity. Moreover, it acknowledges athletes' experiences (often portrayed in the media) that move beyond narratives of trauma, disruption, and discomfort. Tomas's narrative may reflect other aspects of professional athletes' lives and stories that have been discussed by scholars for several decades and may echo in particular some of the existing concerns and assumptions about ageing that abound within the industry (Allen & Hopkins, 2015; Brander et al., 2014). However, Tomas's story offers insights that prompt a different conceptualisation of ageing and its embodiment within sport. For example, the learning undertaken as a result of Tomas's progression and transition in the latter stages of his career was in keeping with literature that conceptualises it as a process of radical identity transformation, change, or reconfiguration (Lavallee, Gordon, & Grove, 1996; Warriner & Lavallee, 2008).

Summary of learning career in sport

At some point in a player's career trajectory, they are forced to consider the end of the professional work and/or contemplate career transition or 'retirement'. These decisions are sometimes precipitated by extreme and/or unforeseen circumstances (e.g., injury, health, contract termination, or personal circumstances) that force a decision to leave the job indefinitely. In other cases, such as that explored in this case study, the end of a player's career may be more gradual and less dramatic. In regard to the latter scenario, a player's decision to retire may involve considerable contemplation as they weigh their post-playing strategies and alternate career options (if any). We review here the earlier acknowledgement made that, in some cases, there is an element of self-control within the conceptualisation of horizons of ageing. While work has recognised that career change is multifaceted and complex and has a high degree of variation (Douglas & Carless, 2009; Warriner & Lavallee, 2008), what is of most interest in this case study are the ongoing processes and personal development/reflection that occur as players learn to adjust and negotiate their life beyond their professional playing careers. Although there has been some organisational interest in athlete welfare and retirement options and opportunities, they are often focused on the effects of the process on athletes and how athletes may need to be supported through this period (Clemmet, Hanrahan, & Murray, 2010; Cosh, Crabb, & LeCouteur, 2013). Many sport organisations have made significant contributions by developing broad-based educational and developmental packages, resources, forums, and mentorship opportunities to assist athletes in the later stages of their careers (e.g., IOC Athlete Career Programme, Athlete Futures (UK), Game Plan (Canada)). Here, it is noteworthy that Tomas, like many of his professional peers, was going through this process (and essentially constructing his horizons) independent of organisational/institutional assistance.

Tomas's story illustrates the extent to which ageing is subjective, as well as tied to the setting in which it is embedded (Johnson, Berg, & Sirotzki, 2007). It provided an insight into the embodiment of ageing that differs from current scholarship and prompts us to consider the inevitability of ageing and the acceptance of this within the professional sport career trajectory. As mentioned above, career transitions and retirements have been conceptualised as a series of phases and milestones that must be 'worked through' and that eventually lead to a point of change in the athlete's identity and understanding of their life circumstances. For Tomas, this is a partial explanation of his situation. The basketball context in which Tomas worked was a setting demarcated by particular cultural norms and assumptions (e.g., in regard to gender construction, work ethic, geopolitical ideas and localised traditions, and commodification cultures). The setting provided Tomas with a distinct cultural environment for deep learning, professional and personal development, and identity work.

This case study has focused on 'Tomas' and the professional context shaping his ageing experiences. His story reflects some of the realities that we have already witnessed, and continue to witness, in professional players' lives in different settings. With the increasingly lucrative nature of professional sport, more extensive/enduring careers of athletes are becoming, if not normative, then more frequent. Moreover, there remains a wide(ning) array of motivations with respect to players' rationales for career continuation (Cosh, LeCouteur, Crabb, & Kettler, 2013). These motivations are also compounded by changing sociocultural perceptions about ageing, the body, career/dual-career/post-career and employment, and well-being. In providing a narrative of athlete ageing, this case study has contributed to needed conversations regarding what sports work entails and the complexities and consequences it might have for individuals, organisations, and wider professional industries.

References

Allen, S. V., & Hopkins, W. G. (2015). Age of peak competitive performance of elite athletes: A systematic review. *Sports Medicine*, *45*(10), 1431–1441.

Allen, S. V., Vandenbogaerde, T. J., & Hopkins, W. G. (2014). Career performance trajectories of Olympic swimmers: Benchmarks for talent development. *European Journal of Sports Science*, *14*, 643–651.

Barker, D., Barker-Ruchti, N., Rynne, S. B., & Lee, J. (2014). 'Just do a little more': Examining expertise in high performance sport from a sociocultural learning perspective. *Reflective Practice*, *15*(1), 92–105.

Bennett, E. V., Scarlett, L., Hurd Clarke, L., & Crocker, P. R. E. (2017). Negotiating (athletic) femininity: The body and identity in elite female basketball players. *Qualitative Research in Sport, Exercise and Health*, 9(2), 233–246.

Benson, A. J., Evans, M. B., & Eys, M. A. (2016). Organizational socialization in team sport environments: Socialization in team sport. *Scandinavian Journal of Medicine and Science in Sports*, *26*(4), 463–473.

Brander, J. A., Egan, E. J., & Yeung, L. (2014). Estimating the effects of age on NHL player performance. *Journal of Quantitative Analysis in Sports*, *10*, 241–259.

Carless, D., & Douglas, K. (2013). Living, resisting and playing the part of the athlete: Narrative tensions in elite sport. *Psychology of Sport and Exercise*, *14*(5), 701–708.

Clemmet, S., Hanrahan, S., & Murray, J. (2010). Transition out of sport: An examination of the loss of athletic careers. *Journal of Science and Medicine in Sport*, *12*(s2), e111.

Cockerill, I. M. (2005). They think it's all over, but it may not be! *British Journal of Sports Medicine*, *39*, 880–883.

Cosh, S., Crabb, S., & LeCouteur, A. (2013). Elite athletes and retirement: Identity, choice and agency. *Australian Journal of Psychology*, *65*(2), 89–97.

Cosh, S., Crabb, S., & Tully, P. J. (2015). A champion out of the pool? A discursive exploration of two Australian Olympic swimmers' transition from elite sport to retirement. *Psychology of Sport and Exercise*, *19*, 33–41.

Cosh, S., LeCouteur, A., Crabb, S., & Kettler, L. (2013). Career transitions and identity: A discursive psychological approach to exploring athlete identity in retirement and the transition back into elite sport. *Qualitative Research in Sport, Exercise and Health*, 5(1), 21–42.

Douglas, K., & Carless, D. (2009). Abandoning the performance narrative: Two women's stories of transition from professional sport. *Journal of Applied Sport Psychology*, *21*(2), 213–230.

Faulkner, J. A., Davis, C., & Mendias, C. L. (2009). The aging of elite male athletes: Age-related changes in performance and skeletal muscle structure and function. *Clinical Journal of Sport Medicine*, *18*(6), 501–507.

Fried, H. O., & Tauer, L. W. (2011). The impact of age on the ability to perform under pressure: Golfers on the PGA Tour. *Journal of Productivity Analysis*, *35*, 75–84.

Gill, D. L. (2007). Gender and cultural diversity. In G. Tenenbaum & R. C. Eklund (Eds.), *Handbook of sport psychology* (3rd edition) (pp. 823–844). Hoboken, NJ: Wiley.

Hodkinson P., Biesta, G. J. J., & James, D. (2008). Learning cultures and a cultural theory of learning. In D. James & G. Biesta, *Improving learning cultures in further education: Improving learning* (pp. 21–37). London: Routledge.

Hollings, S. C., Hopkins, W. G., & Hume, P. A. (2014). Age at peak performance of successful track and field athletes. *International Journal of Sports Science and Coaching*, 9, 651–662.

Johnson, M. K., Berg, J. A., & Sirotzki, T. (2007). Differentiation in self-perceived adulthood: Extending the confluence model of subjective age identity. *Social Psychology Quarterly*, *70*, 243–261.

Kohe, G., & Purdy, L. G. (2016). In protection of whose 'wellbeing'?: Considerations of 'clauses and a/effects' in athlete contracts. *Sport and Social Issues*, 40(3), 218–236. DOI: 10.1177/0193723516633269

Lavallee, D., Gordon, S., & Grove, R. (1997). Retirement from sport and the loss of athletic identity. *Journal of Personal and Interpersonal Loss*, *2*(2), 129–147.

Laz, C. (1998). Act your age. *Sociological Forum*, *13*(1), 85–113.

Laz, C. (2003). Age embodied. *Journal of Aging Studies*, *17*(4), 503–519.

Mallett, C. J., Trudel, P., Lyle, J., & Rynne, S. (2009). Formal vs informal coach education. *International Journal of Sports Science and Coaching*, 4(3), 325–334.

Meijers, F. (1998). The development of a career identity. *International Journal for the Advancement of Counselling*, 20, 191–207.

Phoenix, C., & Smith, B. (2011). Telling a (good?) counterstory of aging: Natural bodybuilding meets the narrative of decline. *Journals of Gerontology Series B: Psychological Sciences and Social Sciences*, 66(5), 628–639.

Phoenix, C., & Sparkes, A. C. (2006). Young athletic bodies and narrative maps of aging. *Journal of Aging Studies*, 30(2), 107–121.

Purdy, L. G., Kohe, G. Z., & Paulauskas, R. (2017). Coaches as sport workers: Professional agency within the employment context of elite European basketball. *Sport, Education and Society*. DOI: 10.1080/13573322.2017.1323201

Purdy, L. G., Kohe, G. Z., & Paulauskas, R. (2018). Changing it up: implications of mid-season coach change on basketball players' career and professional identities, *Sport in Society*.

Ronkainen, N. J., Ryba, T. V., & Nesti, M. S. (2013). 'The engine just started coughing!'—Limits of physical performance, aging and career continuity in elite endurance sports. *Journal of Aging Studies*, 27(4), 387–397.

Rüst, C. A., Knechtle, B., Knechtle, P., Rosemann, T., & Lepers, R. (2012). Age of peak performance in elite male and female Ironman triathletes competing in Ironman Switzerland, a qualifier for the Ironman world championship, Ironman Hawaii, from 1995 to 2011. *Open access journal of sports medicine*, 3, 175.

Rüst, C. A., Knechtle, B., Rosemann, T., & Lepers, R. (2012). Sex difference in race performance and age of peak performance in the Ironman Triathlon World Championship from 1983 to 2012. *Extreme Physiology and Medicine*, *1*(1), 1–15.

Schinke, R. J., & McGannon, K. R. (2014). The acculturation experiences of (and with) immigrant athletes. *International Journal of Sport and Exercise Psychology*, *12*(1), 64–75.

Stambulova, N., Alfermann, D., Statler, T., & Côté, J. (2009). ISSP position stand: Career development and transitions of athletes. *International Journal of Sport and Exercise Psychology*, *7*(4), 395–412.

Tulle, E. (2008). *Ageing, the body and social change: Running in later life*. London: Palgrave Macmillan.

Warriner, K., & Lavallee, D. (2008). The retirement experiences of elite female gymnasts: Self-identity and the physical self. *Journal of Applied Sport Psychology*, *20*, 301–317.

Waskul, D.D., & Vannini, P. (2016). Introduction: The body in symbolic interaction. In P. Vannini (Ed.), *Body/embodiment: symbolic interaction and the sociology of the body* (pp.1–18). London: Routledge.

Chapter 10

The implications of sport attire and culture for Muslim women's participation in elite boxing: A case of a female boxer

Anne Tjønndal

Good Somali girls are not boxers.

Introduction of athlete: Aisha's story

In 2006, when Aisha was 10 years old, her father was killed in the Somali civil war. Fearing for their lives, Aisha's mother took her children and fled from their home in Somalia. Two years later, the family found sanctuary in Norway and made a new home for themselves. During the first years in Norway, Aisha struggled to adapt to her new life. Aisha had a hard time understanding Norwegian culture and language, and she missed Somalia, her father, and the extended family members they had left behind. As a result, Aisha struggled with depression and social anxiety. She was angry, did not do well in school, and isolated herself from everyone around her. Little did Aisha know that she would soon be introduced to boxing and that it would change her life.

Aisha's brother had started boxing, and one day in 2012, Aisha snuck out of her room to go with him. The boxing gym was not like any other place Aisha had ever seen before, but from the time she walked through the doors, she knew she had found a new home. Since her introduction to boxing at the age of 16, she has not missed a training session. Before she started boxing, Aisha had no friends, spent most of her time in her room, and refused to eat regularly. For her, boxing became a way of changing herself and turning a new page in life. Boxing helped her gain new friends, and in a short time, Aisha became more outgoing, did better in school, calmed down, and developed confidence.

I first met Aisha in 2014 at a national boxing tournament we were both competing in. Although I have been a competitive boxer since 2005, watching Aisha fight in 2014 was the first time I saw a Somali girl box. What made me notice Aisha was the way she dressed when she competed. I have always boxed in a standard boxing competition uniform (shorts and singlet) without giving it much thought. Aisha, however, wore full-length tights and a long-sleeved shirt under her competition uniform. Under her head guard, all of her hair and neck was covered in a black hijab.

Eventually, Aisha and I would travel together to training camps and international tournaments, competing for the national team. In all the tournaments we went to together, I never saw any other Somali girl fight. I spent many hours with Aisha during these trips, and talking to her, I realized that while we both experienced barriers connected to our athletic careers as women in a male-dominated sport, her barriers were different and seemed harder to overcome. Today, Aisha is 20 years old, and she has lived in Norway for as long as she has lived in Somalia. She is an elite boxer and competes for the national team.

Using Aisha's learning and career development in elite boxing, this case study will focus on the implications boxing clothing—specifically competition uniforms—and cultural and religious beliefs have for Muslim women's participation in elite boxing. Specifically, the case study discusses how Aisha, as a Somali (and Muslim) woman, struggles to balance the different demands of the elite sport culture of boxing and the traditional cultural/religious beliefs associated with women and the female body in Somali culture. In this way, the case study illustrates how Aisha as an athlete adopts various strategies to manage the demands put upon her by other athletes, coaches, referees, and officials and the demands put upon her by family members and informal networks to be a 'good Somali girl'. In the second half of the chapter, I explore Aisha's learning processes as an elite athlete in boxing. This section is divided into three parts, depicting Aisha's early, middle, and current career phases.

Managing elite sport and Somali culture

In the elite sport context, elitist objectives are normalized and institutionalized in a number of practices that sport organizations adopt to identify and prepare athletes for elite sport success. In this case, boxing culture has institutionalized and normalized a dominant ideal and practices of how elite female athletes should dress when competing. Boxers are normally required to compete in shorts (or skirts) and singlet with a clear line/belt separating the upper body and the lower body, the purpose of the line functioning as a clear visual aid for officials to call fouls in the form of blows below the belt. In Olympic boxing, male athletes compete without a head guard, while female and youth athletes must compete with a head guard. Female athletes are also required to gather all of their hair under the head guard when competing. To do this, most female athletes use a buff,[1] so that no hair is showing outside of the head guard. Furthermore, women can choose to wear protective breast cups and groin protection, while male athletes are required to wear an athletic jock strap in case of low blows.

In competitions, officials commonly enforce the rule that athletes do not cover their legs, arms, or neck—for instance, by wearing long-sleeved shirts or leggings under the standard competition trunks and singlet. A common argument for enforcing such attire regulations is that officials will not be able to see potential injuries sustained by the athletes if they cover these body parts. However, the International Boxing Association's (AIBA) technical and competition rules (2017) and the *AIBA Event Operational Manual* (n.d.) do not specify such restrictions for athlete competition uniforms. As a result, in some competitions, Muslim female boxers are allowed to wear a headscarf that covers both their hair and their neck under their head guard; in others, they are not allowed to wear such covering. In some competitions, they are allowed to wear long-sleeved shirts and tights under their trunks and singlets; in others, they are not allowed to wear them. Some boxing officials might allow Muslim female boxers to wear a T-shirt under the singlet to cover up their shoulders but not a long-sleeved shirt. Hence, Muslim female elite boxers experience many inconsistencies in terms of what they are allowed to wear when competing and what they prefer to compete in.

Learning cultures are governed by a number of written and unwritten rules. With regard to the former, elite boxing is governed by AIBA and international sport organizations such the World Anti-Doping Agency (WADA) and the International Olympic Committee (IOC). On a regional level, national and club-specific policies apply. For Aisha's case, this is the Norwegian Boxing Federation (NBF) and the policies of her local boxing gym. With regard to unwritten rules, sport- or training-specific traditions and ideologies also shape elite sports' learning cultures. Such formal and informal rules mean that elite sport learning cultures produce certain types of athletes—not just in terms of their athletic performances but also in terms of their identity. This entails certain ways of acting, dressing, training, and eating—in other words, how you live your life as an elite athlete. As an individual athlete, Aisha must manage the inconsistencies in how boxing officials enforce and interpret AIBA's rules for competition attire. Hence, material objects like clothing affect not only competition practices in elite boxing but also athletes' horizons for action and horizons of learning. Using this as a starting point, the aim of the analysis in this case study is to describe and discuss the different horizons Aisha develops to handle both the elite boxing and the Somali pressures put on her as an athlete.

Developing an elite boxing career

Migrating to Norway and the introduction to boxing: Early career phase

Because of her turbulent childhood, Aisha's athletic career began late, at the age of 16. Aisha had limited sport and physical activity experience when she came to Norway. In Somali culture, organized sport participation is mainly associated with men and masculinity and is not considered to be important or valuable for girls and women. In addition to her late introduction to boxing, her early career phase was shaped by the conflicting demands of the learning cultures of elite boxing and Somali culture. Hence, an important part of the early career phase for Aisha entailed familiarizing herself with Norwegian sport culture while managing the cultural expectations her family had for her as a Somali girl.

None of Aisha's three sisters compete in sport or play sport at a recreational level. According to Aisha, traditional Somali families do not encourage their daughters to participate in sport because it is considered 'unladylike' and not appropriate for 'good Somali girls':

> When I started, going to the boxing gym was difficult. I had to sneak out of the house and go with my brother, I couldn't tell my mom where I went. It was hard to keep it a secret, and to lie to her. In the boxing gym, there were a few Norwegian girls.... But I have never seen another Somali girl boxing. The Norwegian girls act and dress different than me, they wear shorts and tank tops. I couldn't really relate to them that much. I don't think they understood what it means to be a Somali girl.

Since Aisha came to Norway in 2008, she has lived with her siblings and their mother in a small apartment. In Somali culture, the father is considered the head of the family, having the final word in all matters concerning his family members (Pfister, 2000, 2003; Walseth, 2006). Aisha explained that Somali men are strict, especially with their daughters, and Aisha does not think that she would have been able to become a boxer if her father was still alive. Her mother and her extended family do not approve of her boxing. Her uncles in particular, who also fled to Norway, constantly tell her that boxing is a 'sport for men' and are critical of the ways female boxers dress when they fight. Aisha says that she is lucky to live with her mother and not her uncles because she believes her uncles would forbid her to box. Aisha describes her initial attempts to hide her involvement in boxing and her fear of her mother's reaction upon finding out:

> Eventually, I couldn't sneak out of the house anymore. I had to tell my mom what I was doing.... In the beginning, I told her I was only doing boxing to keep fit, and she accepted it....well, kind of.... At least she didn't demand that I stop. Maybe because she saw that it made me happier, more confident and outgoing.... Somali parents are strict. A lot of my [Somali] friends are afraid of their parents, but I have never been afraid of mom. I know she only wants what's best for me.... But once I started fighting competitively, it was very hard for her, we argued a lot and I thought about quitting boxing. In reality, mom has never approved of me boxing. I think she is worried that I will get hurt because I am a girl. She told me to pick another sport, a sport that respects my religion...but I love boxing, so I didn't want to let religion stop me from doing it.... I don't think it is right.... I don't think God will condemn me for loving boxing, even if I am a girl.... My brother is a boxer, but he is a boy, so she accepts his choice more than she accepts mine.

Even though Aisha's mother is disapproving of her boxing, Aisha says that it is her uncles that are the most difficult to manage in her family:

> My family doesn't like it at all, but they don't really know that much about my boxing either. My uncles are against the clothes I wear when I fight, but I don't listen to them. They tell me it's a 'boys' sport', and that it isn't suitable for girls. But I think that's normal in every culture, that men don't want girls to be involved in boxing.

Aisha's struggle to adapt to boxing culture encompasses challenges connected to religious beliefs and social norms connected to perceptions of the female body in Somali culture. The idea of women boxing clashes with cultural expectations of girls and women in Somali culture, as boxing is traditionally associated with men and masculinity (Hovden & Tjønndal, 2017; McCree, 2015; Tjønndal, 2017; Woodward, 2006). However, as Aisha points out, the sociocultural belief that boxing is an 'inappropriate sport for women' is not unique to Somali culture (or other Islamic cultures) but can be found in many Western cultures (e.g., Carlsson, 2017; Matthews, 2016; Tjønndal, 2016), as well as in other regions of the world (e.g., Kim, Kwon, & Lee, 2015; Kipnis & Caudwell, 2015; Nash, 2017). Moreover, Aisha has to manage specific cultural/religious barriers connected to the clothing worn by competitive boxers in the ring. Somali culture imposes strict social codes for how women should dress in public (Hassan, 2017; Johnson, 2017). For Aisha, this means that her legs, arms, and neck should always be covered, including during training sessions and boxing tournaments. As an elite sport culture, boxing has its own regulations for competition outfits for athletes and covering the legs, arms, and neck is often prohibited. This puts female Muslim athletes such as Aisha in a difficult situation, pressured by both the formal and informal rules of elite sport learning culture and the traditional cultural/religious beliefs of their families.

When Aisha came to Norway, she was struggling with the trauma of escaping the Somali civil war and the loss of her father while being exposed to a foreign country and culture at the same time. As a result, Aisha had a limited horizon for action. Her Somali horizons of learning did not apply in Norway, and because she suffered from anxiety and depression, her isolation (e.g., she did not engage in social interactions with local Norwegians) meant that she had limited possibilities to develop new and workable horizons for action. Her horizon of learning was almost non-existent. Starting her boxing training became a turning point for Aisha, from which point on she felt more comfortable and gained confidence and new friends. The introduction allowed her to develop horizons for action and of learning that gave her hope for something new and positive in her life. It also created a horizon for a boxing future. However, even in her early career phase, this horizon was complicated and conflicted by her Somali culture. This was (and still is) demanding for Aisha as she struggles to negotiate these conflicting horizons.

Developing strategies to cope with elite sport culture: Middle career phase

Since Aisha started fighting competitively in 2013, she has been juggling the pressure to conform to the institutionalized norms of boxing competition attire and the pressure to adhere to cultural/religious expectations of her family. Aisha's uncles have always pressured Aisha's mother to forbid Aisha to continue her training and give up her dreams of becoming a boxing champion. Aisha explains this, describing what her mother and uncles expect of her as a good Somali girl:

> A good Somali girl spends a lot of time at home. She doesn't go to parties and she doesn't drink alcohol. That's all bad things to do as a Somali girl. Good girls stay at home, respect their parents, respect their elders, follow the Somali culture and speak the language.... Education is important. Somali parents are extra strict with the girls. Mom doesn't want me to end up like her—with no education.

While Aisha's mother is concerned that boxing distracts Aisha from getting a good education, the men in Aisha's extended family do not see boxing as a suitable hobby or viable career path:

> My uncle tells me all the time 'You're a good Somali girl. You shouldn't be doing this. When will you stop this foolishness? You're a girl, and girls shouldn't be boxing. You will hurt yourself'. When he says things like that to me, it makes me very upset. I get sad. It makes it hard for me to keep training for the next fight.

In 2015, Aisha became a national champion. In 2016, she moved up to the elite[2] rank and competed in the national elite championship for the first time. After winning her semi-final, Aisha was stopped from entering the ring by an official because of her 'inappropriate' attire:

> I have a lot of issues with my hair and neck in boxing bouts. I usually cover my hair and neck when I'm in public, that's why I wear the hijab. In the final of the national championship in 2016, an official stopped me just when I was about to enter the ring. They wouldn't let me fight because I wore a hijab under my head guard. I felt like giving up, like I should just quit boxing then and there.... But I had to find a solution. In the end, my coach gave me a buff, and I used it to cover my hair and neck. Then it was okay—because it wasn't a hijab, even though it did the same thing as the hijab would have.

Despite her trouble getting into the ring, Aisha managed to win the final, and she gained her first title as an elite boxer and fulfilled her goal of becoming a champion. This situation, where Aisha used a buff to fulfil the function her hijab normally does to be allowed to compete, can be interpreted as an example of how sport-specific traditions and ideologies shape elite sports learning cultures (see, for instance, Kerr, Barker-Ruchti, Schubring, Cervin, & Nunomura, 2017). Such formal and informal rules mean that learning cultures produce certain types of athletes—not just in terms of athletic performance but also in terms of certain ways of acting and dressing as an elite athlete/boxer. For Aisha, at this point of her athletic career, developing strategies to manage the clothing expectations of elite boxing has become a part of Aisha's life as a female Muslim/Somali boxer:

> I have to find solutions all the time. I prefer to wear leggings, hijab and a long-sleeved shirt under my trunks and singlet. Then I feel normal. Sometimes that's okay. Other times the officials won't accept it. They won't accept leggings and long sleeves, but they'll tell me that I can wear long socks up to my knees and a T-shirt under the singlet. I don't understand why they care so much about my clothes. It seems very random—and unfair.

The quotation is an example of how Aisha, as an individual, manages the inconsistencies in how boxing officials interpret AIBA's competition rules and regulations. At a micro level, this entails a learning process through which Aisha tries to manage a sense of who she is, how she can act, and what she can and cannot do as a Somali woman and a boxer. The statements above also indicate that in the middle career phase, Aisha started to develop a horizon for finding solutions to combine her Somali culture with boxing. This indicates a shift in her actions from not knowing how to handle the clothing requirements of competitive boxing to understanding that she has to find her own solutions.

As a Somali woman, Aisha faces strict judgements from her family, particularly the male members of her extended family, when she conforms to the informal dress rules of elite boxing:

> One time, one of my uncles saw a video of my fight on YouTube. In the video, I was boxing with trunks and long socks, so part of my knees and lower thigh was showing. He was furious and called my mom straight away. He told my mom she had ruined me and that no Somali man would marry me. He said I was naked. Somali men call it 'naked-clothing' and they don't accept it at all.

For traditional Somali men and women, integrity is imperative. A central part of this means following Islamic rules about the female body and its presentation in public (Pfister, 2010; Walseth, 2005). For traditional Somali, women's covered bodies are a symbol of Islam and their culture. The anger Aisha's uncle expressed when Aisha did not adhere to these rules can be interpreted as an expression of the cultural belief that women who do not cover their bodies in this way are acting against Islam.

In her middle career phase, Aisha's continued struggle to negotiate the different cultural expectations of elite boxing and Somali culture is a central topic. Her situation is further complicated by her prolonged engagement in boxing. As Aisha continues to develop her career and compete in boxing, she is subjected to more referees and coaches who do not understand the dress codes for Somali girls and who interpret the competition rules of boxing in a way that makes it difficult for Aisha to compete.

Adapting to the elite athlete lifestyle while managing elite sport culture/Somali culture: Current career phase

Today, at age 20, Aisha is at the beginning of her career as an elite boxer. She has a part-time job to help her mother support the family while living out her dream of pursuing a career as an elite athlete. Aisha trains two times a day and competes as often as she can. Since Aisha became a national champion, she has been under the supervision of the national head coach. Since getting on the team, Aisha has had problems getting along with the head coach:

> The national head coach pretends to respect me and my religion, but he really doesn't! He just doesn't understand how I feel, and he isn't fair to me. I don't know if he does it on purpose, or if it's just because he doesn't understand my religion. I just want to respect God…but he talks to me as if I'm a child who doesn't understand anything! Sometimes, he has made me fight without covering my legs and shoulders. That feels so unnatural to me. I'm not comfortable with it, especially not having my neck covered. I would never go out in public without my hijab. For me, my neck and my legs are the most important to cover up. If I have to box in trunks alone, I have to enter the ring with something I'm not comfortable with. It feels like a part of me is missing, and I feel like I am disappointing God and my family.

Sport attire is a highly controversial topic in Islamic gender discourses (Pfister, 2000). For Muslim women, modesty through covering their bodies signals submission to God (Pfister, 2010). Thus, modesty by covering the body signals solidarity with Islamic traditions (Pfister, 2003). The discomfort Aisha feels when her (ethnic Norwegian) coach forces her to fight without leggings, hijab, and a long-sleeved shirt can be interpreted as going against Islamic/Somali traditions. Aisha is torn between the one-dimensional identities often associated with elite sport learning cultures (e.g., Barker-Ruchti & Schubring, 2016; Barker-Ruchti & Tinning, 2010; Carless & Douglas, 2013; Johns & Johns, 2000; Lang, 2010; McMahon & Penney, 2012; Warriner & Lavallee, 2008) and her ethnic identity/background as a Somali woman.

In 2015, AIBA announced a permanent removal of the head guard for male elite boxers. The change in AIBA's competition rules was prompted by research done by the association's Medical Commission, through which AIBA studied the outcome of 'more than 11,000 bouts in major boxing competitions' and concluded that 'the number of concussions showed a significant drop of 43% from 2013 to 2015' (AIBA, 2016). Although there is research indicating that there are no differences in cognitive and neurological functions between male and female Olympic style boxers (Stojsih, Boitano, Wilhelm, & Bir, 2008), AIBA has removed the head guards for elite men's competitions only. In 2017, however, rumors started to spread that AIBA might remove the head guard for elite women as well. Aisha fears that AIBA will impose the new rule for women's competitions:

> If they make women box without a head guard, like the men, I won't be able to cover my neck anymore, and I have to quit boxing. That's the end of competitive boxing for me, and most Somali girls.

A sport-specific rule change such as removing the head guard for women's competitions will potentially affect the learning culture of elite boxing. Individual athletes such as Aisha must manage such instabilities, which entails learning at a micro level (e.g., Hodkinson, 2008; Hodkinson, Biesta, & James, 2008). For Aisha, a dramatic change in the rules of competition equipment is impossible to adjust to without going against Islamic/Somali culture (e.g., Hassan, 2017; Pfister, 2010). Thus, female Muslim boxers might hope to influence the activities of boxing as a learning culture so that the culture of elite boxing may evolve. However, as Barker-Ruchti points out in Chapter 3, individuals cannot invent culture at will. Indeed, the chances of female Muslim boxers, such as Aisha, influencing AIBA's rule changes are slim. In a local context, Aisha still struggles to influence the learning culture of her own boxing gym, and she often argues with the local coaches:

> Recently, one of the coaches in my club told me that I'm wasting my life. That I shouldn't believe in 'my stupid religion'. He told me everything I believe in is shit, and that Ramadan is nonsense.... He didn't like that I covered up in the boxing gym. It made me angry with him. It isn't his place to tell me about my religion, or my life. His job is to teach me boxing.... In our culture it's very important to respect your elders, but what do you do when an older person speaks to you like that? None of the other coaches did anything about it. It was a very difficult situation for me to handle.

Becoming a part of the national team constituted a turning point in Aisha's athletic career. That is, her horizons needed adjusting because the national team coach is different from her club coaches and has a different (and even less sensitive) understanding of the Muslim culture. Based on Aisha's actions when confronted with the views of the national coach, one could argue that Aisha's horizon for Muslim religion is not strong enough to determine her conduct, as she allows the national coach to disregard her own wishes for competition attire.

Summary

As an athlete, Aisha's career development has been remarkable. Aisha did not start boxing until she was 16 years old. At that age, most Norwegian boxers already have an extended fight record. Despite the late introduction to sport, Aisha managed to win her first national title only two years after she began her training. The year after, Aisha won her first title as an elite boxer. Unlike most ethnically Norwegian athletes, Aisha's learning has been concerned not just with developing the sport-specific skills required to become an elite boxer. Her learning has equally been about adapting to Norwegian elite sport culture and managing the learning culture of elite boxing and Somali culture and traditions.

As illustrated in this case study, Aisha's struggle to gain acceptance in elite sport (represented by coaches, fellow athletes, and officials) and in her family is multifaceted. On one side, Aisha struggles to gain acceptance that she, as a woman, wants to participate and compete in a hypermasculine sport that many view as 'unsuitable' for women. However, this is not unique to Somali culture or Islamic cultures but represents a barrier many women in Western cultures experience during their boxing careers. On the other side, Aisha struggles to combine her identity as an elite athlete/boxer with her ethnic identity as a Somali girl. Good Somali girls are not boxers. Aisha's athletic career path clashes with many aspects of Somali culture. Firstly, Somali girls are expected to stay at home and not spend a lot of time in public. For Aisha, this is impossible to combine with the lifestyle of an elite boxer. Secondly, as a Somali girl, Aisha is expected to cover her legs, arms, and neck at all times when she is in public. These Islamic rules for the presentation of women's bodies have followed Aisha's athletic career, causing many arguments between Aisha and her family, as well as between Aisha and her boxing coaches and officials at tournaments and championships.

At a micro level, Aisha's learning as an athlete consists of managing both her sport-specific development and the dualities of her identity as an elite athlete/boxer and a Somali Muslim woman. As demonstrated in this case study, Aisha does her best to adjust to the changing demands put upon her by coaches and boxing officials while still staying true to her Somali roots and Islamic beliefs. In this way, Aisha is interpreting and negotiating practices of what it means to be a Muslim female boxer. This reflexivity between being structured (by elite boxing culture and Somali culture) and structuring her personal and athletic development grants some individual agency, and in some cases, Aisha has been able to compete in the clothes she feels comfortable in. However, as expressed by the arguments Aisha has with both her family and her coaches, she still struggles to adjust to the one-dimensional identities associated with elite sport/elite athletes (Barker-Ruchti & Schubring, 2016; Carless & Douglas, 2013).

To summarize, the early, middle, and current phases of Aisha's career demonstrate how both her horizons for action and her horizons of learning have changed. In her early career phase, Aisha's horizons for action were limited. She had little sport and physical activity experience from Somalia, and when she first came to Norway, she struggled with anxiety and depression caused by her traumatic childhood. The introduction to boxing became an initiating turning point that helped Aisha to expand her horizons for action as a Somali woman in Norway. It gave her confidence, helped her to become familiar with Norwegian culture and people, and enabled her to create a new horizon of learning. Aisha's early, middle, and current career phases are characterized by her struggle to manage the expectations put upon her by boxing culture and by Somali culture and religious beliefs. Over the course of Aisha's career, these struggles intensified as she was introduced to new officials and referees who do not understand Somali culture. Despite this, Aisha managed to adapt to the rules and regulations of boxing competition attire by finding her own solutions to cover her body more than the boxing trunks and singlets allow. Aisha's actions demonstrate her determination to stay in boxing and also represent new horizons of learning for her as an elite athlete. Lastly, in her current career phase, her horizon for action is challenged by the national team coach, as she faces more pressure to compete in sports attire that does not cover her body the way she prefers to.

Notes

1. A buff is headwear in the shape of a tubular piece of fabric. It is multifunctional and can be worn as a scarf, bandana, headband, beanie, face mask, tube top, helmet liner, wristband, cap, pirate, Sahara style, and other variations.
2. Boxers aged 19-40 are called 'elite boxers'.

References

AIBA. (2016). *AIBA confirm Rio 2016 Olympic Games will be headguard-free for the first time in 32 years*. Available at http://www.aiba.org/blog/aiba-confirm-rio-2016-olympic-games-will-be-headguard-free-for-first-time-in-32-years/. Retrieved 2 March 2018.

AIBA. (2017). *AIBA technical rules*. Available at https://d152tffy3gbaeg.cloudfront.net/2015/02/AIBA-Technical-Rules-April-26-2017.pdf. Retrieved 22 May 2018.

AIBA. (n.d.). *AIBA event operational manual*. Available at https://aiba.s3.amazonaws.com/2015/02/AIBA_EVENT_OPERATIONAL_MANUAL.pdf. Retrieved 22 May 2018.

Barker-Ruchti, N., & Schubring, A. (2016). Moving into and out of high-performance sport: The cultural learning of one women's artistic gymnast. *Physical Education and Sport Pedagogy*, *21*(1), 55–68.

Barker-Ruchti, N., & Tinning, R. (2010). Foucault in leotards: Corporal discipline and coaching practice in women's artistic gymnastics. *Sociology of Sport Journal*, *27*(3), 229–250.

Bjørndal, C. T., Ronglan, L. T., & Andersen, S. S. (2015). Talent development as an ecology of games: A case study of Norwegian handball. *Sport, Education and Society*, 1–14.

Carless, D., & Douglas, K. (2013). Living, resisting, and playing the part of athlete: Narrative tensions in elite sport. *Psychology of Sport and Exercise*, *14*(5), 701–708.

Carlsson, H. (2017). Researching boxing bodies in Scotland: Using apprenticeship to study the embodied construction of gender in hyper masculine space. *Gender, Place and Culture*, *24*(7), 939–953.

Hassan, A. (2017). The impact of transnational remittances on the transformation of Somali gender roles. *Journal of Somali Studies*, 4(1-2), 43–63.

Hodkinson, P. (2009, Winter). Understanding career decision-making and progression: Careership revisited. *Career Research and Development*, no. 21, 4–17.

Hodkinson, P., Biesta, G., & James, D. (2008). Understanding learning culturally: Overcoming the dualism between social and individual views of learning. *Vocations and Learning*, *1*, 27–47.

Hovden, J., & Tjønndal, A. (2017). The gendering of coaching from an athlete perspective: The case of Norwegian boxing. *International Review for the Sociology of Sport*, 1–17.

Johns, D. P., & Johns, J. S. (2000). Surveillance, subjectivism and technologies of power: An analysis of the discursive practice of high-performance sport. *International Review for the Sociology of Sport*, 35(2), 219–234.

Johnson, A. (2017). Getting comfortable to feel at home: Clothing practices of black Muslim women in Britain. *Gender, Place and Culture*, *24*(2), 274–287.

Kerr, R., Barker-Ruchti, N., Schubring, A., Cervin, G., & Nunomura, M. (2017). Coming of age: Coaches transforming the pixie-style model of coaching in women's artistic gymnastics. *Sports Coaching Review*. DOI: 10.1080/21640629.2017.1391488

Kim, Y. J., Kwon, S. Y., & Lee, J. W. (2015). Resisting the hegemonic gender order? The accounts of female boxers in South Korea. In A. Channon & C. R. Matthews (Eds.), *Global perspectives on women in combat sports—Women warriors around the world* (pp. 204–218). Hampshire: Palgrave Macmillan.

Kipnis, H., & Caudwell, J. (2015). The boxers of Kabul: Women, boxing and Islam. In A. Channon & C. R. Matthews (Eds.), *Global perspectives on women in combat sports—Women warriors around the world* (pp. 41–57). Hampshire: Palgrave Macmillan.

Lang, M. (2010). Surveillance and conformity in competitive youth swimming. *Sport, Education and Society*, *15*(1), 19–37.

Matthews, C. R. (2016). The tyranny of the male preserve. *Gender and Society*, 30(2), 312–333.

McCree, R. (2015). The fight outside the ring: Female boxing officials in Trinidad and Tobago. In A. Channon & C. R. Matthews (Eds.), *Global perspectives on women in combat sports—Women warriors around the world* (pp. 104–119). Hampshire: Palgrave Macmillan.

McMahon, J. A., & Penney, D. (2012). (Self-) surveillance and (self-) regulation: Living by fat numbers within and beyond a sporting culture. *Qualitative Research in Sport, Exercise and Health*, 5(2), 1–22.

Nash, M. (2017). Gender on the ropes: An autoethnographic account of boxing in Tasmania, Australia. *International Review for the Sociology of Sport*, 52(6), 734–750.

Pfister, G. (2000). Doing sport in a headscarf? German sport and Turkish females. *Journal of Sport History*, *27*(3), 497–525.

Pfister, G. (2003). Women and sport in Iran: Keeping goal in the hijab. In I. Hartmann-Tews & G. Pfister (Eds.), *Sport and women: Social issues in international perspective* (pp. 207–223). London: Routledge.

Pfister, G. (2010). Outsiders: Muslim women and Olympic Games—Barriers and opportunities. *International Journal of the History of Sport*, *27*(16-18), 2925-2957.

Stojsih, S., Boitano, M., Wilhelm, M., & Bir, C. (2008). A prospective study of punch biomechanics and cognitive function for amateur boxers. *British Journal of Sports Medicine*. DOI: 10.1136/bjsm.2008.052845

Tjønndal, A. (2016). Pugilistic pioneers—The history of women's boxing in Norway. *Sport History Review*, *47*(1), 3–25.

Tjønndal, A. (2017). Modern female fighters: Barriers women face in boxing. In A. Milner & J. H. Braddock (Eds.), *Women in sports—Breaking barriers, facing obstacles*. Westport, CT: Praeger.

Walseth, K. (2005). Young Muslim women and sport: The impact of identity work. *Leisure Studies*, *25*(1), 75–94.

Warriner, K., & Lavallee, D. (2008). The retirement experiences of elite female gymnasts: Self identity and the physical self. *Journal of Applied Sport Psychology*, *20*(3), 301–317.

Woodward, K. (2006). *Boxing, masculinity and identity*. Abingdon, Oxon: Routledge.

Chapter 11

The experience of an international female rugby player

Francesca Cavallerio and Katrina McDonald

> I just enjoyed that I was learning something new.

This case study aims to portray the experience of an elite female rugby player, Paola, examining her journey from the start of her career—moving from football to rugby—through the experience of playing internationally and finally starting to consider retirement and a career in coaching. Paola's story was collected using a method of narrative inquiry, the life story interview (McAdams, Josselson, & Lieblich, 2013), which facilitated the gathering of detailed information about her sport career experiences through a series of consecutive interviews.

Paola is a 31-year-old athlete. While the focus of the case study will be on her athletic career, it is important to keep in mind that throughout her experience, Paola was also a PhD student initially and a sport coaching lecturer later on. She started playing rugby at 25 years old, being immediately fast-tracked into the elite level. Learning to adapt to a completely new environment and a different sport culture was challenging, and further challenges are currently on the horizon, as disappointment and deselection forced Paola to reflect on her life choices, where rugby might take a different position in the future.

Rugby is respected as one of the sports across the world where men and women play under the same rules. The development of women's rugby is not well documented but full of stories of resistance: from a school game for boys in the UK to the inclusion of the sport in the 2016 Olympic Games with both male and female Rugby Sevens teams and with the Women's Rugby World Cup officially recognised by World Rugby in 1998. The development of the sport has attracted women from various nations, including developing ones. At the same time, it has also pushed the boundaries of this once amateur sport and, in the lead up to the World Cup in Ireland in 2017, saw more financially supported players than ever before.

Theoretical lens

Transitions through and out of sport have been widely recognised as a challenging and potentially stressful experience for many (Lally, 2007). Much of the literature in this area emerged from the field of sport psychology and sees these transitions as *normative* and *non-normative* events (Stambulova, Alfermann, Statler, & Côté, 2009). The former are moments such as moving up through age categories, moving from recreational to professional level, and retiring from sport (when planned); the latter are unexpected events that can happen during the athletic career (e.g., injury, deselection) (Stambulova et al., 2009). This unpredictability has been related to the increased challenges athletes face when dealing with these episodes and the negative emotions stemming from them (Alfermann & Stambulova, 2007). Difficulties encountered by athletes include decreased self-confidence, emotional difficulties such as depression and eating disorders, and substance abuse (Blinde & Stratta, 1992; Papathomas & Lavallee, 2006; Stirling, Cruz, & Kerr, 2012). Initially conceptualised as single events, clearly delimited in time, transitions are nowadays described as being dynamic, more like a process than a unique event (Wylleman, Rosier, & De Knop, 2016). Moreover, the perspective from which these processes have been studied moved from simply focusing on the sport-specific career to encompassing different aspects of an athlete's life, adopting a holistic point of view (Wylleman & Lavallee, 2004). The Developmental Model of Transitions Faced by Athletes (Wylleman & Lavallee, 2004) identifies several areas in an individual's life (e.g., academic, psychosocial, athletic), each with their own challenges and transitions, and highlights how experiences happening in one area of an athlete's life can impact the others.

Literature in the area of transitions in sport has increasingly focused on retirement from sport and specifically on the role played by self-identity during this final transition (Lally, 2007; Lavallee & Robinson, 2007; Sparkes, 1998; Warriner & Lavallee, 2008). Identity has been defined as a 'multidimensional view of oneself, that is both enduring and dynamic' (Lally, 2007, p. 86). Individuals can have numerous dimensions, but when one becomes dominant (e.g., athletic dimension), investment in it means neglect for the others. This phenomenon, known as identity narrowing or identity foreclosure (Markus, 1977), represents a risk factor for identity issues following the loss of the dominant dimension (e.g., athletic retirement). These difficulties have been identified in many competitive athletes, especially when retirement was not being planned and prepared for, like in the case of severe injuries or deselection from a programme (e.g., Blinde & Stratta, 1992; Sparkes, 1998).

The psychological nature of the majority of studies looking at transitions in sport in the literature meant that the metaphors more widely used are those of 'acquisition' and 'transfer', which underpin the idea of learning through sport as a simple cognitive activity as outlined in Chapter 2 (Barker-Ruchti & Schubring, 2016). In other fields though, learning is now understood as a process that is mainly experienced on a subconscious level, based on relationships, and inevitable when there is a change in circumstances, as outlined in Chapter 3 (Hodkinson, Biesta, & James, 2008). This learning process adopts the metaphor of *becoming*, which underlines the idea of learning through social practices, such as taking part in sport (Hodkinson et al., 2008).

As outlined in Chapter 3, Hodkinson and Sparkes's (1997) sociological theory of career development brings forward the concepts of *horizons for action* (i.e., how a learning culture and an individual's background and experiences indicate what individuals perceive they can become) and *horizons of learning* (i.e., how individual dispositions to knowledge and learning preferences shape a person's orientation towards learning; Bloomer & Hodkinson, 2000) and the idea of 'turning points'.

Therefore, when individuals experience changes, their horizons need to be reshaped to fit the new situations. This process of change and adaptation and the following experience of learning as becoming are portrayed in this case study through Paola's story. Her learning journey through sport is presented in the following sections: firstly, her first year moving from football to rugby (24-25 years old). Secondly, her experience being selected and then deselected to play for her country (26-30 years old). Lastly, Paola's current experiences as a rugby coach and a Premier League player (30-31 years old). Paola realised herself, during her interview, how each of these times provided many learning experiences, which changed her into the person she is today.

Should I kick, or should I throw?

Paola is a European athlete who was born in [Country X] but grew up with her parents in [Country Y], which to her is 'home'. She moved to [Country X] again to complete her master's degree and has been living there ever since. At the age of 11, she started to play football and did so for about 10 years. At the age of 24 years, she started to grow bored of the sport and annoyed with her club coach, with whom she felt she was not improving any further and who was not selecting her to play often. Paola had never played rugby before, but when she was 25, a friend from University invited her:

> ...one of my best friends was like 'oh, why don't you try rugby, we've got this friendly game for like freshers', and they didn't have enough people, so they needed more people to make up...she said, 'come along and have a go at it'. So...they didn't teach me anything about how to play or how to tackle... but I knew a little bit of rugby beforehand because I watched it on TV and I really enjoyed it, even though I didn't really know that women's rugby was a thing, to be honest. So I knew the rules, and I had a rugby ball before then, so I knew how to pass and stuff.... So I played in that game and it was...ha, it was like full-contact game and the first time somebody ran at me and I was supposed to tackle I just tried to shoulder barge her, as you do in football...that wasn't very successful, so then they scored a try and someone in my team taught me how to tackle in the try area, behind the posts...so I learned how to tackle by another teammate...during a game, basically!

Paola really enjoyed playing, as she was naturally gifted for the sport, and soon started training with the team for the freshers (i.e., new people) at the university. The social side of rugby immediately surprised her:

> Because I was a postgraduate I was older than other people, when…it was like I didn't want to make friends. I was like 'I have all my friends already, I am not interested in the social side of the game, I just wanna give it a go, like try and learn a new sport'…but then rugby people are so…like friendly and supportive, there's something about the game, 'cause you have to… like…touch people in quite intimate places, first you like hit people hard and then…yeah, it's basically like hugging and stuff…and I just made friends without even trying to.

Nowadays, Paola still mentions her best friends all being from rugby, so she clearly got involved into the social side of the game and started to create important emotional bonds, which increased the pleasure she was feeling every time she played. Compared to her football experience, she felt appreciated in rugby, by both teammates and coach, and she enjoyed learning new things:

> The captain at the time was like 'yeah, you can do this, you've got so much potential' and so I just kept doing it and ended up being good at it without really knowing what I was doing! […] I can't remember when I gave up football completely, I just remember that I was enjoying rugby…I just enjoyed that I was learning something new. There are so many rules to learn, and different positions so I was learning different roles…so much to learn and I really enjoyed it. It gave me more than football, that I had been playing for something like 10 years, and I wasn't feeling like I was progressing…I just wasn't really enjoying it that much, so… I kinda switched.

Changing sport did not only mean that Paola had to learn new rules and roles; it also meant she had to start training her body differently, teaching it new ways of working (out):

> Training wise…yeah… you have to learn and go to the gym. I never really used to go to the gym before I took up rugby… training for football it's just more running, and they would just insert some training in the football session. Also, I wasn't playing like at a high level there. I find it much more in rugby, that people, even if not at high level, are going to the gym, to just get stronger and stuff. […] I remember when I was starting I had like pain in the biceps area…someone in my team said that maybe that's because my arms weren't strong enough. So I was like 'Ok, I obviously need to get a bit stronger!' That kind of started the process of getting me into the gym and getting quite stronger.

Becoming stronger was an experience that Paola feels changed her 'inside out', not just from an outside perspective. The change in her body and the ways her body was being used in her new sport impacted her psychologically as well:

> There's a whole body image and a whole 'body living the sport' going on there… I mean, even just the little things in rugby, like we wear short shorts. In football we wear long shorts. I remember thinking like 'OMG, these shorts look *so* small!' I felt so self-conscious, I could see my thighs! But now I love short shorts! I guess they have just become part of the…well, I learn that… yeah, I'm just comfortable now. But also, like, you use your whole body so much more, and in a quite aggressive way in rugby. So there's that as well, like…body confidence. And being comfortable enough to be really close to other people's bodies…like you have to keep them on your shoulders, and then stuff like scrums, you place your face next to people's bums…ahah! And even, related to that, stuff like…in football people don't tend to shower after the game. In rugby they do! Because you get really muddy, and then people shower and come out of showers and…like, people are naked! At the start I was just worried about that! I had to be naked in front of people! But nowadays that's become such a normal thing, and overall with my body I like going to the gym and being strong and I'm also kind of proud of seeing how good I can make my body in terms of strength and muscles. I would have never done that before, I think.

Paola's experience of transitioning from football to rugby, although happening later in her life, had a huge effect on her identity and personal development. She found herself not only learning new technical and tactical aspects related to the game, but also relating herself to new—often younger—friends in social circles and mostly seeing her body under a new light, which positively affected her self-confidence.

Analysis

Paola's entrance into the rugby environment affects her horizon for action and horizon of learning, which had become stale in football but were re-energised by a new enthusiasm for learning the game of rugby. This change developed through an *initiating turning point* (Barker-Ruchti, Lindgren, Hofmann, Sinning, & Shelton, 2015), which is an event made possible by other people's intervention (i.e., her friends inviting Paola to the freshers' game). Following the initial involvement with rugby, Paola falls into a confirmatory routine, which is a routine that endorses decisions taken in the past (Hodkinson & Sparkes, 1997)—in this case, moving from football to rugby. Paola's transition from one sport to another can be understood through the concept of learning as becoming within a transitional process of boundary crossing (Hager & Hodkinson, 2009). Previous authors looked at learning transfer through the metaphor of participation (in sport, in our case; Lave & Wenger, 1991), where the new learner appears so integrated in a social process of learning that she loses personal history and individual agency (Billett, 2001). Learning as becoming, on the other hand, maintains the learner's agency and highlights the process of learning as social as well as embodied (Hodkinson et al., 2008). This holistic perspective of learning integrates practical, physical, cognitive, and emotional learning.

Through Paola's *becoming* experience, moving from a football to a rugby player, several aspects are highlighted: Firstly, there is a cognitive aspect of her learning, which relates to the new technical and tactical information she receives and has to store, understand, and put into practice. Soon Paola's horizons start transitioning from an athlete who knows the rules of football to one who knows, understands, and can implement them. Her enjoyment of the game is enhanced through her learning experience (Balyi & Williams, 2010), and this enjoyment enhances her motivation to participate in the game, illuminating the close relationship between horizons for action and horizons of learning. Secondly, Paola quickly finds herself immersed in the social world of rugby, making friends despite her thinking of 'not needing them' and an age difference. The open and friendly environment embraces Paola as part of the group. As a consequence, she starts getting used to and adhering more and more to the *horizon for rugby*: From the 'short shorts' to the 'people are naked!' Paola becomes accustomed to the ways of rugby. The last aspect of Paola's becoming experience relates to the embodied aspect of learning (Shilling, 2016), which emphasises the connection among cognitive, practical, and sensory knowledge in the process of learning. The cultural/cognitive aspect of short shorts and naked people in the shower, together with a new-found engagement with physical training in the gym and with weights, meant Paola's body became stronger and better shaped for the game but at the same time also a source of confidence, something she grew used to, and something to be proud of. The development of Paola's horizons for action started by the process of becoming a rugby player impacted her horizons of learning far more than just in sport, giving new shape to her personality, with increased self-confidence and pride in her strong body.

Interestingly, Paola's story seems to defy the common idea of gender-role conflict, which women athletes playing a 'masculine sport' appear to be expected to experience (Allison, 1991). Existing research (e.g., Fallon & Jome, 2007; Howe, 2010; Krane, Choi, Baird, Aimar, & Kauer, 2004) discusses the idea of uneasiness, struggles, and emotional pain stemming from the idea of violating cultural norms and expectations in relation to body image. Paola's cultural learning through rugby though seems to have the opposite effect, as her horizon of learning evolves to appreciate and take care of her body more than before. This experience aligns with literature on the notion of *positiveness* of body satisfaction, which increases the more women's bodies appear to adhere to the physical requirements of each sport (Russell, 2004).

The roller coaster that is 'playing for your country'

A year into playing rugby, Paola was immersed in it, playing both for her university and for a club. One day she received an invitation for the selection of a Sevens' team of exiled players (i.e., players from her 'home' country who were not living there), and she decided to give it a go:

> The email said, 'If you are interested just email us and come along to this training day in [city]'. I thought 'Ok, I'll do that, why not? See what it's like…'. I was also really keen on learning new stuff, 'cause I was still very new. Then the day arrived, and I was really nervous, not really sure what to expect. I got the train to [city], and there were only eight people there! We just did some training and stuff, but like a couple of people there already played for the national team. I was like 'OMG, that's crazy!'

After that first experience, Paola was not immediately selected but started being invited to a few more training sessions in her 'home' country. Every time she would throw herself into the adventure, looking forward to learning and developing as a player, until she unexpectedly found herself playing against her same 'home' country just to help some friends:

> They gave me someone's trainers that were too small for me! So off I went and played against them. And we actually scored a try against them! Which is unbelievable! And then I got speaking to their players after that and they recognised me from the trials and were like 'Oh you know, you should come along to the 15's stuff'. I saw the coaches there, who also obviously remembered me and were like 'You should come up to the 15's stuff later' and I was 'yeah, yeah', not really believing they would have invited me.

But in the following months, Paola actually received an invitation to the Friday games called '[Country Y] Series', and soon found herself invited to the national team's training camps:

> I think they liked that I had only been playing for a year, because it meant that they could…like I had this sort of physical attributes almost…the potential, you know? So they could see that they could train me in a way that suited them.

Paola started playing internationally and, after a couple of years, she was selected to play for her 'home' country in the Six Nations. As Paola herself admitted, this was a huge learning experience: Not only was she challenged technically, but also she had to learn to organise her life—and her new job as a university lecturer—to fit around the huge physical, organisational, and emotional burden of the experience:

> Obviously, you're representing your country and everyone's very proud of you and it makes you very proud of yourself. You put everything into every game

that you play, you're in camp for like a few days beforehand but you actually build up to it [the Six Nations] through the whole season, from September right through to January, with everything focused towards that. Then the few days before you're really focusing on the game and what you're gonna do to win and each time we think we're gonna win—because you play to win—and then we end up losing heavily each time. You build yourself up so much and put everything into it and you almost feel like you're letting people down, and yeah, it's like a massive comedown basically. And then for example I had to come back here and deliver a lecture. I once got back at 10:30 at night after being on three flights after the game, and I had made the mistake to teach at 9 am the next day. I hadn't prepared anything and stayed up until after midnight preparing my slides and when I started the lecture there were like 20 people there and I was just, 'This is miserable, huh'. So, yeah, it's just like massive highs and then massive lows, and then up again I guess, after not much time.

After a second experience in the Six Nations, playing with a new coach and in an environment with an overall climate that Paola enjoyed more than before, her name disappeared from the list of those selected to play:

I do really like the culture they've got at the moment and think he's [the coach's] good, but he's not very good at communicating and I don't think he's going to select me, basically. That's what he's been like the past two years, I've not been selected, and he's not really communicated that to me or given me concrete reasons why. He said it was just 'preference'. So, yeah, even though I like the way he is like, the atmosphere and the culture that he created in the team, personally it's not really worked out that well for me, probably because I'm not living there [in Country Y].

After years of emotions and sacrifices, Paola found herself at a turning point after receiving an invitation to a camp for exiled players and realising she was not sure she was interested in getting involved:

The previous year, before the Six Nations I had done all the training and I was part of all the training camps and I was really fit…I did everything they asked of me. We had this test challenge, which is like a running test and I had the best time of any of the forwards and the second-best time in the whole squad and I still didn't get selected. Yes, I know there's a lot more to blame than just fitness, but it seemed to be quite a big thing they wanted to improve for the whole squad, so we could play at a higher tempo for longer… I put everything into it, I don't think I could have done anything differently and I still didn't get selected. And they didn't even tell me that, so you find out reading about other people having been selected and your friends have to come up to tell you. So—you know—I know how much effort that takes and,

> well I don't really have a lot of motivation to do that again. This way of doing, it really killed my desire to be part of it [the national team].

Despite the sadness and disappointment for this situation—still painfully raw—Paola realised that she was lucky because she had developed an identity that went beyond rugby. She had her PhD, a job, a career, and she knew these were important aspects of a balanced life, which not all the players had, with some of them being professional athletes with nothing outside of the sport.

Analysis

Paola's career as a rugby player developed quickly, moving from a confirmatory routine to a *contradictory* and *dislocating* one (i.e., a routine that expresses regret and disappointment and in which Paola disagrees with what is required from her—for example, having to keep training and putting in effort without being selected or not receiving a clear rationale for her deselection). Initially, she experiences some *structural turning points*, initiated by external structures related to the institutions involved (Hodkinson & Sparkes, 1997): for example, when she is selected to play for the national team and she starts taking part in all the training camps and the preparation for the Six Nations and also when she finishes her PhD and has to move from playing university rugby to Premier League rugby. In contrast, the experience of deselection falls under the *forced turning point* category, as it is determined by the actions of others (Hodkinson & Sparkes, 1997). As a consequence of the experience of deselection, Paola is also creating a (partially) *self-initiated turning point*, when she is considering not joining the newly created group of exiled players who are planning to train again. Her decision is based on the disappointment of not having been selected for the recent Six Nations but also on previous learning: knowing how much effort getting into shape requires and being aware of the emotional risks related to lack of selection.

Paola's horizon for action as an international rugby player is closing down due to deselection and maybe even age, when in her 30s she feels it is hard to keep up against young, 18-year-old players. She is struggling to see herself training again as hard as she did previously and to imagine herself in an environment that—despite the positive coaching climate—has proved to be missing clear communication, which Paola highly values. Meanwhile, Paola feels lucky because she knows she can see new horizons for action related to her experience as a club player (and captain), as well as to her professional career in academia. The idea of horizons for action in relation to turning points in an athlete's career can also be linked to narrative studies of athletic career and retirement (e.g., Cavallerio, Wadey, & Wagstaff, 2017; Douglas & Carless, 2006).

Douglas and Carless (2006) identified three main types of narratives athletes fall under in their career: *performance*, *relational*, and *discovery*. Athletes whose only horizon for action concerns their sport, who do not develop any other interests or relationships outside of it, fall under the performance narrative. Those whose horizon for action involves participating in sport in order to be with another person (e.g., best friend) fall under the relational narrative, while those whose horizon comprehends different sides of their identity (e.g., athletes, students, friends) represent the discovery narrative. Cavallerio and colleagues (2017) highlighted a potential link between the narratives of athletes' careers and the ones identified following their retirement: *entangled* (from a performance narrative), *making sense* (from a relational narrative), and *going forward* (from a discovery narrative). Paola's awareness of 'everything else she has' beyond rugby places her in the last narrative, where athletes are able to see themselves in new situations and to develop new horizons for action. This narrative is the most sought after by athletes following retirement, as it tells a story of successful adaptation to a new life. Paola's story sees her developing new horizons for action when she opens up to the new experience in rugby, which in turns affects her horizon of learning (e.g., from a 'horizon for running' in football training to a 'horizon for upper body strength' in rugby) and the way she feels more confident in herself and her body. Once her rugby career seems to draw to a close, the positive past experiences appear to help Paola to believe in the importance of keeping her horizons open, rather than looking back. It is also possible that Paola's initial upbringing, moving between two countries, allowed her to develop horizons for action and of learning that were flexible, allowing space for change, development, and discovery. Finally, maybe due to her late start as an elite rugby athlete, Paola had a chance to develop different horizons before her involvement at a high level in sport, which seems to protect her from low functional narratives.

Learning to pay it forward

During the first years of her career as a rugby player, Paola completely devoted herself to playing, both at university and club levels and then internationally. Over the past few years though, Paola started coaching a local university rugby team, using her previous experience in football and the understanding of coaching developed through her PhD. In the interviews, she discussed how this addition to her life provided one more layer 'of interest' for rugby, as she started using what she was learning in different ways:

> I gained a great amount of technical knowledge or tactical knowledge through being coached. Also, from the last coach, I learnt about the culture and the atmosphere of the systems that they created, which is very practical stuff. I mean, I catch myself noticing those things and almost storing them up for my coaching, or like...even though it's sort of transferred more into actual training, but also just the way things are run, generally. That was the first thing I started to realise, I was thinking 'I would do that when I'm coaching' or when I come to be in charge of something—like a head coach—sometimes when I am training at my club there is some particular stuff that we'll do or like key points and I'll be like 'yeah I'm gonna use that or remember for when I coach'. Even when I am training with [Country Y] actually, it's more

> the…not necessarily technical stuff but just like the activities that we do there, those are things you can take, adapt, and use.

Coaching has taken over a particular role in Paola's life, especially in recent times, which saw her motivation to continue training wavering after the tough disappointment of missed selection. Despite the fact that the treatment she received 'killed her motivation to participate', Paola is still playing nationally at club level, and she explains:

> The other thing is just wanting to be involved! I continue being involved at a high level because I want to keep collecting more knowledge to help with my coaching as well.

Paola's learning experience as a player is not just influencing her coaching knowledge and style but also working the other way around, with her experience as a coach influencing her role as a rugby player:

> Well, [name of the club] made me captain this year and I think that has potentially a bit to do with the fact that they know I can analyse the game… take a step back and provide feedback to people. I think it's probably because of the way I interact with people, which I think partly comes from coaching…well, teaching I suppose as well!

Paola's motivation to coach is also related to a reflection on her own experience and how she is hoping to allow future girls to walk down a similar path, to somehow give back what she received:

> Take the girls I coach at the moment… they're like… I don't know…they see me as a major role model! Yeah, it's good, at least I feel proud, but a little bit like… I'm just a player like you! But then I suppose that's why I got interested in coaching in the first place, because I mean that could have been me… these girls could be me… just started playing at Uni and then ended up playing international rugby and that's pretty amazing! So I figured out if someone else could do that, that would be cool!

Analysis

The third phase of Paola's athletic career to date highlights what we could call *horizons for reinvention*, which refers to horizons for action and horizons of learning that encourage an *evolutionary* routine (i.e., one characterized by successful movement from one career to another; Hodkinson & Sparkes, 1997) brought about by *self-initiated turning points*. Paola explains how the decision to start coaching related to her passion for rugby, but also her choice of doing a PhD in education, and pushed her to evolve further in her experience as a rugby player.

On the one hand, by becoming a rugby coach, Paola started to learn to look at things (e.g., her experiences as a rugby player) differently, asking herself critical questions and trying to 'store' the information in order to be able to use it when she was coaching. On the other hand, her new role as a coach also impacted her game because she developed a more analytical approach and an ability to interact and communicate with the (other) players. In turn, this experience impacted her horizon for action, as she became the captain of her club's team, seeing the skills developed for one role recognised and valued for another one.

While Paola's initial horizon for rugby was to play and win, now her horizon of learning is more instrumental—she participates in order to develop her coaching. This highlights once again the flexibility of Paola's learning as becoming, where she is able to deal with a negative situation (i.e., non-selection) in a way that still constitutes a resource for her personal development.

Conclusion

Throughout Paola's career in rugby, from her beginning as a 'late starter' through the different stages, her horizons for action and horizons of learning have constantly evolved. Her initial experience with rugby, arriving at an older age than the usual involvement in sport, heavily impacted her development as an athlete and as a person. Through the process of learning as becoming, Paola's athletic life changed due to her increased technical and tactical knowledge of the sport—but even more thanks to the new social and embodied experiences in the rugby culture that she was immersed in. A further turning point for Paola arrived when she was selected to play for her country's 15 team. She learnt to manage the physical and emotional requirements to play at high level, as well as to balance the time dedicated to training and playing with the other commitments she had, first the PhD and then a job in academia. Finally, when dealing with the experience of deselection, Paola had to revise her engagement with rugby. Becoming a coach provided a way for her to expand and shift her horizons of learning and horizons for action by investing time and effort in a new career, which allows her to still enjoy her sport but also to prepare for a future retirement from playing.

Paola's story is unique to her situation, but the key lessons that she experienced can help others understand their own journey through sport and the learning that takes place. It also highlights the importance of 'reinvention' so that individuals' education through *becoming* can continue.

References

Alfermann, D., & Stambulova, N. B. (2007). Career transitions and career termination. In G. Tenenbaum, & R. C. Eklund (Eds.), *Handbook of sport psychology* (3rd edition) (pp. 712–736). New York: Wiley.

Allison, M. T. (1991). Role conflict and the female athlete: Preoccupations with little grounding. *Journal of applied sport psychology*, 3(1), 49–60.

Balyi, I., & Williams, C. (2010). *Coaching the young developing performer*. Leeds: Coachwise.

Barker-Ruchti, N., Lindgren, E. C., Hofmann, A., Sinning, S., & Shelton, C. (2015). Tracing the career paths of top-level women football coaches: Turning points to understand and develop sport coaching careers. *Sports Coaching Review*, *3*(2), 117–131.

Barker-Ruchti, N., & Schubring, A. (2016). Moving into and out of high-performance sport: The cultural learning of an artistic gymnast. *Physical Education and Sport Pedagogy*, *21*(1), 69–80.

Billett, S. (2001). *Learning in the workplace: Strategies for effective practice*. St. Leonards: Allen & Unwin.

Blinde, E. M., & Stratta, T. M. (1992). The 'sport career death' of college athletes: Involuntary and unanticipated sport exits. *Journal of Sport Behavior*, *15*(1), 3.

Bloomer, M., & Hodkinson, P. (2000). Learning careers: Continuity and change in young people's dispositions to learning. *British Educational Research Journal*, *26*(5), 583–597.

Cavallerio, F., Wadey, R., & Wagstaff, C. R. (2017). Adjusting to retirement from sport: Narratives of former competitive rhythmic gymnasts. *Qualitative Research in Sport, Exercise and Health*, 9(5), 533–545.

Douglas, K., & Carless, D. (2006). Performance, discovery, and relational narratives among women professional tournament golfers. *Women in Sport and Physical Activity Journal*, *15*(2), 14–27.

Fallon, M. A., & Jome, L. M. (2007). An exploration of gender-role expectations and conflict among women rugby players. *Psychology of Women Quarterly*, *31*(3), 311–321.

Hager, P., & Hodkinson, P. (2009). Moving beyond the metaphor of transfer of learning. *British Educational Research Journal*, *35*(4), 619–638.

Hodkinson, P., Biesta, G., & James, D. (2008). Understanding learning culturally: Overcoming the dualism between social and individual views of learning. *Vocations and Learning*, *1*(1), 27–47.

Hodkinson, P., & Sparkes, A. C. (1997). Careership: A sociological theory of career decision making. *British Journal of Sociology of Education*, *18*(1), 29–44.

Howe, P. D. (2001). Women's rugby and the nexus between embodiment, professionalism and sexuality: An ethnographic account. *Football Studies*, *4*(2), 77–92.

Krane, V., Choi, P. Y., Baird, S. M., Aimar, C. M., & Kauer, K. J. (2004). Living the paradox: Female athletes negotiate femininity and muscularity. *Sex Roles*, 50(5-6), 315–329.

Lally, P. (2007). Identity and athletic retirement: A prospective study. *Psychology of Sport and Exercise*, 8(1), 85–99.

Lavallee, D., & Robinson, H. K. (2007). In pursuit of an identity: A qualitative exploration of retirement from women's artistic gymnastics. *Psychology of Sport and Exercise*, 8(1), 119–141.

Lave, J., & Wenger, E. (1991). *Situated learning: Legitimate peripheral participation*. Cambridge: Cambridge University Press.

Markus, H. (1977). Self-schemata and processing information about the self. *Journal of Personality and Social Psychology*, 35(2), 63.

McAdams, D. P., Josselson, R., & Lieblich, A. (2013). *Identity and story: Creating self in narrative*. Washington, DC: American Psychological Association.

Papathomas, A., & Lavallee, D. (2006). A life history analysis of a male athlete with an eating disorder. *Journal of Loss and Trauma*, *11*(2), 143–179.

Russell, K. M. (2004). On versus off the pitch: The transiency of body satisfaction among female rugby players, cricketers, and netballers. *Sex Roles*, *51*(9-10), 561–574.

Shilling, C. (2016). Body pedagogics: Embodiment, cognition and cultural transmission. *Sociology*, *51*(6), 1205–1221.

Sparkes, A. C. (1998). Athletic identity: An Achilles' heel to the survival of self. *Qualitative Health Research*, 8(5), 644–664.

Stambulova, N. B., Alfermann, D., Statler, T., & Côté, J. (2009). ISSP position stand: Career development and transitions of athletes. *International Journal of Sport and Exercise Psychology*, *7*, 395–412.

Stirling, A. E., Cruz, L. C., & Kerr, G. A. (2012). Influence of retirement on body satisfaction and weight control behaviors: Perceptions of elite rhythmic gymnasts. *Journal of Applied Sport Psychology*, *24*(2), 129–143.

Strauss, A. (1962). Transformations of identity. In A. M. Rose (Ed.), *Human behaviour and social processes: An interactionist approach*. London: Routledge.

Warriner, K., & Lavallee, D. (2008). The retirement experiences of elite female gymnasts: Self-identity and the physical self. *Journal of Applied Sport Psychology*, *20*(3), 301–317.

Wylleman, P., & Lavallee, D. (2004). A developmental perspective on transitions faced by athletes. In M. Weiss (Ed.), *Developmental sport and exercise psychology: A lifespan perspective* (pp. 507–527). Morgantown, WV: Fitness Information Technology.

Wylleman, P., Rosier, N., & De Knop, P. (2016). Career transitions. In R. J. Schinke, K. R. McGannon, & B. Smith (Eds.), *Routledge international handbook of sport psychology* (pp. 111–118). London: Routledge.

Chapter 12

An auto-ethnographic account of one athlete's journey to reconciling gender diversity through elite boxing: A case of a gender nonbinary boxer

Ali Greey and Natalie Barker-Ruchti

> As my sense of self-worth improved I seemed to be losing my desperation to fight.

In this case study, we present an auto-ethnographic account of Ali Greey's experience of 'becoming' (Hodkinson, Biesta, & James, 2008) an elite, international boxer. Ali, one of the authors, describes how their[1] athletic career progressed, beginning as a multisport recreational athlete before emerging as an elite-level volleyball player and finally becoming an internationally competitive boxer in the women's division. Ali's account reveals how their becoming within and beyond sport was not only mutually constitutive but also interdependent.

Ali's auto-ethnographic reflections are informed by their recollection of events (Markula & Friend, 2005), as well as unstructured journal entries (Plummer, 2001) they kept from 2003 until 2018. These journals provide a record of Ali's feelings, memories, concerns, aspirations, and account of events. Rather than presenting their story as an empirical or objective truth, Ali's account draws on memory as a tool for constructing meaning through remembering experience (Markula & Friend, 2005).

Our collaboration on this project was initiated while Natalie, the other author, was a visiting scholar at the University of Toronto. Ali began the writing process by detailing their auto-ethnographic account, to which Natalie offered reflections and suggestions for starting points for analysis. Our email discussions, after Natalie had returned to Gothenburg, allowed us to continue to deepen our analysis and interpretation of Ali's story.

Background

Despite the fact that women's participation in boxing dates back to the 1720s, women's competitive boxing was illegal in many nation-states until the late 1990s (Kipnis & Caudwell, 2015). Although men's boxing has been included in the modern Olympic Games since 1904, citing "medical safety concerns," the International Olympic Committee (IOC) excluded women boxers until the 2012 Olympics (Godoy-Pressland, 2015).

Athletes and scholars alike have argued that the IOC's reluctance to admit female boxers into the Olympics had less to do with medical concerns than with anxieties surrounding femininity and masculinity, which arose from the incursion of women in a sport widely understood to be the domain of men. Revealingly, in 2009, directly after announcing that female boxers would compete in the next Olympiad, the Association Internationale de Boxe Amateur (AIBA) mandated that all women boxers compete in skirts, rather than shorts, to help audiences distinguish between the female and male boxers (Godoy-Pressland, 2015). Justifying this decision, AIBA's president, Wu Ching-Kuo, who was working closely with the IOC, reported that he had "heard from fans who couldn't tell women from men when fighters wear protective headgear" (Godoy-Pressland, 2015, p. 32). This decision was eventually reversed after many amateur boxers in the women's division sharply criticized the mandate. Once women were finally permitted to compete, the IOC limited women's boxing to only 3 of the 10 weight divisions available to men: flyweight (48-51 kg), lightweight (57-60 kg), and middleweight (69-75 kg) (Jennings & Cabrera Velázquez, 2015).

Whether inside or outside of the boxing ring, violence and aggression are widely associated with masculinity. Hegemonic constructions of gender, which associate aggression with masculinity and passivity with femininity, are widespread in sports media (Burstyn, 1999). In these representations, boxing is commonly presented as an athletic expression of masculine toughness and an ability to fight despite pain or injury (Young & White, 1995).

The competitive female boxer directly challenges the link between boxing and masculinity. Halbert (1997) describes the professional woman boxer as a "triple threat" to boxing: to the social order, sport, and boxing industry (p. 8). Scholars have described the unique challenge that women boxers issue to the hegemonically masculine sport of boxing (e.g., Caudwell, 2008; Godoy-Pressland, 2015; Halbert, 1997), but scholars are yet to examine how transgender and gender nonbinary boxers negotiate heteronormative demands to demonstrate binaric expressions of gender. Ali's case offers an account of the complexity of strategies that a gender nonbinary elite boxer may use to navigate a sporting environment and society that expects binaric expressions of gender.

A number of scholars in fields ranging from biology to gender studies have asserted that the fluidity and complexity of humanity's expressions of biological sex and social gender cannot be adequately conceptualized within a two-sex, male/female binary (Blackless et al., 2000). Despite this scholarship, binaric gender remains ubiquitously assumed within Western society. Nowhere, arguably, is the male/female divide more rigorously enacted than in elite sport. An emerging body of scholarship has attended to the ways in which trans athletes, at both recreational and elite levels, cope with structural and social barriers to their participation (e.g., Lucas-Carr & Krane, 2011). This scholarship suggests that individuals who do not conform to the gender binary face significant barriers to competing in elite sports and struggle to access physical activity at recreational levels. Beyond sport, a number of studies suggest that compared to "normatively" gendered individuals, transgender and gender nonbinary individuals face elevated rates of violence and psychological distress (Effrig, Bieschke, & Locke, 2011) and are more likely to consider or attempt suicide (Mathy, 2003).

In the following sections, we use Ali's words to chronologically present their three sporting career phases: first, their entrance into sport and volleyball; second, their entrance and progression in boxing; and, finally, their retirement from elite boxing and transition into university studies.

I grew up with the conviction that, when it came to sports, anything was possible for me

In my earliest memories, most of them at least, I am moving and playing sport: kicking a soccer ball with my dad in the schoolyard, spending hours alone throwing a ball against the wall of our house where I grew up. As a child, one who tended toward hyperactivity, my parents put me in as many activities as their schedules would permit. In our middle-class, dual-income earning family, I never heard the words "we just can't afford that activity right now." I excelled at sports and I thrived playing them. I grew up with the conviction that, when it came to sports, anything was possible for me.

My primary school classmates often called me a *tomboy* to explain my preference for climbing trees alone in the park by my house and for wearing my dad's shirts, which were baggy on my young lanky frame. At a young age, I learned that gender was something I didn't understand and couldn't figure out how to play. I still remember another child asking "Mommy, is that a boy or a girl?" when I was six. I darted from my mother's reach and ran, feet pounding the pavement, until I disappeared behind the grove of trees that lined the schoolyard. I remember hoping that my flight could somehow answer the child's question. For me, speed was an antidote; it gave me freedom and power.

My dad passed away suddenly when I was 13 years old. More than ever, sport became my safe haven. The year following his death, I competed on six teams for my middle school. When I was 16, my high school gym coach sat me down and said: "Look… you're one of the most gifted athletes I've seen in my entire career. But if you're going to excel you need to settle on one sport." Competing at the Olympics had been my dream for as long as I could remember, so I took her advice to heart. But I couldn't figure out how to settle on only one sport. A couple of months later, the same coach sent me to a volleyball camp in western Canada. Most of the other athletes at the camp were either provincial team members or junior national team athletes. Though I was initially outclassed by these elite athletes, as the camp progressed, I developed confidence in my ability to train and compete. Upon the recommendation of a coach I worked with at the camp, when I returned home I contacted Sharon,[2] the head coach of a women's volleyball program at a local university. Sharon immediately responded to my email and arranged for me to begin playing on an elite team that her assistant coach, Quan, coached.

Three times each week, I rode the subway for an hour to meet Quan, and then he would drive me an additional hour to practice. Although I was the youngest and least experienced player on the team, I immediately felt accepted by the other athletes. Quan never yelled at me and he rarely substituted me off the court so I quickly grew accustomed to taking risks at this new level of competition. I enjoyed playing volleyball with this team, and although I felt uncomfortable in spandex shorts, I was confident that I had finally found my sport.

It was that same year, at age 17, that I fell in love for the first time. Her name was Sarah, and she was another member of my volleyball team. I had no words to describe what was happening to me or to identify how this experience might shape my sexuality. All I knew was that I was hopelessly attracted to a girl who didn't seem to reciprocate or notice. I began attending house parties with the team almost every other weekend. When Sarah would disappear to spend time with her boyfriend, I would drink liquor to drown out my confusion and disappointment. Our team continued to succeed provincially and even travelled to compete at nationals. Likely because of my infatuation with Sarah, I grew a reputation on the team for making homophobic jokes.

In about October of that year, I realized that if I was going to spend the summer with Sarah before she left on a full scholarship to the United States, I would need to earn a spot on Team Ontario, which she was a member of. I began training with devout discipline. On evenings that I didn't have practice with Quan's team, I would train with Sharon and her athletes at the university. Sharon's coaching style was demanding. She expected her athletes to be 100% present during training. Sharon was also a very empathetic coach. I remember on one occasion Sharon suggested I train in the squash courts with a senior athlete, Katja. We set the ball back and forth so many hundreds of times that the paint on the ball wore off onto our fingers. When Katja and I went upstairs to Sharon's office to show her the paint on our fingers, she chuckled at our amazement and delight.

That spring, I was selected for Team Ontario and spent the summer training with Sarah. I never told her about my feelings for her. When September came and she left for university, I was devastated. Around this time, I began visiting Toronto's gay neighbourhood and self-identifying as queer. Sharon introduced me to an LGBTQ counsellor at the university, and they both listened patiently to my emerging concerns about my sexuality. That fall, I also began working more closely with Sharon and playing for her elite youth team. She switched me from middle blocker to setter position, and though I initially worried that I wouldn't be able to make the transition, with her patient and encouraging coaching style, I soon found myself confident in my new role leading the team. In the midst of this, I came out to my family, school, and team and received only support. Sharon's team was a strict homophobia-free environment. No one made gay jokes, and if they did, they faced reprimand directly from Sharon.

I began spending more and more time in Toronto's gay neighbourhood. In the evenings, including often after practices and matches, I would drop by the local gay bar where everyone knew me by name, despite the fact that I was using a fake ID with a stranger's name on it to gain entrance to the bar!

I started university and became the starting setter for my team, which Sharon also coached. By the end of the season, I was named the provincial Rookie of the Year. I was also selected as a member of the Canadian All-Rookie Team.[3] Despite this success on the court, I was struggling. I kept my habit of smoking weed and drinking a secret from Sharon, with whom I shared many other aspects of my athletic and academic life. I had trouble focusing during practice, and I felt anxious when I stepped onto the court. With only two months remaining before my second year of university began, I quit the team. I couldn't imagine enduring the pressure that I put on myself to perform perfectly for another year. Sharon, who didn't have a setter to replace me, was shocked but accepted my decision when I told her.

After I quit the team, my drinking accelerated. A year later, at 20, I dropped out of university and moved to Vancouver, where I began working in organic farming and landscaping and later as a bike courier. I had trouble keeping a job. I wasn't in touch with my family very much, and they were often worried about me.

Over the two years that followed, I became aware that I was unable to moderate my drinking. I felt lost and directionless. I quit my job and moved back to Toronto to try out for Sharon's university team. I re-enrolled part-time as a student just to try out for the team. I had not picked up a volleyball in years, and I was, energetically, a bit of a loose wire. I didn't make the team, and I was devastated. Over the following two years, I became physically inactive and gained about 25 pounds as a result.

When I was 22, a friend recommended I try Ashtanga yoga, a physically demanding yoga practice that relies on arm strength. Six days a week, practitioners perform a sequence, which takes roughly 1.5 hours to complete. I threw myself into Ashtanga yoga, sometimes doing the sequence twice in one day. The repetitiveness of the practice soothed my mind. My body grew physically stronger and leaner. The silence in the practice room gave me an opportunity to experience a new level of internal focus and reflection. Through this practice, I began to observe a deep anger within myself. I'm not certain when it arose or where it came from, but inside I felt sheer rage.

The rage I felt startled me and seemed to explode without provocation. Often, when I was in public with a romantic partner, men regularly invited themselves into our conversations or took the opportunity to comment on our relationship. This behavior awoke a fury in me, and I would respond aggressively. I felt I was moving upstream against the current of the world. An unspeakable, unlocatable rage accompanied me everywhere.

Analysis phase I

Ali's first phase illustrates how their horizon for sport, horizon for sexuality and gender diversity, and horizon for "being on edge" emerged and took shape. We begin by interpreting the former two horizons in order to illustrate how the three horizons interacted upon one another. Ali's horizon for sport was shaped by Ali's athletic giftedness and disposition for being physically active at an early age. They enjoyed climbing trees and became a successful athlete on a number of sports teams at school. Their athletic achievements garnered praise, particularly from a high school coach, reinforcing Ali's self-identity as a gifted athlete. Their sense of self was, from a young age, constituted by sport. On the occasion when Ali participated in the elite volleyball training camp, their horizon of learning began to expand to include the possibility of excelling in elite sport. This turning point also introduced Ali to "being on edge." Ali's volleyball coach, and arguably teammates, viewed risk-taking on the court as necessary for athletic improvement and therefore did not reprimand Ali's mistakes. Ali's horizon for sport thus not only began to shift into a horizon for elite sport but also was characterized by performing on edge and risk-taking.

In terms of Ali's horizon for sexuality and gender diversity, their childhood experiences suggest an inability to articulate tensions surrounding their sexuality and gender. While Ali processed much of this conflict "in their head," encounters that destabilized their gender identity sent them, literally, running. At an early age, Ali's horizon for learning did not include sexuality or gender diversity, as they had not yet developed the conceptual tools necessary to understand and react to societal expectations of masculinity and femininity. Nonetheless, these societal expectations were clearly unsettling for Ali. The antidote, or reconciliation, for these expectations was Ali's physicality. Upon Ali's father's death, the value of sport-as-antidote took on even greater meaning.

With regard to Ali's horizon of "being on edge," Ali's story demonstrates a number of occasions that encouraged the development of this horizon. First, the line between health and ill health is fine in elite sport. Risking injury and performing while experiencing pain or injury are normalized within elite sport (Schnell, Mayer, Diehl, Zipfel, & Thiel, 2014). Although Ali's volleyball coaches did not encourage athletes to risk their physical health, the environment of elite athletics cultivated in Ali a familiarity with competing "on edge." Second, Ali's training environments encouraged them to exert maximum effort. This training was physically and mentally demanding and perhaps taught Ali how to compete on edge. Finally, Ali's experiences of sexuality and gender (e.g., societal expectations of sexuality/gender and falling in love with Sarah) and their perception that physicality represented an antidote to these societal expectations fueled their determination to train to succeed. We argue that Ali's athletic prowess, the elite volleyball training environment, and the societal expectations of sexuality and gender impressed upon Ali interacted to shape their horizon for being on edge, a horizon that is characterized by risk-taking.

Towards the end of Ali's account of the life phase presented above, they express an inability to continue enduring the internal pressure to compete. Without notice, they quit the sport. At this stage, their horizon for elite sport, which represented a significant part of Ali's sense of self, became temporarily disrupted. The time following this self-initiated turning point was characterized by an absence of physical activity, as well as emotional difficulty and feeling "directionless."

My career accelerated meteorically after that fight

In 2012, at age 25, six years after I quit volleyball, a friend recommended that I watch women's boxing make its Olympic debut. I went to a local sports' bar to tune in. I found myself engrossed with the speed, strength, and athleticism of the women I saw competing on the screen. During her match, the Canadian boxer appeared stunned and was, for the most part, motionless as the Chinese fighter pummeled her with punches. As the fight continued, I felt a growing sense of resolve. I had never laced up a pair of boxing gloves, much less watched a boxing match before this one, but as the Chinese athlete's hand was raised in victory, I felt stirred. I would join a boxing gym tomorrow, I decided. And I ordered another pint of beer to celebrate my decision.

I started the following day with my regular Ashtanga practice; in the afternoon, I would see about joining a boxing gym. I did a quick calculation. 365 × 4 = 1,460 days until the next Olympics. I wrote that number on a piece of paper and taped it to the wall inside my closet. I arrived at Sully's, a small gym that smelled of sweat and leather. When I arrived, I was directed to the women's change room, a curtained-off area the size of a broom closet.

I was eager to tell the coach, Toby, that I would be the next Olympic champion in the 75 kg women's division. "Is that so?" he responded, looking up briefly between bites of his smoked meat sandwich. "Well, I'm going to put you to work with Carlos then. He'll have you whipped into shape in no time." From then on, I spent every spare moment at the gym working with Carlos, skipping in the parking lot of my apartment, or running up hills at Christy Pitts Park. Despite my new regime, I continued drinking. When I got home from practice, I would reward myself with a drink, which felt like a horizon of relief at the end of each day.

A month after I first entered the gym, I approached Toby to ask if I was ready for my first fight. He responded: "Look, kid, you won't be ready to fight for another six months. *At least*." I left the next day and joined a women's gym named The Toronto Knockouts. After two months of training there every day, I begged the coach for the opportunity to compete in my first fight, and she agreed. So my career as an amateur boxer began.

I won my first four fights and moved to the border city of Windsor, Ontario, to begin training with an internationally recognized coach named Eddie. After my fifth win and much pleading, Eddie moved me from "novice" to "open" class. A short time later, after more begging, he accepted a fight on my behalf against Claressa Shields, the reigning Olympic champion from Flint, Michigan. Whether it was her undefeated record or the reputation that Flint had as a black urban slum, Claressa could not find an opponent in North America. Claressa was throwing a boxing gala to fundraise for her youth camp, and our match was to be the main event. I was elated. If I won, I would make *history*! Officials from Boxing Canada tried to intervene in the match. Eddie reported that one official had called the pairing "a joke." This only strengthened my resolve as I continued to prepare for the fight.

With only 10 months of experience boxing, I stepped into the ring to compete against the reigning Olympic champion. Ten seconds into the first round, I was knocked down with a shot harder than any I'd been hit with before. I was stunned but still fully in command of my faculties. I popped back up and finished the round. In the corner between rounds, Eddie worried over my eye: "It's swelling a mile a minute. Kiddo, this is a code red. The referee *will* stop the fight if you take another shot like that to the head, and if this fight gets stopped, that means a six-month suspension, so no nationals." Eddie was referring to Boxing Canada's safety protocol for suspending boxers who have received a KO or a TKO.[4] Pressing my lips closed, I tried to take command of my breathing. I knew that if I was going to have a shot at the 2016 Olympics, I had to win nationals that year.

When the bell rang, Claressa charged. She was hungry to knock me out in front of her home crowd. I moved unceasingly. For the remaining three rounds, I raised my guard in order to protect my eye and let her throw to my body. When the final bell rang, Eddie jumped into the ring in celebration. I had lost the fight, but I had gone the distance with an Olympic champion.

My career accelerated meteorically after that fight. I knocked out my first opponent at nationals with a body shot in the first round. The following day, I beat my second opponent, the reigning Canadian champion, to win the gold medal. I found out afterward, while I was at the bar celebrating, that my opponent had been admitted to the hospital with a serious concussion. Ignoring Eddie's advice, I went, a little drunk, to visit her in the hospital. Shortly after nationals, I moved back to Toronto and began training with another internationally recognized coach, Andreas.

At 27, I began competing for Canada and travelling around the world. I won three consecutive Canadian championships; the second I won competing with a broken foot. I reached the top eight in international rankings after winning a silver at the Continental Championships and a gold at a tournament in the Balkans. When the Olympic trials were held in Montreal, Quebec, I was invited to compete. In my first match, I beat the boxer I had seen on TV four years before. I lost in the finals against the young woman who would compete for Canada at the 2016 Olympics. Although Andreas disputed the judging of the fight, I felt satisfied. Even though I would not be going to the Olympics, I was selected as the Olympic alternate; I felt that I had done my best to prepare and that I had competed with pride and heart.

Analysis phase 2

In the account presented above, Ali's horizon for elite sport reaches its peak. Ali's success in the boxing ring appeared to be earned not only through training and hard work but also through a willingness to take risks. Throughout this life phase, Ali's propensity for risk-taking begins to shift into recklessness. Ali's recklessness is suggested by their decisions to compete with a broken foot and to fight a significantly more experienced athlete. Although this horizon for recklessness appears to have worked for Ali—for example, accelerating their career from rookie boxer to Olympic alternate in under four years—other factors appear to be at play in

Ali's horizon for risk-taking/recklessness. Ali's alcohol use remains a persistent theme throughout their account.

Ali's horizon for sexuality and gender is less prominent throughout this phase of their athletic career. There exists an absence, within Ali's account, of descriptions of difficulty navigating society's expectations of sexuality and gender. This absence could affirm the assertion made in the "Analysis phase 1" section that Ali's involvement in elite sport acted as an antidote with regard to these aspects of their identity. Additionally, many boxers in the women's division challenge conventional notions of femininity and masculinity. It is also plausible to infer that, for Ali, being surrounded by these athletes was affirming and allowed them to focus their energy on competing. It is also plausible to infer that Ali's role in elite boxing enabled them to place a primacy on their athletic identity, as a boxer, rendering their gendered identity secondary.

As my sense of self-worth improved, I seemed to be losing my desperation to fight

At 28, a number of changes were occurring in my life. For the first time since I quit my university volleyball team, I finally felt deserving of respect from my family and friends. To prepare for the Olympics, I had begun receiving financial sponsorships from small donors for my training and competition costs. For three years, the provincial government awarded me financial carding. This funding was very competitive, and my ability to garner financial support through boxing made me feel proud and competent.

Physically, my body was changing from my training; it became leaner and more angular. One Saturday, I visited my hairdresser and asked her to cut my hair short. She shaved the sides into a fade and trimmed the top. I was thrilled. Now, as I moved through the world, I was often perceived as male. When I walked down the street, people addressed me with "sir," "pal," and "bud." Even though I hadn't consciously intended to, I began to pass as male. I quickly realized that being perceived as male was a relief. I no longer received stares or had to struggle to claim space for myself. In my muscular body and with my new hair, I finally felt as though I had found a home in my body.

As soon as I began presenting as masculine, I started having trouble when I entered women's change rooms. I often received stares from women when I entered the space. They would regularly turn to watch me walk past. The entrance was the most scrutinized area. I would hear the words "excuse me" followed by directions to the men's change room. If I was coming out of the change room when a woman was preparing to come in, she would often apologize and go to the other change room or turn to inspect the sign more closely. I had to be careful if I was exiting the change room while a man was passing by; often he would automatically turn to enter through the door I had exited from.

Other changes were happening in my life, too. I was abruptly sober. I had tried many, many times to moderate or quit drinking on my own. Often during international competitions, I would vow to myself that I would stay dry until I returned to Canada, only to find myself on the second day sneaking out of the lodgings, with toothpaste in hand, for a couple of beers. Even then I didn't realize that I had a problem. I had always imagined alcoholics to be people who lived under bridges and drank from paper bags. I couldn't have a drinking problem. I was top eight in the world, for goodness sakes! Nonetheless, at age 27, I finally admitted that I had a drinking problem that I could no longer handle on my own. Following the guidance of a 12-step group, I not only became and stayed sober but also made a thorough list of past misconducts and offered amends to those whom I had disrespected. Additionally, I began visiting a therapist who assisted me in finally grieving my father's passing. The group encouraged me to, independently, forge a spiritual relationship to the world and to use this relationship to find balance in my life. The rage that I had felt since I was 17 years old finally began to dissipate.

As a result of these changes, I began to see my boxing as independent from my worth as a person. The journals I kept at the time shift from focusing entirely on boxing to exploring other topics. The negative self-talk that I recorded in previous journals also began diminishing at this time. Initially, this separation of my self-worth from my success at boxing helped me improve my patience during matches and made me a smarter fighter. As my sense of self-worth improved, however, I seemed to be losing my desperation to fight and dedication as a fighter. I was no longer willing to take unnecessary shots to prove my commitment to the sport. I also no longer saw myself as invincible or indestructible. Nevertheless, I continued boxing.

At 28, I returned to university to complete the degree that I had begun nearly 10 years prior. This time I found myself excelling at academics. I applied the same discipline and focus that I had used in boxing to approach my schoolwork.

In 2016, I travelled with the Canadian women's boxing team to Astana, Kazakhstan, to compete in the Women's World Championships. I lost my quarter-final match against Morocco. My heart wasn't in the match. I decided to retire from boxing—not with resignation or disappointment but with excitement for whatever direction would come next.

Today, at age 31, I am physically active every day. I still practice Ashtanga and compete in at least one triathlon a year. I enjoy volunteering my time as a boxing coach at The Toronto Knockouts. I have completed my undergraduate degree and begun a master's degree. My research uses participatory research methods to consult transgender and gender nonbinary individuals to create a set of practical and effective strategies for making change rooms more accessible for members of my community. I have also come to proudly identify as gender nonbinary myself.

Analysis phase 3

Ali's account presented above signals a striking shift in their horizon for sexuality and gender as Ali begins presenting as masculine. It is worth emphasizing that although Ali notes that they began "passing as male" at this time, they began identifying as *gender nonbinary*, rather than as male or female. Ali describes the "relief" that they experienced in their new gender presentation; this turning point was accompanied by other notable shifts, both within and beyond the boxing ring. Shifting to expressing an authentic gender presentation and becoming sober, for example, are closely linked temporally within Ali's account. Despite the synchronous timing of these turning points, Ali dispels a causal explanation between sobriety and gender presentation by crediting a 12-step group for the former's emergence in their life.

Ali's sobriety impacts not only their horizon for recklessness, which Ali describes as diminishing through this life phase, but also their horizon for elite sport. Ali's drive as a boxing athlete appeared to be ebbing as aspirations for other opportunities emerged. Ali reflects on the internal changes and emotional growth that accompanied their involvement in the 12-step group and sobriety. It's possible that Ali's emotional growth drained much of the rage that was fuelling their boxing and ultimately led them to retire. Ali's retirement represents another horizon of learning; they embraced this horizon with excitement for future academic and activist projects, which build upon their own experiences as a gender nonbinary athlete.

Conclusion

In this case study, three horizons of learning emerge and develop throughout Ali's three life phases. Examining the connections and interactions among these three horizons is foundational to developing an understanding of Ali's becoming as an elite athlete. Central to a study of how these three horizons informed Ali's learning as an athlete is a longitudinal or diachronic perspective. Centring this approach is essential for establishing an understanding of how the horizons interacted to shape Ali's becoming as an elite athlete.

Notes

1. Ali uses the gender-neutral singular pronouns *they*, *them*, and *their*. This is a widely used practice and is consistent with the *Oxford English Dictionary*'s usage of the pronoun.
2. Pseudonyms are used throughout this text to safeguard confidentiality and anonymity.
3. Being named as a member of the Canadian All-Rookie Team is an award offered to outstanding first-year athletes around Canada. Approximately seven athletes are selected from across Canada each year.
4. KO is boxing terminology for a *knockout*; this occurs when an athlete cannot stand before the referee has finished counting to 10. A TKO is boxing terminology for a *technical knockout*; this occurs when the referee stops the fight because they deem that one athlete is no longer able to safely compete in the match.

References

Blackless, M., Charuvastra, A., Derryck, A., Fausto-Sterling, A., Lauzanne, K., & Lee, E. (2000). How sexually dimorphic are we? Review and synthesis. *American Journal of Human Biology*, *12*, 151–166.

Burstyn, V. (1999). *The rites of men: Manhood, politics, and the culture of sport*. Toronto, ON: University of Toronto Press.

Caudwell, J. (2008). Girlfight: Boxing women. *Sport in Society, 11*(2-3), 227–239.

Effrig, J. C., Bieschke, K. J., & Locke, B. D. (2011). Examining victimization and psychological distress in transgender college students. *Journal of College Counseling, 14*(2), 143–157.

Godoy-Pressland, A. (2015). Moral guardians, miniskirts and Nicola Adams: The changing media discourse on women's boxing. In A. Channon & C. R. Matthews (Eds.), *Global perspectives on women in combat sports: Women warriors around the world* (pp. 25–40). Basingstoke, UK: Palgrave Macmillan.

Halbert, C. (1997). Tough enough and woman enough: Stereotypes, discrimination, and impression management among women professional boxers. *Journal of Sport and Social Issues, 21*(1), 7–36.

Hodkinson, P., Biesta, G., & James, D. (2008). Understanding learning culturally: Overcoming the dualism between social and individual views of learning. *Vocations and learning, 1*(1), 27–47.

Jennings, G., & Cabrera Velázquez, B. (2015). Gender inequality in Olympic boxing: Exploring structuration through online resistance against weight category restrictions. In A. Channon & C. R. Matthews (Eds.), *Global perspectives on women in combat sports: Women warriors around the world.* (pp. 89–103). Basingstoke, UK: Palgrave Macmillan.

Kipnis, H., & Caudwell, J. (2015). The boxers of Kabul: Women, boxing, and Islam. In A. Channon & C. R. Matthews (Eds.), *Global perspectives on women in combat sports: Women warriors around the world* (pp. 41–56). Basingstoke, UK: Palgrave Macmillan.

Lucas-Carr, C., & Krane, V. (2011). What is the T in LGBT? Supporting transgender athletes through sport psychology. *Sport Psychologist, 25*, 532–548.

Markula, P., & Friend, L. A. (2005). Remember when... Memory-work as an interpretive methodology for sport management. *Journal of Sport Management, 19*(4), 442.

Mathy, R. M. (2003). Transgender identity and suicidality in a nonclinical sample. *Journal of Psychology and Human Sexuality, 14*(4), 47–65.

Plummer, K. (2001). *Documents of life 2: An invitation to a critical humanism*. London: Sage.

Schnell, A., Mayer, J., Diehl, K., Zipfel, S., & Thiel, A. (2014). Giving everything for athletic success! Sports-specific risk acceptance of elite adolescent athletes. *Psychology of Sport and Exercise, 15*(2), 165–172.

Young, K., & White, P. (1995). Sport, physical danger, and injury: The experiences of elite women athletes. *Journal of Sport and Social Issues, 19*, 45–61.

Part III

Informing research and practice

Chapter 13

Insights and implications for research and practice

Natalie Barker-Ruchti

In this chapter, I present key scientific insights and consider the implications the cultural perspective of learning has for research and practice. The question that guides this chapter is: If we are to understand athlete learning as shaped by context, biography, individual dispositions, subjectivity, and serendipity, how then can scientists research and practitioners influence learning in (elite) sport? The chapter first presents implications for research, which I illustrate with the experiences I and the case study authors have had writing their chapters. Second, I propose key insights and implications for sport organisations, officials, coaches, and coach educators (from here 'sport stakeholders') and elite sport practice. My main aim of presenting this understanding is to provide readers with practical knowledge on how to conduct research on and support elite athletes' learning.

Implications for research

Thinking about athletes' learning from a cultural perspective has a number of implications for research and researchers. In the following, I first outline how athlete learning research informs sport coaching science and then present methodological, ethical, political, and analytic implications the cultural perspective of learning generates.

Athlete learning research for sport coaching science

Existing sport coaching literature predominantly examines coaching from the perspective of the coach. Key research foci have been coach behaviour and thinking (for a literature review, see Gilbert & Trudel, 2004), coach learning (for a literature review, see Cushion et al., 2010), learning in sports coaching (e.g., Nelson, Groom, & Potrac, 2016), coaches' personal and career development (e.g., Nash & Sproule, 2009), and sites of coach learning (e.g., Rynne, Mallett, & Tinning, 2010). Only rarely have coaching researchers taken the perspective of the athlete to understand and inform coaching. This neglect surprises, since scholars from research areas similar to coaching, particularly education, argue that to develop teaching (read coaching), 'a prerequisite must be an appropriate understanding of the nature of learning and of learning careers, and the wider lives of the young people we are trying to help' (Bloomer & Hodkinson, 2000a, p. 74). In this spirit, this book's focus on elite athletes' learning represents an important contribution to sport coaching science.

Foregrounding athlete learning as the primary research topic has implications for sport coaching scholars. First, the integration of the athlete learning perspective adds further complexity to a research topic that is already multifaceted. Practically, it will demand researchers to develop projects that examine different contexts, manifold practices, and multiple actors. This is likely to require an integration of scientific disciplines (e.g., sociology, pedagogy, psychology), which is demanding to develop, finance, and conduct (Bouffard & Spencer-Cavaliere, 2016). Second, scholars who foreground athlete learning may find that the gained knowledge does not obviously generate implications for coaching practice. Indeed, I have found the process of applying knowledge about athlete learning to practice challenging, as I did not want to assume or generalise applicability or effectiveness. One productive way forward may thus be for scholars to involve sport stakeholders by asking them to interpret cases or examples of athlete learning to develop with them context-specific best practice implications. Finally, in order for researchers to make knowledge about athlete learning pertinent, the chosen research methodology needs to allow contextualisation, temporalisation, and attention to the individual.

Contextualisation, temporalisation, and attention to the individual

A key implication of the cultural perspective of learning is that researchers must pay close attention to a person's life. The methodology that allowed the case study authors to focus on a single person and generate multidimensional, longitudinal data was *case study inquiry*. Yin (2012, p. 4, emphasis mine) argues that case study inquiry generates 'a(n) (up-) close or otherwise in-depth understanding of a single or small number of "cases," set in their *real-world contexts*'. Similarly, but with regard to conducting case study research on learning, Flyvbjerg (2006) argues that the closing in on learning as it *unfolds over time*, while contextualising the case (or cases), creates the 'nuanced views of reality' generative to understanding learning.

Both Yin (2012) and Flyvbjerg (2006) propose a number of criteria for successful case studies. A first criterion is *inclusion of theory*.[1] Case study inquiry advocates agree that theory should guide design and data collection methods. For this book, I have taken this criterion to heart by sketching the landscape of elite sport in Chapter 1, adopting a multidimensional and longitudinal conceptualisation of learning (Chapters 2 and 3), and purposefully selecting athlete case studies for Chapters 4-12. The case study authors then drew on the cultural perspective of learning to interpret the data they had produced on their athlete.

A second criterion for successful case studies is *purposeful sampling*. Flyvbjerg (2006) argues that paradigmatic and extreme cases are well suited to produce information on unusual or particularly problematic cases and, through this single focus, get a point across effectively. If multiple such extreme cases are brought together, the significance of different circumstances and outcomes within a particular cultural context can be demonstrated particularly well. In this book, a central aim was to evidence elite athletes' realities and the individual learning this constitutes. Thus, in following Flyvbjerg's argument that paradigmatic and extreme cases have the greatest potential to demonstrate social phenomena, I purposefully contacted authors that could work with athletes from different sports, countries, and cultures. These authors in turn recruited suitable (available) elite athletes and decided on the specific relevant athletic career experiences (e.g., ageing, illness) they intended to foreground in their case studies.

A third case study quality criterion is *proximity to reality*. By proximity, Flyvbjerg (2006) means for researchers to have gained concrete and context-dependent experience of a particular cultural context or social phenomenon. This author argues that such proximity is a prerequisite for advanced-level interpretation of case study materials. In this book, the case study authors had gained closeness to athletes through long-standing personal experience with the sports the case studies represented. Other authors had gained proximity through observing athletes in training and competition and forming personal relationships with them. Moreover, all authors had gained familiarity with national cultures and sporting contexts through having grown up or lived in these settings or having sought collaboration with cultural and/or sport-specific experts.

Researchers can also gain proximity to reality through available literature. The elite sport landscape presented in Chapter 1 is based on literature that demonstrates how the commodity orientation infiltrates the purpose of sport and training, the view of athletes and the coach-athlete relationship, and the type of knowledge employed to understand how coaching and sport performance are influenced. Collecting national and sport-specific policy documents and including social and other media texts (e.g., athlete blogs, biographies) represent additional means that can highlight values and norms, social memory, systems and organisational practices, relationships and practices, and individual experiences (for a useful example of such a methodology, see Barker-Ruchti, Schubring et al., 2017).

The case study authors indicated that their proximity to the sport and athlete was essential to understand learning. One of the authors commented that the 'sustained academic involvement and personal engagement with the individuals, the sport, and the countries in which the research was conducted' that her author team had gained allowed them to bring 'a deeper and more nuanced sensitivity and sensibility to the topic'. Another comment from an author team was that their gaining of cultural proximity had been essential 'to explore how their athletes' embodied learning was deeply shaped by the shifting contexts in which they were situated'. Evidently, the proximity to reality these authors had established had taken time and effort. The result of improved 'research quality and the ability to better speak to the communities that we claim to represent', however, was reported as rewarding.

Lastly, a fourth case study quality criterion is *attention to the individual*. A number of scholars write that researchers should favour presenting dense case studies because their details generate '*real* expertise' (Flyvbjerg, 2006, p. 239, emphasis in original) and enhance the impact they can have on practitioners and social theorists (Peattie, 2001). To generate insight into elite athletes' lives and learning, common data production methods are the life story or life history interview (Atkinson, 1998), narrative interview (Bochner & Riggs, 2014), and oral history (Thompson, 2017). If such interviews allow interviewees to freely articulate their biographies, voice their views of relevant systems and practices, and describe their ideas, dreams, and values, much individual detail can be gained (Baddeley & Singer, 2012; Clandinin, 2007). In this book, life reconstruction interviews were the main approach that the authors used to trace the athletes' biographies and hear their subjectivities. Some of the authors interviewed their athletes once; others talked to them on several occasions.

Two additional research methods that can generate attention to the individual, and that were employed by two of the case study authors, are biographical mapping (Parry, Thomson, & Fowkes, 1999; Wilson, Cunningham-Burley, Bancroft, Backett-Milburn, & Masters, 2007) and memory work as part of auto-ethnography (Markula & Friend, 2005). Biographical mapping entails a grid or matrix on which research participants map (selected aspects of) their lives for a particular time span. The participants then evaluate these according to perceived individual and/or career development importance (Bell, 2005; Berney & Blane, 2003; Wilson et al., 2007). This tracing of a period during one's life is likely to reveal key life transitions and turning points (Parry et al., 1999; Sheridan, Chamberlain, & Dupuis, 2011).

Memory work as part of auto-ethnography is a method that allows researchers to produce case materials on themselves (Markula & Friend, 2005). Memory work is particularly suitable to illustrate and analyse personal experiences that are, or were, meaningful at one point. Memory work requires detailed, but discrete, recollections of lived experiences, which can be made either retrospectively through taking notes, perhaps with the help of photo albums or videos, or prospectively through keeping a diary. One case study author employed memory work. This author found the process giving, as it provided an opportunity to diachronically analyse a sporting past. However, the author also found it challenging to overcome insecurities over scientific rigor. These doubts required this author to reflect over paradigmatic differences, differing scientific quality criteria, dominant positivist research quality criteria, and what Sykes (2017) calls the 'positivist claw' that scholars new to memory work may experience.

Ensuring anonymity and opportunity for awareness raising

Researching athletes' learning using case study inquiry has ethical and political implications. With regard to ethics, a key implication is anonymity. Generally, anonymity demands that researchers remove 'information about any individual or research site that will enable that individual or research site to be identified by others' (Walford, 2005, p. 85). Indeed, ethical vetting boards demand that researchers remove or obscure contextual, temporal, and individual details. However, in elite populations, such as in elite sport, this demand is difficult to achieve. Even if researchers exclude specific names, a narrowing down of possible settings or individuals is likely (Bickford & Nisker, 2015). Further, stripping a case study of contextual, biographical, and individual detail is likely to fall short of the quality criteria outlined above (Nespor, 2000).

In this book, all case study authors faced the challenge of anonymity. In order to ensure that their athletes could not be identified, the common strategy was to omit names, locations, and years. For some authors, however, additional safeguarding strategies were necessary. A strategy that one author adopted was to conflate several athletes into one fictional athlete character. Such composite narratives, according to Willis (2018), provide researchers with a means to keep contextual detail, yet ensure anonymity. Another strategy that some authors adopted related to an 'ethics of social life'. Ethics of social life is less concerned with protecting individuals from harm (especially in the sense of medical harm) and more with enabling research to be critical and unmask social and political injustice and suffering (Bickford & Nisker, 2015). First, this form of ethics made sense to a number of case study authors because a number of athletes found it a relief to tell their story (for similar finding, see Schubring, Barker-Ruchti, Post, & Pettersson, under review). Second, some authors commented that their athletes were politically motivated to share their story. For these athletes, raising awareness of elite sport realities and the challenges and injustices these can entail was important. Third, telling their story generated in the athletes (further) important reflections (Phoenix & Smith, 2011), which several authors felt influenced the athletes in positive ways. For one athlete, the reflections contributed to reconciling with the past. Lastly, hearing the athletes' experiences provided the authors with insight and created important learning, which they interpreted as a privilege and inspiring.

In this political spirit, several of the case study authors tackled anonymity with additional safeguarding measures, including reflecting critically on ethical dilemmas and risks, discussing ethical safeguarding and risk of identification with the case study athletes, and providing case study athletes with drafts and finished copies of their chapter. These strategies were helpful for authors and athletes to weigh risks of identification, discuss the importance of communicating their cases, and agree that the included information could be published as was presented in the case studies.

Levels of inquiry and theory-driven interpretation

Researching athletes' learning using the cultural perspective of learning has analytic implications. Specifically, the perspective demands researchers to examine and move between levels of inquiry and to research these levels over time.

According to Säljö (2009, p. 206), it is through attending to this 'what, where, who and when of learning' that 'we might understand how practices evolve and what happens to people in terms of their capacities, intellectual repertoires and identities as part of such processes'.

Analytic 'gymnastics' is demanding. The case study authors noted that identifying changes in individuals was particularly challenging. One author stated that 'notions of being, becoming and horizons are very messy constructs and do not necessarily "fit" nicely within an easily definable narrative'. Indeed, the authors found it tricky to discern whether an individual's preference for something 'was already there or whether it developed at a particular time' because the fact that an athlete 'didn't mention a certain thought/idea at a certain age doesn't mean it was not there previously'. Further, several of the case study authors noted that following an athlete through habitual routines and multiple turning points was not something with which they were familiar or which they found easy. Bloomer and Hodkinson (2000) wrote that the interpretive dilemma of influence and effect is common in constructivist (read also cultural) discussions of learning. These authors acknowledge that it may be difficult to specify reasons for why individual dispositions change—not because evidence for change is lacking but because 'their relations with transforming perceptions and evaluations were of such complexity as to defy simple description or causal explanation' (Bloomer & Hodkinson, 2000b, p. 592).

Regardless of interpretative challenges or concerns, the case study authors commented that they found relating their athletes' sporting contexts, biographies, and horizontal development (i.e., learning as becoming) valuable. One insight was how career decisions relate to both contextual factors and available expectations, experiences, meanings, and options. One author commented that she found the cultural perspective particularly giving, since her athlete participated in starkly different cultures. This author proposed that the cultural perspective of learning is well suited for researchers studying athletes who have to learn to manage the expectations of multiple cultures. Another appreciated insight was that the longitudinal perspective on athletes' careers allowed them to notice changes and outcomes in the athletes' career pathways, contexts, relationships, and practices, as well as the reflection and decision-making this initiated. One author reported that the 'process a person goes through in life is useful when combined with following the person to see how their future actually pans out'. Indeed, the diachronic emphasis was felt to alleviate the limitations a focus on particular events or periods would impose.

In summary, the cultural perspective of learning proposed in this book implies that researchers adopt the principles of case study inquiry, engage in ethical deliberation, and are flexible with and connective in the analytical phase of research. These principles are challenging and require time—but are rewarding. Certainly, the case study chapters presented in this book significantly contribute to current research methodology and understanding of athlete learning in elite sport.

Key insights and implications for practice

The contents presented in this book, and the case studies particularly, produce important insights for sport stakeholders. In the following, I outline five insights the cultural perspective has generated and propose implications for practice.

Insight 1—Elite sport is constituted by a way of life

According to the cultural perspective of learning, culture exists because of routinely performed practical, social, and intelligible activities that individuals perform because of a *way of life* that is meaningful in a specific context. The case studies illustrated elite sport ways of life and demonstrated how greatly they may differ. They were, however, also similar. These similarities related to athletes needing to adjust to the elite sport way of life when they entered elite sport and to all athletes enjoying the elite sport way of life during their beginning years (regardless of age and background), which motivated them to invest time and effort. Further common features were that the elite sport way of life was more or less bound and prescribed and that acceptance of its demands and practices was necessary and for some even demanded. Lastly, all athletes experienced transitions, such as when moving from one sport to another, when progressing to a higher performance level, or when preparing to retire from sport, and all nine athletes experienced incidents and conflict that impacted the elite sport way of life.

> *Implication:* In recognising that elite sport is a way of life, sport stakeholders will foreground practical, social, and intelligible activities (rather than spaces, locations, teams, or individuals). In doing so, the focus will illustrate that individuals' actions relate to local, sport-specific, situational, circumstantial, career-specific, and individual factors. This relationality will demonstrate that *all* sport stakeholders (not just athletes), as well as rules/regulations, facilities, and materials, are implicated in creating the elite sport way of life.

Insight 2–The elite sport way of life is shaped by the commodity orientation

As argued in Chapter 1, the commodity orientation is a consistent force that ubiquitously shapes the elite sport way of life. The performance investment narrative, which entails the 'single-minded dedication to sport performance that justifies, and even demands, the exclusion or relegation of all other areas of life and self' and which is understood as a necessary investment in return for future athletic success, is the most dominant way of life that athletes adopt (Douglas & Carless, 2014, p. 73). The case studies demonstrated the narrowly defined demands athletes experience and the relegation strategies they may adopt in order to adjust to and cope with the stresses. The compromises affected the athletes' childhood, education, enjoyment of sport, family, health, religion, and professional life.

> *Implication:* In recognising that the elite sport way of life is bound by the commodity orientation, sport stakeholders will come to understand the limited options individual actors (especially athletes) have in negotiating their elite sport way of life. This recognition will offer understanding for why some actors may struggle to accept the demands of elite sport and adopt problematic strategies (e.g., doping, abusive coaching) in order to cope with the pressure to adhere to a commodity-driven elite sport way of life.

Insight 3—The elite sport way of life is precarious

A number of internal and external factors shape sport into an exceptionally precarious context. While not all athletes experience these factors to the same extent and athletes do experience steady and successful periods, elite sport's precariousness is omnipresent. The case studies showcased the myriad of challenges athletes experience during an athletic career. While day-to-day demands of training were challenging, more serious difficulties related to physical functionality (i.e., illness, injury, performance stagnation, overtraining), difficult living arrangements (e.g., billeting, boarding), cultural differences and conflict between athletes and sport stakeholders, non-/deselection, transgressions of ideals, and emotional turmoil. For some of the athletes, the challenges were temporary, and return to training and competition was possible. For others, the challenges resulted in coping or survival strategies that negatively impacted athletic performance, long-term health, and well-being and that had career-ending effects. Thus, the case studies presented in this book indicate that elite athletes are a population at risk of significant problems, most prominently ill health and emotional distress, and require continuous and individualised care.

> *Implication:* In recognising that the elite sport way of life is precarious, sport stakeholders will come to understand the risks athletes must manage on a continuous basis. This recognition will explain why athletic and personal development is for most athletes not linear. It will further offer insight as to why athletes may adopt survival strategies (rather than performance enhancement ones) that are likely to be detrimental to athletic performance, health, well-being, and career longevity. This recognition will identify where sport stakeholders can develop support systems to provide the care elite athletes need.

Insight 4—Athletes negotiate their elite sport way of life

Elite athletes do not adopt or replicate the elite sport way of life. Rather, athletes continuously negotiate activities in relation to the assemblage of social, cultural, situational, circumstantial, biographical, and individual factors they face within and outside of elite sport. This negotiation occurs through intelligible actions such as reflecting over what and how to do things, considering options and outcomes, judging possible consequences, and developing meaning. The case studies documented the reflection and meaning making athletes may engage in during their careers. These descriptions showed that negotiation was easiest during the athletes' beginning sport years because during this time their participation was not yet strictly bound and pressure to perform was light. The athletes enjoyed sport and were looking forward to the elite sport way of life. As elite sport expectations tightened, the majority of the nine athletes needed to adopt the elite sport way of life, which they began to rationalise with hard work, investment, and competition/replacement logics. This rationalisation compromised personal needs and other aspects of life. Yet, and importantly, some athletes, at least some of the time, enjoyed agency or were able to access agency to develop idiosyncratic elite sport ways of life (e.g., horizon for a dual career, horizon for self-health care, horizon for enjoying repetitive training drills, horizon for ageing). While this freedom did not omit sport-specific rules, the training ethos, or performance expectations, the ability to self-regulate horizons for action provided the athletes with means to enjoy and be more satisfied with their elite sport ways of life (for similar findings, see Barker-Ruchti, Kerr, Schubring, Cervin, & Nunomura, 2017; Carless & Douglas, 2013).

> *Implication:* In recognising that athletes negotiate their ways of life, sport stakeholders will realise that athletes are cognitively and emotionally engaged in constructing and reconstructing their realities. This negotiation may be normalising (i.e., athletes accept and adapt to demands); entail friction, conflict, and compromise; and be self-driven. While freedom and support to self-regulate the elite sport way of life should be encouraged because it has been shown to positively affect health, well-being, performance, and career longevity, any negotiation requires emotional engagement and, during difficult times, can be challenging and energy-consuming.

Insight 5—The elite sport way of life shapes individuals

According to the cultural perspective of learning presented in Chapter 3, performing the negotiated activities of a particular way of life shapes individuals. The sense of self this creates in turn creates the 'dispositions people have towards themselves, life and learning' (Biesta, Field, Goodson, Hodkinson, & Macleod, 2008, p. 20). The case studies demonstrated how the nine athletes developed idiosyncratic senses of self and how these in turn shaped the athletes' continued participation, performance, experiences, meaning making, and learning. In some instances, the athletes' activities affected the practices of their sporting contexts, although not necessarily with positive transformative effects (e.g., lack of religious sensibility in Norwegian boxing context). However, having a coherent and resilient sense of the elite athlete is vital for athletes to be able to commit to the demands of the elite sport way of life.

Implication: In recognising that the elite sport way of life shapes individuals, sport stakeholders will realise the interconnectedness of learning as self-development, athletic performance, and career longevity. This understanding will point to the importance of athletes being able to develop a sense of self that entails dispositions to manage the elite sport demands and likely changes to their careers and lives. This recognition will support sport stakeholders in identifying ways that help athletes to develop a coherent and resilient sense of self.

Conclusion

In this chapter, I have argued that case study inquiry informed by a cultural perspective of learning offers a framework to comprehensively research athlete learning in elite sport. Implications of this approach include an additional interpretative step to demonstrate how athlete learning informs sport coaching science, a demanding research methodology (including analysis), concerns regarding anonymity, and potential for political engagement. The five insights presented in the latter section of the chapter reveal how commodity-driven elite sport creates a precarious context that places athletes at risk of ill health, emotional distress, and lack of proper care. The insights further reveal that athletes' learning is normalising, entails friction and conflict, and may be agentic. Two key implications of these insights are that (a) learning relates to context, biography, and subjectivity and (b) self-regulated elite sport ways of life benefit athletes' selves, performance, enjoyment, and career longevity. The main practice recommendation is for sport stakeholders to view each athlete from a holistic perspective and develop means that allow these athletes to self-regulate their elite sport ways of life.

Note

1. With theory, I refer to sociocultural theories that are 'typically defined as a logically interrelated set of propositions that provide explanations of human actions, interactions and meaning-making processes', which represents a key task social science researchers perform in the process of data interpretation (Pringle & Thorpe, 2018, p. 32).

References

Atkinson, R. (1998). *The life story interview*. Thousand Oaks, CA: Sage.

Baddeley, J., & Singer, J. A. (2012). Charting the life story's path: Narrative identity across the life span. In D. J. Clandinin (Ed.), *Handbook of narrative inquiry: Mapping a methodology* (pp. 177–202). Thousand Oaks, CA: Sage.

Barker-Ruchti, N., Kerr, R., Schubring, A., Cervin, G., & Nunomura, M. (2017). 'Gymnasts are like wine, they get better with age': Becoming and developing adult women's artistic gymnasts. *Quest*, 69(3), 348–365.

Barker-Ruchti, N., Schubring, A., Aarresola, O., Kerr, R., Grahn, K., & McMahon, J. (2017). Producing success: A critical analysis of athlete development governance in six countries. *International Journal of Sport Policy and Politics*, 1–20. DOI: 10.1080/19406940.2017.1348381

Bell, A. J. (2005). 'Oh yes, I remember it well'! Reflections on using the life grid in qualitative interviews with couples. *Qualitative Sociology Review*, *1*(1), 51–67.

Berney, L., & Blane, D. (2003). The lifegrid method of collecting retrospective information from people at older ages. *Research Policy and Planning*, *21*(2), 13–22.

Bickford, J., & Nisker, J. (2015). Tensions between anonymity and thick description when 'studying up' in genetics research. *Qualitative Health Research*, *25*(2), 276–282.

Biesta, G., Field, J., Goodson, I., Hodkinson, P., & Macleod, F. (2008). Learning lives: Learning, identity and agency in the life-course. *Teaching and learning research briefing* (51). Available at https://s3.amazonaws.com/academia.edu.documents/42420193/190224.pdf?AWSAccessKeyId=AKIAIWOWYYGZ2Y53UL3A&Expires=1535710098&Signature=fh6aOfzx9w4wt6CZx%2FN5oMG0wfU%3D&response-content-disposition=inline%3B%20filename%3DLearning_lives_learning_identity_and_age.pdf.

Bloomer, M., & Hodkinson, P. (2000a). The complexity and unpredictability of young people's learning careers. *Education + Training*, *42*(2), 68–74.

Bloomer, M., & Hodkinson, P. (2000b). Learning careers: Continuity and change in young people's dispositions to learning. *British Educational Research Journal*, *26*(5), 583–597.

Bochner, A., & Riggs, N. A. (2014). Practicing narrative inquiry. In P. Leavy (Ed.), *The Oxford handbook of qualitative research* (pp. 195–222). New York: Oxford University Press.

Bouffard, M., & Spencer-Cavaliere, N. (2016). Interdisciplinarity in adapted physical activity. *Quest*, 68(1), 4–14.

Carless, D., & Douglas, K. (2013). Living, resisting, and playing the part of athlete: Narrative tensions in elite sport. *Psychology of Sport and Exercise*, *14*(5), 701–708.

Clandinin, D. J. (2007). *Handbook of narrative inquiry: Mapping a methodology*. Thousand Oaks, CA: Sage.

Cushion, C., Nelson, L., Armour, K., Lyle, J., Jones, R., Sandford, R., & O'Callaghan, C. (2010). *Coach learning and development: A review of literature*. Leeds: sports coach UK.

Douglas, K., & Carless, D. (2014). *Life story research in sport: Understanding the experiences of elite and professional athletes through narrative*. London: Routledge.

Flyvbjerg, B. (2006). Five misunderstandings about case-study research. *Qualitative Inquiry*, *12*(2), 219–245.

Gilbert, W. D., & Trudel, P. (2004). Analysis of coaching science research published from 1970-2001. *Research Quarterly for Exercise and Sport*, *75*, 388–399.

Markula, P., & Friend, L. A. (2005). Remember when... Memory-work as an interpretive methodology for sport management. *Journal of Sport Management*, *19*(4), 442–463.

Nash, C. S., & Sproule, J. (2009). Career development of expert coaches. *International Journal of Sports Science and Coaching*, *4*(1), 121–138.

Nelson, L., Groom, R., & Potrac, P. (2016). *Learning in sports coaching theory and application*. New York: Routledge.

Nespor, J. (2000). Anonymity and place in qualitative inquiry. *Qualitative Inquiry*, 6(4), 546–569.

Parry, O., Thomson, C., & Fowkes, G. (1999). Life course data collection: Qualitative interviewing using the life grid. *Sociological Research Online*, 4(2). Available at http://www.socresonline.org.uk/socresonline/4/2/parry.html.

Peattie, L. (2001). Theorizing planning: Some comments on Flyvbjerg's *Rationality and power*. *International Planning Studies*, 6(3), 257–262.

Phoenix, C., & Smith, B. (2011). Telling a (good?) counterstory of aging: Natural bodybuilding meets the narrative of decline. *Journals of Gerontology, Series B: Psychological Sciences and Social Sciences*, 66(5), 628–639.

Pringle, R., & Thorpe, H. (2018). Theory and reflexivity. In M. L. Silk, D. L. Andrews, & H. Thorpe (Eds.), *Routledge handbook of physical cultural studies* (pp. 32–41). Abingdon: Routledge.

Rynne, S. B., Mallett, C. J., & Tinning, R. (2010). Workplace learning of high performance sports coaches. *Sport, Education and Society*, *15*(3), 315–330.

Schubring, A., Barker-Ruchti, N., Post, A., & Pettersson, S. (Under review). Researching athletes' health behaviour in 'real time': Insights from a prospective study on Olympic hopefuls.

Sheridan, J., Chamberlain, K., & Dupuis, A. (2011). Timelining: Visualizing experience. *Qualitative Research*, *11*(5), 552–569.

Sykes, H. (2017, 2 November). Personal communication between Ali Greey and Heather Sykes at the North American Society for the Sociology of Sport Conference.

Säljö, R. (2009). Learning, theories of learning, and units of analysis in research. *Educational Psychologist*, *44*(3), 202–208.

Thompson, P. (2017). *The voice of the past: Oral history*. New York: Oxford University Press.

Walford, G. (2005). Research ethical guidelines and anonymity. *International Journal of Research and Method in Education*, 28(1), 83–93.

Willis, R. (2018). The use of composite narratives to present interview findings. *Qualitative Research*. DOI: 10.1177/1468794118787711

Wilson, S., Cunningham-Burley, S., Bancroft, A., Backett-Milburn, K., & Masters, H. (2007). Young people, biographical narratives and the life grid: Young people's accounts of parental substance use. *Qualitative Research*, *7*(1), 135–151.

Yin, R. K. (2012). *Applications of case study research* (3rd edition). Thousand Oaks, CA: Sage.

Chapter 14

Final reflections

Natalie Barker-Ruchti

This last chapter aims to conclude the book with final reflections. I structure these reflections by first considering the potential the cultural framework offers to understand athlete learning in elite sport and then outlining the alternative questions the cultural framework evokes for research and practice. Finally, I invite readers to engage with the book's contents. With these reflections, I hope to close this book with ways forward to think about, research, and influence athletes' learning in elite sport.

Potential of the cultural framework

I see the cultural framework of learning to have three major potentials for understanding learning. The first potential is *authentic and compelling stories*. The case studies generated uniquely captivating stories that have significant potential to enlighten and emotionally engage readers (Denison & Markula, 2003). This authenticity and engagement enhances scientific trustworthiness and promises to impact readers.

The second potential is *insight into learning*. Drawing on the cultural perspective of learning, particularly the concepts of horizons for action and horizons of learning, the case studies offered specific points of analysis, which revealed how the elite athletes developed, transformed, and let go of beliefs, ambitions, expectations, and practices. This longitudinal insight demonstrated how athletes' learning continuously entails intelligible negotiation and requires significant time and effort. The focus on horizontal development also offered a productive means to discern the relational nature of learning. The elite athletes' stories documented how an incredible range and complex combination of social, local, sport-specific, biographical, and dispositional factors shaped horizontal development. While such relationality is messy and essentially complicates scientists' work, it has the potential to create more pertinent research findings. Ultimately, the relationality that the case studies exposed illustrated the complexity behind the nine athletes continuing, changing, and ending their elite sport careers.

The third potential is the *longitudinal methodology*. Through the research conducted for this book, the longitudinal case study approach demonstrated the omnipresence of elite sport's precariousness and the diverse ways of life this context creates. This longitudinal insight is important, as it can demonstrate why contextual changes and unexpected incidents occur, how athletes experience them, and what reactions, decisions, and transformations the events generate. Such longitudinal knowledge is, in my view, essential to understand athletes' learning and to develop implications for how sport stakeholders can provide athletes with the guidance and support they need throughout their careers.

Alternative questions for research and practice

For researchers and practitioners to capitalise on the potential of the cultural framework of learning, they must ask alternative questions. At present, the commodity orientation directs elite sport research, systems, and practice towards questions of prediction, effectiveness, and productivity. Questions of worth receive much less attention. Yet, I agree with Hodkinson, Biesta, and James (2008) that such questions are important to generate performance, ensure athlete welfare, stimulate individual citizenship, and fulfil social responsibility. Two alternative questions of worth, which I have adopted from Hodkinson and colleagues (2008), are as follows: What is/should be the valuable learning in any particular elite sport culture or for any particular elite athlete or group of athletes? In other words, what is it that elite athletes should learn to ensure performance, health and well-being, career longevity, and citizenship? Following this focus, the second question is: How can researchers, sport organisations, sport stakeholders, and coach educators enhance the likelihood of the valuable learning identified for specific individuals and groups? In other words, what can sport stakeholders do to ensure that athletes learn what they (meaning stakeholders and athletes) have identified as valuable? Clearly, these questions contrast with existing outcome questions such as how coaches can be more effective and what the best way is to produce competitive results. They require a reorientation of underlying commodity values to create a logic that values process, authenticity, emancipation, and ethics (Barker-Ruchti, Barker, & Annerstedt, 2014). While this may appear counter-intuitive, the case studies have provided some examples of alternative ideals and practices that support the emerging vision that elite sport can be successfully conducted in sustainable ways (for similar results, see Annerstedt & Lindgren, 2014; Barker, Barker-Ruchti, Wals, & Tinning, 2014; Barker-Ruchti, Kerr, Schubring, Cervin, & Nunomura, 2017). These counter-stories are significant, but further research and practice examples are necessary to confirm—and, importantly, explicate—the positive links among questions and practices of worth, performance results, and positive personal development.

Invitation for readers to engage in the book's contents

My last reflection builds again on Enright and Gard's (2016) response to Hodkinson and colleagues' (2008) cultural perspective of learning, and particularly their suspicion that "'learning" is a necessarily and inevitably elusive concept and that partial and highly situated understandings [of learning] are as much as we can aspire to' (p. 53). I agree that this book offers one possible way to think about athletes' learning in elite sport and that further 'playing with theory' is necessary to advance understanding of elite athletes' learning (Thomas, 2007). It is thus important that readers reflect on, critique, and adapt the cultural framework to advance understanding of learning in elite sport. Indeed, Flyvbjerg (2006) proposes that readers of case study reports are *required* to 'make different interpretations and draw diverse conclusions regarding the question of what the case is a case of' (p. 238). These interpretations are likely to differ among readers: Some will recognise the book's contents and analyses, perhaps because they have produced similar research findings or have had similar athletic experiences. Others will relate only partially or not at all to the presented framework and findings. Regardless, the engagement promises two potentials: First, as Tracy (2010) writes, the material may generate 'critical intelligence' or moral critique. I believe that the book's focus on athlete learning as self-development and the case study materials create important counter-stories that challenge underlying assumptions about elite sport and learning and raise important critical questions about today's elite sport landscape and practices. Second, Smith (2018) writes that readers who consider how research findings and interpretations resonate with their own experiences and understanding can generate naturalistic generalisation. That is, as presented materials 'ring true' or speak to readers in other ways, they gain qualitative validity. I trust that the case study materials offer opportunities for readers to connect their thoughts, experiences, and understanding with those presented here. This connection, as Flyvbjerg (2006) and others (Peattie, 2001; Smith, 2018) have argued, generates social impact. It is my hope that current and future practitioners find the book's contents useful for their work.

I would like to close this book by encouraging students and scientists to research athletes' learning in (elite) sport. For me, to think about and research elite athletes' learning in today's commodity-driven elite sport has great potential to advance sport coaching science and elite sport practice. I would further like to appeal to sport stakeholders to take seriously elite sport's ways of life and the learning these generate for athletes and to critically reflect over (their) athlete development systems, training and coaching practices, and athlete safeguarding efforts.

References

Annerstedt, C., & Lindgren, E.-C. (2014). Caring as an important foundation in coaching for social sustainability—A case study of a successful Swedish coach in high-performance sport. *Reflective Practice*, *15*(1), 27–39.

Barker, D., Barker-Ruchti, N., Wals, A. E. J., & Tinning, R. (2014). High performance sport and sustainability: A contradiction of terms? *Reflective Practice*, *15*(1), 1–11.

Barker-Ruchti, N., Barker, D., & Annerstedt, C. (2014). Techno-rational knowing and phronesis: The professional practice of one middle-distance running coach. *Reflective Practice*, *15*(1), 53–65.

Barker-Ruchti, N., Kerr, R., Schubring, A., Cervin, G., & Nunomura, M. (2017). 'Gymnasts are like wine, they get better with age': Becoming and developing adult women's artistic gymnasts. *Quest*, 69(3), 348–365.

Denison, J., & Markula, P. (2003). *Moving writing: Crafting movement in sport research*. New York: Peter Lang.

Enright, E., & Gard, M. (2016). Media, digital technology and learning in sport: A critical response to Hodkinson, Biesta and James. *Physical Education and Sport Pedagogy*, *21*(1), 40–54.

Flyvbjerg, B. (2006). Five misunderstandings about case-study research. *Qualitative Inquiry*, *12*(2), 219–245.

Hodkinson, P., Biesta, G., & James, D. (2008). Understanding learning culturally: Overcoming the dualism between social and individual views of learning. *Vocations and learning*, *1*(1), 27–47.

Peattie, L. (2001). Theorizing planning: Some comments on Flyvbjerg's *Rationality and power*. *International Planning Studies*, 6(3), 257–262.

Smith, B. (2018). Generalizability in qualitative research: Misunderstandings, opportunities and recommendations for the sport and exercise sciences. *Qualitative Research in Sport, Exercise and Health*, *10*(1), 137–149.

Thomas, G. (2007). *Education and theory: Strangers in paradigms*. Maidenhead: McGraw-Hill Education.

Tracy, S. J. (2010). Qualitative quality: Eight 'big-tent' criteria for excellent qualitative research. *Qualitative Inquiry*, *16*(10), 837–851.

Index